# ETHICS AND PROFESSIONALISM

*The Keys to Building and Maintaining a Successful Law Practice*

JEANNE HUEY, EDITOR

AMERICAN BAR ASSOCIATION
Litigation Section

Cover design by Mary Anne Kulchawik/ABA Design



Printed in the United States of America.

30 29 28 27 26 5 4 3 2 1

A catalog record for this book is available from the Library of Congress.

# Contents

# Preface

**To Our Colleagues and Contributors**

This book exists because a remarkable group of lawyers believed their stories, struggles, and ideas were worth sharing. To those authors, thank you. Your willingness to reflect, be honest, and challenge others is the essence of professional leadership.

To the members, editors, and leadership of the American Bar Association, your commitment to elevating the profession and providing a platform for these voices to be heard made this work possible. Because of your stewardship, this book is stronger, and our profession is better.

To the reader: These pages are only the beginning of a conversation that belongs in every law office, classroom, and courtroom. Take what resonates with you and leave what doesn't. But don't leave unchanged. Because professionalism is not something we master—it's something we practice, refine, and pass on. And it's something the profession needs from each of us—now more than ever.

# Introduction

Professionalism is the foundation of our work as lawyers. It is the architecture that shapes how we serve clients, interact with colleagues, and uphold the integrity of the legal system, not just as advocates for individual clients but also as officers of the court and guardians of the justice system. Because of a lawyer's unique role, the public's trust in the rule of law largely depends on how we conduct ourselves—on our civility, competence, and commitment to fairness. Maintaining the highest levels of professionalism is how we demonstrate that public trust is well placed.

There is no single way to be a great lawyer. The essays in this book reflect that truth, each rooted in a different experience, voice, and insight. However, no matter where we are in our careers, there is always room for improvement. We may not have always been as civil as we could be with opposing counsel. We may have neglected opportunities to reach out to colleagues in need, avoided bar service, or dismissed pro bono work as something we did not have time for. But professionalism is not a box to check—it is a mindset, a commitment, and a choice we can make at any time. It is never too late to raise our standards and those at our firm, to engage more fully with our profession, and to do our part in strengthening the legal community and the rule of law itself.

This book explores several key aspects of professionalism—our duties to clients, our role in regulating and shaping the future of the profession, and our service to one another and the public. The following essays are organized around these themes, offering practical guidance, personal reflections, and informative challenges to think differently about the meaning of professionalism in the practice of law.

There is something here for every lawyer: Whether you are looking to make small changes or start anew, we hope this book inspires and encourages you to take that step. Our profession will be better for it when you do.

# Authors

**Paige L. Adamczyk**, Adamczyk Legal PC, 1237 Victoria Avenue #256, Oxnard, CA, paige@adamczyklegal.com, www.adamczyklegal.com

**Emil J. Ali**, McCabe/Ali LLP, 13337 South Street, Suite 555, Cerritos, CA, emil@mccabeali.com, www.mccabeali.com

**John M. Barkett,** Shook, Hardy & Bacon LLP, 201 South Biscayne Boulevard, Suite 3200, Miami, FL, jbarkett@shb.com, www.shb.com

**Dominika Borek**, Fried Frank Harris Shriver & Jacobson LLP, New York, NY, dborek@penncareylaw.upenn.edu

**Hon. Tiffany Williams Brewer (Ret.),** 2025–26 Chair, American Bar Association Litigation Section, Howard University School of Law, tiffany.brewer@howard.edu, https://profiles.howard.edu/tiffany-williams-brewer

**Hon. John Browning (Ret.)**, Fifth District Court of Appeals (Texas), Distinguished Jurist in Residence, Faulkner University School of Law, Montgomery, AL, jbrowning@faulkner.edu

**Hon. Christopher C. Conner (Ret.)**, Saxton & Stump, 4250 Crums Mill Road, Suite 201, Harrisburg, PA, cconner@saxton stump.com, www.saxtonstump.com

**Professor Susan Fortney**, Texas A&M University School of Law, 1515 Commerce Street, Fort Worth, TX, sfortney@law .tamu.edu, www.law.tamu.edu

**Mary Gately,** DLA Piper LLP, 500 Eighth Street NW, Washington DC, mary.gately@us.dlapiper.com, www.dlapiper .com

**Bruce A. Green,** Fordham University School of Law, 150 West 62nd Street, New York, NY, bgreen@law.fordham.edu, www .fordham.edu/school-of-law

**Erica Grigg, MEd, LPC, LCDC**, Erica Grigg Counseling Services, PLLC, 2901 Bee Caves Road, Suite J, Austin, TX, erica@grigg-counseling.com, www.ericagriggcounseling.com

**Lauren Grinder** , DLA Piper LLP, 1900 North Pearl Street, Suite 2200, Dallas, TX, lauren.grinder@us.dlapiper.com, www .dlapiper.com

**Gregory R. Hanthorn,** Jones Day (Ret.), P.O. Box 1790, Mableton, GA, grhanthorn@icloud.com

**Kathleen Balthrop Havener**, The Cullen Law Firm, PLLC, 1101 30th Street NW, Suite 500, Washington, DC, kathleen@ cullenlaw.com, www.cullenlaw.com

**Alicia Hickok**, DLA Piper LLP, One Liberty Place, 1650 Market Street, Suite 5000, Philadelphia, PA, alicia.hickok@ us.dlapiper.com, www.dlapiper.com

**Rebecca Howlett**, The Legal Burnout Solution LLC, 3841 North 123rd Street, Kansas City, KS, becky@legalburnout.com, www.legalburnout.com

**Jeanne M. Huey**, Hunt Huey PLLC, 17304 Preston Road, Suite 800, Dallas, TX, jhuey@hunthuey.com, https://hunthuey.com/

**Richard M. Hunt** , Hunt Huey PLLC , 17304 Preston Road, Suite 800, Dallas, TX, rhunt@hunthuey.com, https://hunthuey.com/

**Jan L. Jacobowitz,** Legal Ethics Advisor, Jan@JacobowitzLaw.com, www.legalethicsadvisor.com

**Allegra Lawrence-Hardy,** Krevolin & Horst, LLC, One Atlantic Center, 1201 West Peachtree Street, NW, Suite 3500, Atlanta, GA, Lawrence@khlawfirm.com, www.khlawfirm.com

**Michael S. LeBoff**, Klein & Wilson LLP, 4770 Von Karman Avenue, Newport Beach, CA, leboff@kleinandwilson.com, www.kleinandwilson.com

**Roberta D. Liebenberg,** Fine Kaplan & Black, One South Broad Street, Suite 2300, Philadelphia, PA, rliebenberg@finekaplan.com, www.finekaplan.com

**Hon. Barbara M.G. Lynn (Ret.)**, Lynn Pinker Hurst & Schwegmann, 2100 Ross Avenue, Suite 2700, Dallas, TX, blynn@lynnllp.com, www.lynnllp.com/legacy

**Maya Mallya**, Judicial Intern, February–August 2024, Senior United States District Judge Barbara M. G. Lynn

**Jon May**, Jon May, Inc., P.O. Box 970006, Boca Raton, FL, jonmay@jonmaycriminaldefense.com, www.jonmaycriminal defense.com

**Michelle McClafferty**, Krevolin & Horst, LLC, One Atlantic Center, 1201 West Peachtree Street, NW, Suite 3500, Atlanta, GA, mcclafferty@khlawfirm.com, www.khlawfirm.com

**Lucian Pera**, Adams and Reese LLP, 6075 Poplar Avenue, Suite 700, Memphis, TN, Lucian.Pera@arlaw.com, www.adams andreese.com

**Jayne R. Reardon** , Fisher Broyles LLP, 203 North LaSalle Street, Suite 2100, Chicago, IL, jayne.reardon@fisherbroyles .com, www.fisherbroyles.com

**Tiffany A. Rowe**, Parker Poe, 900 7th Street NW, Suite 700, Washington, DC, tiffanyrowe@parkerpoe.com, www.parker poe.com

**Paul Mark Sandler**, Shapiro Sher Guinot & Sandler (ret.), pmsandler@gmail.com

**Stephanie A. Scharf, Ph.D**, Scharf Banks Marmor LLC, 30 West Hubbard Street, Suite 500, Chicago, IL, sscharf@scharf banks.com, www.scharfbanks.com

**Teresa Schmid,** Consultant: Legal Ethics, Lawyer Regulation, Association Management, www.linkedin.com/in/teresajschmid

**David B. Seserman,** Seserman Law LLC, 3900 East Mexico Avenue, Suite 300, Denver, CO, dseserman@seserman.law, www.seserman.law

**Cynthia Sharp,** The Legal Burnout Solution LLC, 3841 North 123rd St., Kansas City, KS, cindy@legalburnout.com, www.legalburnout.com

**Tiffany Shimada**, Greenberg Traurig, LLP, 222 South Main Street, Suite 1730, Salt Lake City, UT, Tiffany.shimada@gtlaw.com, www.gtlaw.com

**Abigail Stone**, Greenberg Traurig, LLP, 222 South Main Street, Suite 1730, Salt Lake City, UT, Abigail.stone@gtlaw.com, www.gtlaw.com

# Chapter 1

## Rethinking Civility: A Professional Imperative

Professionalism begins with civility—in how we treat others when disagreement is inevitable regardless of the hat we are wearing. Whether we are acting as a counselor, negotiator, or advocate, how we treat clients, colleagues, and court personnel shapes not only our own credibility but also the strength of the system we work within.

In a world where rudeness can sometimes appear as confidence, making a conscious effort to lead with civility in every circumstance requires judgment, restraint, and a clear sense of purpose. Civility is not just a relic of the past; it is a professional advantage that allows lawyers to serve clients effectively while preserving the integrity of the legal system.

# Civility Homecoming: A Lawyer's Call to Action to Return to Civility

*Hon. Tiffany Williams Brewer (Ret.)*

Civility is a lawyer's home. As former U.S. Supreme Court Justice Anthony M. Kennedy has stressed: "Civility is the mark of an accomplished and superb professional, but it is more even than this. It is an end in itself. Civility has deep roots in the idea of respect for the individual."[1] On the other hand, the deterioration of civility, according to former ABA President Lee Cooper,

> interrupts the administration of justice. It makes the practice of law less rewarding. It robs a lawyer of the sense of dignity and self-worth that should come from a learned profession. Not least of all, it . . . brings with it all the problems . . . that accompany low public regard for lawyers and lack of confidence in the justice system.[2]

---

1. Justice Douglas S. Lang & Haleigh Jones, *Can Courts Require Civil Conduct?*, 6 St. Mary's J. Legal Mal. & Ethics 222, 226 (2016) (quoting Louis H. Pollak, *Professional Attitude*, 84 A.B.A. J. at 66 (Aug. 1988) (quoting Justice Kennedy)).

2. United States District Court for the District of New Jersey, Appendix R, Guidelines for Litigation Conduct, https://www.njd.uscourts.gov/sites/njd/files/AppR.pdf (quoting Lee Cooper).

In examining the etymology of the term "civility," its meaning lies close in similarity to the meaning of the word "citizen," suggesting that civility is linked to the state of being a citizen or demonstrating good citizenship. Civility has also been defined as a code of decency that characterizes a civilized society. Evaluation of these meanings and the common understanding of the role of civility in the legal profession has become the centerpiece of our ethical obligations as lawyers and the standard by which we believe we should do what we do. As a means to our end, civility can also define the manner in which we practice and reveal why we practice. Most importantly, civility can reveal the level of integrity and character that lawyers bring to their work.

The D.C. Bar Voluntary Standards of Professional Responsibility give a good backdrop of the understanding of the meaning of civility in the legal profession:

> Our judicial system is a truth-seeking process designed to resolve human and societal problems in a rational, peacefully, and efficient manner and designed to be perceived as producing fair and just results. We must be careful to avoid actions or statements that undermine the system or the public's confidence in it.
>
> The organized bar and the judiciary, in partnership with each other, have a responsibility to promote civility in the practice of law and the administration of justice. Uncivil conduct of lawyers or judges impedes the fundamental goal of resolving disputes rationally, peacefully and efficiently. Such conduct may delay or deny justice and diminish the respect for law, which is a cornerstone of our society and our profession.
>
> Civility and professionalism are hallmarks of a learned profession dedicated to public service. These standards are designed to encourage us, as lawyers and

> judges, to meet our obligations of civility and professionalism, to each other, to litigants, and to the system of justice.[3]

## Civility Myths

In order to fully embrace the meaning of civility and its continuing role in the legal profession, it is equally important to debunk myths about civility. Jane Reardon, former executive director for the Illinois Supreme Court Commission on Professionalism, exposited several aspects of confusion about civility in carving out the borders of civility's core:[4]

- Civility is not the same as agreement.
- Civility is not the absence of criticism.
- Civility is not the same as liking someone.
- Civility *should not be equated with politeness or manners alone.*[5]

In busting the myths that civility means agreement and complete acquiescence, we are able to focus on the role of civility within the adversarial system where advocates using varied strategies are seeking to gain tactical advantage for their clients. Civility means we can still agree to disagree and demonstrate the highest forms of persuasion and unrelenting advocacy for our position. The presence of civility, however, implicates a respect for listening to our adversary's position, refraining from seeking only to be heard ourselves. Civility also means

---

3. *Preamble, D.C. Bar Voluntary Standards of Civility in Professional Conduct*, DCBar.org, https://www.dcbar.org/for-lawyers/legal-ethics/d-c-bar-voluntary-standards-of-civility-in-profess.

4. *See* Jayne R. Reardon, *Civility as the Core of Professionalism*, Bus. L. Today (Sep. 18, 2014), https://www.americanbar.org/groups/business_law/resources/business-law-today/2014-september/civility-as-the-core-of-professionalism.

5. *Id.*

that while we have permission to sharply disagree with our opponents and to vociferously express our disagreement, we can choose a communication style whose tone is not offensive, off-putting, or odious. A civil lawyer can be a lawyer that others do not like, and a civil lawyer need not be popular at the water cooler. Nonetheless, a civil lawyer should be a lawyer that garners respect for emotional self-control, creative consensus-building, and mannerly comportment.

## Ethical Considerations for Civility Under the Model Rules

Civility intertwines directly with a lawyers' professional responsibility under the ABA Model Rules of Professional Conduct. Review of the Model Rules reveals that civility is rooted in our ethical obligations as lawyer-advocates, public citizens, and officers of the court. Foundationally, the Preamble to the Model Rules describes the role of lawyer as a public citizen, setting the stage for the role of civility in maintaining the integrity of the profession:

> As a public citizen, a lawyer should seek improvement of the law, access to the legal system, the administration of justice and the quality of service rendered by the legal profession. . . . [A] lawyer should further the public's understanding of and confidence in the rule of law and the justice system because legal institutions in a constitutional democracy depend on popular participation and support to maintain their authority.[6]

The Preamble maintains that even in client dealings, counsel is expected to show respect for the legal system in his or

---

6. *See* ABA Model Rules of Pro. Conduct, Preamble ¶ 6.

her role as advisor, negotiator, or evaluator.[7] The Preamble also encourages lawyers to resolve the conflicts inherent in duties owed to client, the legal system, and the lawyer's own interest through the exercise of discretion and judgment "while maintaining a professional, courteous, *and civil attitude* toward all persons involved in the legal system."[8]

Courts also remain concerned with diminishing public confidence or tainting the legal process:

> *All* lawyers, by virtue of their licenses, enjoy the status of officers of the court. That status brings with it the responsibility to refrain from conduct unbecoming such officers, to uphold the rule of law, and *to enhance public confidence in that rule and the legal system set up to safeguard it.*[9]

The U.S. Supreme Court has even weighed in, adding that:

> [A] lawyer belongs to a profession with inherited standards of propriety and honor, which experience has shown necessary in a calling dedicated to the accomplishment of justice. He who would follow that calling must conform to those standards.[10]

In addition to the Preamble, the text of the Model Rules speak to a lawyer's duties to maintain the integrity of the profession and prescribes that "[i]t is professional misconduct for a lawyer to . . . engage in conduct that is prejudicial to the administration of justice."[11] In describing the standard of diligence

---

7. *See id.* at cmt. 5.

8. *See id.* at cmt. 9 (emphasis added).

9. *In re* Pyle, 283 Kan. 807, 829–30 (2007) (emphasis added).

10. *In re* Sawyer, 360 U.S. 622, 646–47, 79 S. Ct. 1376, 3 L. Ed. 2d 1473 (1959) (Stewart, J., concurring).

11. *See* Model Rules of Pro. Conduct r. 8.4(d).

that a lawyer must demonstrate in handling client matters, the Model Rules require that a lawyer pursue client matters despite "opposition, obstruction or personal inconvenience to the lawyer, and take whatever lawful and ethical measures are required to vindicate a client's cause or endeavor. A lawyer must also act with commitment and dedication to the interests of the client and with *zeal* in advocacy upon the client's behalf."[12] In exercising diligence, the Model Rule comment suggests that zealous advocacy should still be lawful and ethical advocacy—implying that the standard of professionalism in pursuing client matters zealously does not dispense with civility, but rather continues in requisite degree as the degree of advocacy increases.

"A lawyer is not bound, however, to press for every advantage that might be realized for a client. . . . The lawyer's duty to act with reasonable diligence does not require the use of offensive tactics or preclude the treating of all persons involved in the legal process with courtesy and respect."[13]

Model Rule 1.16(b)(4) roots civility in the decision to withdraw from client representation by providing that a lawyer may withdraw if the client insists upon taking action that the "lawyer considers repugnant or with which the lawyer has a fundamental disagreement." Further, Model Rule 3.1 addresses the civility in avoiding frivolity in the practice. It specifically provides that a lawyer cannot abuse legal procedure by frivolously bringing or defending a proceeding, or asserting or controverting an issue. Finally, Model Rule 8.4(d) allows for the most egregious forms of incivility to fall within conduct prejudicial to the administration of justice.

12. Model Rules of Pro. Conduct, Diligence r. 1.3 cmt. 1 (emphasis added).

13. *Id.*

## Why Is Civility the Goal? Why Is It Our Home as Lawyers?

Incivility remains pervasive in the profession and has an impact on the administration of justice, attorney well-being, and the public's confidence in the legal system. According to a 2007 Illinois Bar study, 71 percent had reported experiencing rudeness in the form of sarcastic and condescending comments, swearing, or inappropriate interruption while speaking.[14] The survey also revealed uncivil behaviors by opposing counsel that lawyers perceived to have been employed strategically to an advantage in the proceedings, such as deliberate misrepresentation of facts, failing to agreeing to reasonable requests for accommodation, frivolous pleadings, and use of inflammatory language in legal writing.[15] Judges often spend needless time moderating disputes that are rooted in uncivil behavior at depositions, in the exchange of discovery, in motion practice, and at trial.

Conversely, embracing and demonstrating civility has a positive impact on the public's confidence in the legal system, the furtherance of democratic values, and on attorney well-being. Civil lawyers have the capacity to be more effective and achieve better outcomes and superior service for their clients.[16] Leading with civility can help lawyers build better professional reputations for achieving excellence and can lead to fewer disciplinary charges. Some states are resorting to bringing formal

---

14. Survey on Professionalism, A Study of Illinois Lawyers, Ill. Sup. Ct. Comm'n on Professionalism (Dec. 2007), https://www.2civility.org/wp-content/uploads/2014/07/surveyonprofessionalism_final.pdf.

15. *Id.*

16. *See* Reardon, *supra* note 4 ("Research also shows that superior service, in which relationship abilities are central, increases client retention rates by about one third. Effective client service and positive relationships, in turn, increase profit to the lawyers by about the same rate.").

disciplinary action against lawyers under their state rules of professional conduct as well as under the auspices of failing to uphold civility oaths taken when entering the practice. For example, in South Carolina and Illinois, lawyers were disciplined for incivility under ethics rules and the lawyer's oath taken upon admission to the bar that contained a civility pledge.

Additional benefits of advancing civility include increased job satisfaction and reduced negative outcomes risked by incivility on the psyche of a judge when there is a close call on an issue, or by a jury/factfinder during a trial. It cannot be emphasized enough that civility reduces stress and increases lawyer well-being in a context where lawyers are more than twice as likely as the general population to suffer from mental illness and substance abuse. Most importantly, civility can eliminate bias in the legal profession and reduce the stress of lawyers who find themselves on the receiving end of incivility that is rooted in bias and discrimination, which may cause diverse attorneys to be subject to disproportionate stress.

## How Can We Embrace This Civility Homecoming?

The most compelling strategy to the proliferation of civility in the legal profession is for members of the bar to take personal responsibility in offering thought leadership about civility, performing training, and setting the atmosphere of civility in the workplace. As a self-governed profession we should continue to foster accountability within the bar association structure and in state disciplinary boards, including enacting civility standards with peer accountability. In 1996, after the Conference of Chief Justices adopted a resolution calling for the courts of the highest jurisdiction in each state to take a leadership role in evaluating lawyer professionalism, the supreme courts of 14 states established commissions on professionalism to promote professionalism and civility. In addition to professionalism commissions, several states have formed bar association or court committees focused on addressing professionalism issues in the profession and developing aspirational principles of ideal behavior for lawyers. Other courts have established peer mediation models to address complaints against lawyers and judges failing to comport with aspirational standards.

One early model was developed by the DC Bar, in the form of Voluntary Standards of Professional Responsibility. In South Carolina, Florida, and California, the attorney oath taken upon admission to the bar was amended to include a pledge of civility and courtesy to judges, opposing parties and their counsel, and court personnel. Some jurisdictions have also amended their disciplinary rules to provide that a violation of the civility oath could be grounds for discipline.

Finally, lawyers ultimately have a responsibility to actively model and teach civility to the next generation of lawyers, whether supervising law students on internships, discussing civility in guest lectures and panels at law schools, sponsoring professionalism awards to law students, or simply emphasizing law students' roles in treating classmates, professors, and staff with respect while serving as a student. Lawyers could also support and assist law schools in establishing professionalism curriculum and centers, such as the Dean's Professionalism Certificate at Howard University School of Law in Washington, DC, the Parris Institute for Professional Excellence at Pepperdine Caruso School of Law in Malibu, California, and the Holloran Center for Ethical Leadership at University of St. Thomas School of Law in Minneapolis, Minnesota.

To my fellow brothers and sisters of the bar, I urge you to take up this call to return to our roots of professionalism and civility, and I say to you, "Welcome Home!"

# Everyone Deserves Civility: Why It Matters Across the Legal System

*Michael S. LeBoff*[1]

The story of how I became managing partner of my law firm here illustrates why litigators should maintain a professional, courteous, and civil attitude toward everyone involved in the legal system.

More than ten years ago, my then firm and my current firm were on opposite sides of a very contentious joint venture dispute. For nearly three years, we battled on every issue from the meaning of the joint venture agreement, the applicable law, the proper scope of discovery, and admissibility of expert testimony. Ultimately, the parties settled the case on the courthouse steps minutes before we started picking a jury.

Both relieved and disappointed about losing the chance to try the case, I moved on to other cases. Then, a few years later, I received a call out of the blue from my former opponents. The firm was looking to expand and thought I was what they needed. They were impressed by my skills as a litigator but, more importantly, they were impressed with my ethics and civility in the conduct of a very contentious case.

---

1. Michael S. LeBoff is a trial lawyer with Klein & Wilson in Newport Beach, California, focusing on commercial disputes and legal malpractice cases.

Though it was a difficult decision to leave my old firm, I accepted the opportunity and quickly became the first new partner in the firm's 25-year history. A few years later, I became managing partner. These career developments not only benefited me financially but, more importantly, reinvigorated my enjoyment of the practice of law.

Every lawyer's story is unique, but I never would have had these opportunities had I acted like a jerk during the case. Treating opposing counsel, judges, clients, and everyone else in the litigation system with courtesy and respect won't guarantee a corner office, but it will have immediate practical benefits.

## Being a Jerk Is Not Zealous Advocacy

There are numerous benefits to getting along with opposing counsel. First and foremost, the practice of law is more enjoyable when you can shake hands and have professional conversations with opposing counsel. Instead of fighting over who said what and whether actions were taken in good faith, your conversations can focus on the law, facts, and achieving a resolution. When there is a level of trust between counsel, you can better serve your client by discussing settlement without worrying that anything you say can and will be used against you. And you can do this without compromising your client's position or being a less effective advocate.

This is a key point, as many lawyers are taught that opposing counsel is the enemy and to best represent your client, you need to go to "war" with opposing counsel. Twenty-five years of litigating has taught me nothing could be further from truth, and most effective lawyers are the ones that can persuade through solid legal arguments and fact development. While from time to time, bullying and abusive tactics may intimidate a less confident or experienced attorney, most litigators are not affected by such behavior. To the contrary, such tactics build a culture of distrust that harms the parties and the administration of justice.

Further, being a jerk may signal weakness in your case. There is an adage in the law that, if you are strong on the facts, pound the facts. If you are strong on the law, pound the law. And, if you have nothing else, pound the table. So, when attorneys do nothing but pound the table, it indicates their case is weak on the facts and laws. On the other hand, lawyers who confidently and civilly present the law and facts often get the best result.

Civility and professionalism also tend to lower the costs of litigation, as clients can avoid the costs of unnecessary motions and discovery disputes. In a similar vein, inevitably, during a lawsuit, your clients will need an extension on discovery, to reschedule a deposition or hearing date, or get a short trial continuance. You are far more likely to get these accommodations from opposing counsel without an expensive fight if you treat them and their client with civility.

On a final note, as it relates to opposing counsel, civility and professionalism extend beyond attorneys. Regardless of how you feel about opposing counsel, you should always treat their staff with courtesy. Nothing upsets me more than when opposing counsel treat my staff with even the slightest disrespect. By and large, these are hard-working and often underpaid employees who do not deserve to be mistreated.

## Developing a Reputation for Civility Is Good Business

Your biggest asset when it comes to business development is your reputation. Treating opposing counsel with respect and civility only enhances that reputation. Attorneys talk about attorneys. If you give your opposing counsel negative things to say about you, word will get out in your legal community.

Your legal reputation is something that takes years to build, but only seconds to destroy. Further, every year, lawyers (including myself) trot out faux accomplishments like Super Lawyers, Best Lawyers, and the like. Right or wrong, these lists are effective marketing tools, but at their core, are just popularity contests.

I am also proud to say I have received numerous referrals from former opposing counsel. I consider this a tremendous compliment. Lawyers tend to refer cases to people that they like and trust. I take pride in the fact that I can develop those feelings during adversary relationships. As most cases have at least one opposing counsel, acting like a jerk in litigation effectively eliminates a large group of lawyers from your referral base. And again, I am not selling out my clients for the chance of getting a later referral. You can be a good advocate and civil, and, in fact, the best advocates are typically the most civil.

Civility and professionalism can also benefit you in billing disputes as well, as illustrated in the recent California case *Snoeck v. Exaktime Innovations, Inc.*,[2] where the appellate court affirmed a negative 0.4 multiplier in an attorney's fee award based on the attorney's "lack of civility throughout the entire course of this litigation." In that case, the attorney made ad hominem attacks unnecessary for the zealous representation of his client, accused opposing counsel of telling the courts lies, committing fraud and engaging in "sleazy" and "cringeworthy" conduct. As to the court, the attorney's tone was "belittling and antagonistic" and "verged on the contemptuous." The attorney also belittled the court in his emails to opposing counsel, claiming defense counsel made "a total fool of," "exploited," and "duped" the trial court, and treated the trial court as an "easy mark." Based on this conduct, that attorney's chronic incivility cost him $457,683 in attorney's fees.

---

2. Snoeck v. Exaktime Innovations, Inc. 96 Cal. App. 5th 908 (2023).

Sadly, the *Snoeck* case is not alone in providing newsworthy examples of incivility toward opposing counsel. In a recent case out of San Diego, a litigator was referred to the State Bar for saying "See You Next Tuesday" (an apparently familiar code for a misogynistic term) to two female lawyers. Most of us have also seen the classic YouTube clip of Texas lawyers challenging each other to a fight during a deposition. In another example out of my home state of California, an attorney sent his adversary over 100 profane and insulting emails, including telling opposing counsel to "eat a bowl of dicks." There is no place for this conduct in our profession.

## Treat the Court and Its Staff Like They Will Be Judging Your Case

Every judge I have spoken to cringes when an attorney utters the words "With all due respect" or "Respectfully, your honor[.]" These phrases are better demonstrated than said aloud. Nevertheless, treating the judge that is deciding your motion or your case with respect and civility seems like a no-brainer. Yet, I am constantly amazed at how frequently lawyers disrespect the bench.

Judges will grant or deny motions or decide cases based on the law and evidence—not on their opinions of counsel. Yet, civility enhances your chances of success, as it gets a judge to focus on what you are saying instead of how you are saying it. It further enhances your credibility as an advocate. A judge's decision does not always come down to a rigid application of the law to the facts and sometimes, as lawyers cannot nail down every single point the way we might like to, because of time or page limits. In those cases, the judge's perception of reliability, trustworthiness, and integrity matters, and being rude or abusive is just as bad as being ignorant or sloppy in terms of how reliable our arguments appear. As seen in the *Snoeck* case, it is a tall order to present an attorney fee motion to a judge you treated with "chronic incivility" throughout the case.

Civility toward the bench also helps at trial, as juries typically like the judge. So, if the jury sees you treat the judge with respect, and the judge reciprocates, the jury is more likely to like you and, by extension, your client. If the jury sees you treat the judge with disrespect, the jury is less likely to like you and, by extension, your client. Thus, treating the bench with proper respect during trial is the best way to be a zealous advocate for your client.

I have been told judges talk about attorneys behind closed doors. I have no knowledge if that is true and doubt any judge would admit that backroom chatter impacts any of their judicial decisions. But judges are human. And, if an attorney has a negative reputation with some judges, that is likely to spread to other judges. In other words, incivility in one case can impact you in future cases for years to come.

Lastly, as with opposing counsel, treating the court staff with courtesy and respect is imperative. Judges are far more likely to get angry with a lawyer that mistreats the judge's staff then the judge itself. Even if the judge is not on the bench when it occurs, she will hear about it. Plus, court staff is the gateway to the judge. Attorneys often need things from court staff, so maintaining a good relationship with the judge's clerks can make your life much easier.

## Clients and Prospective Clients Want Civility and Results

A significant amount of my practice deals with representing clients in disputes with their former attorneys, either large-dollar fee disputes or legal malpractice claims. In doing this work, I have noticed a very important trend: Clients rarely sue lawyers they like. This is true even if the results are not as expected.

In my experience, the clients that sue their lawyers (or do not pay their bills) are the ones that feel disrespected or unheard. It is not enough to do the work, send the invoices, and expect payment. Attorneys have an ethical obligation to communicate with their clients, and this where many fall down on the job.

ABA Model Rule 1.4 generally requires attorneys communicate with their clients about significant matters and developments concerning their case. This includes things about what is happening in the case, costs and budgets, legal strategy, and other key matters. It is not just a matter of what you say to the client, but also how and when you say it. Clients want to be a partner in deciding their own legal fate. They are the ones that must live with the results of their cases—not the attorneys who get to walk away and move on to the next case. Therefore, it is important when communicating with clients to engage in a discussion, listen to their ideas, and patiently explain aspects of the legal process they do not understand. If a lawyer tries to dictate legal strategy to the client, the client will not hesitate to hold the attorney liable when things go wrong.

In addition, lawyers tend to forget that legal matters, be it a lawsuit, divorce, or potential criminal liability, can be incredibly stressful for clients. When people get stressed, they can be short, rude, demanding, or even, at times, insulting. While lawyers are not required to—and should not—accept insulting or demeaning behavior from clients, they also should not react to such behavior in kind. Lawyers need to remember the emotional and mental toll the legal process takes on ordinary people. Lawyers need to address such conduct calmly and take the time to explain the process to the client, why things are happening and what limitations exist. Often, the client will calm down and apologize, and the relationship should move forward. If it does not, the lawyer needs to end the relationship. But always, the lawyer should treat the client respectfully and with civility, even if not reciprocated.

Treating clients with civility also helps set the tone and expectations for the entire litigation process. Many clients think they want a "pit bull" to represent them, at least at the beginning of the case, because their goal may be to inflict maximum pain on the other side. This is where lawyers need to step in to set the client's expectations early that the litigation will be conducted with civility and professionalism. This is a lawsuit, not a bar fight. Clients need to understand the difference.

Going back to my belief that clients do not sue attorneys they like; civility and courtesy are in the attorney's own self-interest. This is true for potential clients as well, who have social media and the internet to fight against incivility in lawyers. Unhappy clients, or potential or former clients, can easily jump on a message board and bad mouth you online. Your duty of confidentiality limits your ability to respond. But, if you are polite and courteous when you are declining a case or terminating a representation with a client, that person is far less likely to take to the message boards to complain about the attorney who politely declined to accept their case.

I think most lawyers will agree there is a civility problem in this profession. Yet, most lawyers will also refuse to admit that they treat others discourteously. The problem, at least in most lawyers' minds, is with the other person: "Opposing counsel is a jerk." "My client is an idiot." "The court clerk is rude and angry." "That potential client is crazy." We need to get out of the blaming mindset and focus on how you treat people regardless of how they treat you, because that is all you can control.

Treating all people with civility can open you up to new opportunities, increase your productivity, make you more money, avoid malpractice claims and fee disputes, and generally improve the practice of law. But that is not why you should treat people with civility and respect. You should do it because it is the right thing to do.

# A Case for Civility in the Modern Day

*Hon. Barbara M.G. Lynn (Ret.)*
*and Maya Mallya*

Uncivil behavior plagues our nation, indeed the world. People openly express disdain for one another and permit without disapproval conduct that was once grounds for censure. Mere disagreements explode into threats. The omnipresence of technology and social media has magnified incivility, which has then spilled over into legal discourse. Acerbic emails between lawyers seem to be the norm and are often attached to conflicting motions to compel or for sanctions. This breakdown in civil behavior comes at a cost, for it undermines respect for our profession and our system of justice. Unfortunately, some lawyers believe that civil behavior is a sign of weakness or lack of confidence and that to be adverse means you are hostile.

Pleas for civility in politics and law have become so commonplace that they are often just background noise treated by many as mere nostalgia for the values of a bygone era. Civility is, however, as necessary and relevant today as it ever was. It is worth remembering that incivility and efforts to curb incivility are long-standing American traditions. Outright violence, such as that which occurred at the end of Reconstruction, may have decreased, but poison-pen letters, the casting of aspersions, and general vitriol remain. Before we can discern how to restore and renew civility, it is worthwhile to consider its meaning.

## Civility's Meaning and Origins

Today, "civility" is generally used to mean formality, politeness, and courteousness in both behavior and speech. A straightforward example of civility in the legal profession is the common reference of lawyers to one another in the courts of Britain, Hong Kong, New Zealand, Australia, and Canada. Barristers routinely designate opposing counsel as "my learned friend," thereby recognizing the opponent's training and expressing collegiality and respect. Aspects of historical precedent for civility in the American court system derive from the UK justice system, wherein the social conventions are far more firmly enshrined. Polite address is an obvious form of courtesy, but civility means much more than just being polite. The term "civility" is primarily derived from the Latin *civilis,* meaning "relating to public life, befitting a citizen." It is the treatment by one citizen of another and is fundamental to democracy. Equally important, civility shares the same root as "civilization." As the Institute for Civil Civic Engagement, based at the University of San Diego, expresses it, civility is more than courtesy and politeness; it embodies proper conduct in human relationships through concepts of friendship, altruism, responsibility, dignity, and justice.

What is the origin of such an important kind of behavior? Aristotle saw civility as originating primarily from friendship, but he recognized the existence of a kind of advantageous friendship that combines varying degrees of self-interest with altruism. In contrast, Thomas Hobbes expressed skepticism that humans could genuinely sympathize with others, and instead believed that humans operate purely out of self-interest, with civility arising only from its utility. David Hume, however, found that humans were naturally sympathetic and that reason and custom influence benevolence. No matter the reasoning, as John Rawls put it, in a democratic society, we have a "duty of civility" to the people around us.

Questions of intrinsic human nature will not be resolved with a simple plea for civility. Rather, civility, whether a natural or a learned behavior, whether based on true and genuine empathy or a desire to conform to professional norms, is an essential aspect of citizenship and of the practice of law.

## Can Civility Be Legislated?

Philosophers differ over whether the imperative toward civility emanates from nature or rule; it is not surprising then, that many jurisdictions have attempted to legislate civility by imposing rules or codes. The American Bar Association lists over 100 legal organizations and courts that have adopted nonbinding civility and professionalism codes. In 1887 the Alabama State Bar Association was the first to adopt a code of ethics and the ABA issued its *Canons of Professional Ethics* in 1908. The fact that these were composed so long ago stands as a reminder that navigating civility concerns is a perennial endeavor.

The American Bar Association's Center for Professional Responsibility "provides leadership and guidance to the legal profession and the judiciary by developing, interpreting and promoting the implementation of policies and standards that govern the conduct and regulation of lawyers and judges[.]"[1] The ABA's website also provides a list of all American professionalism codes, standards, and guidance.[2] They generally emphasize the same points: Lawyers owe candor, diligence, and the utmost respect to the judiciary, as well as a duty of courtesy and cooperation to opposing counsel. For instance, the

1. Am. Bar Ass'n, About Us, https://www.americanbar.org/groups/professional_responsibility/about_us/#:~:text=Share:,the%20History%20of%20Professional%20Responsibility (last visited Jan. 22, 2026).

2. Am. Bar Ass'n, Professionalism Codes, https://www.americanbar.org/groups/professional_responsibility/resources/professionalism/professionalism_codes/ (last updated Mar. 2017).

Standards for Civility in Professional Conduct of Idaho state that lawyers "will not request an extension of time solely for the purpose of unjustified delay."[3] The Colorado Principles of Professionalism provide that "A client has no right to demand that counsel abuse any participant in the judicial system or indulge in offensive conduct" as "[e]ffective advocacy requires neither."[4] Other courts and bar associations around the country employ similar language and concepts.

Despite these efforts, incivility persists. The Illinois Supreme Court Commission on Professionalism, in 2021, found in a statewide survey of lawyers that 54 percent of them had recently experienced uncivil or unprofessional conduct from another lawyer. From lawyers interrupting judges or each other, using impolite tone or address, making personal attacks, to ignoring the court's deadlines—there seems to be no shortage of ways to cause annoyance or offense. High-profile examples of needless incivility in the legal profession underscore how ubiquitous the problem is. As lawyers, we have professional obligations to the court and clients, but also to courtesy, justice, humanity, and the rule of law.

## Civility and Advocacy: A Delicate Balance

While some lawyers' conceptions of civility may be shaped by philosophical approaches, it is uncertain to what extent most

3. Idaho State Bar, U.S. Dist. Ct. of Idaho & Cts. of the St. of Idaho, Standards for Civility in Professional Conduct, https://isb.idaho.gov/wp-content/uploads/standards_for_civility.pdf (last visited Jan. 22, 2026).

4. Colo. Bar Ass'n, Colo. Principles of Professionalism, https://www.cobar.org/For-Members/Committees/Professionalism-Coordinating-Council/Principles-of-Professionalism#9712573-colorado-principles-of-professionalism (last visited Jan. 22, 2026).

people are informed about the underpinnings of civility. The average client likely falls into one of two camps, believing either that (1) the best lawyer is the most congenial and respected or (2) the best lawyer is the one who seeks to win at all costs. Lawyers in the first category value civility, while lawyers in the second category view civility either as an impediment or as irrelevant to achieving their objectives for their clients.

The language of most professionalism codes is generally aspirational, and violations of codes are rarely grounds for disciplinary action. A respected lawyer upholds the values of the legal profession and honors the advocate's responsibilities to clients by working toward the best possible outcome. This means balancing zealous advocacy with respect for opposing counsel and the court. Overt personal hostility to opposing counsel likely prevents solutions, leading to delay, cost, and stress to everyone involved. While an uncivil lawyer might engage in such inappropriate behavior in an attempt to win, they must recognize that behaving uncivilly may actually be a lose-lose strategy. The legal sphere is small and lawyers' commitments to honoring their oaths to their clients and colleagues is a significant part of building a reputation as well as gaining and retaining clients. It is a safer bet to maintain a professional, civil demeanor since lawyers rely on a relatively small circle of clients and colleagues and word of mouth for business. Recently, I witnessed an attorney recommend his opposing counsel to a potential client—a dramatic example of how civil behavior led to an unexpected positive relationship.

## The Important Role of Judges

It is important to recognize that judges can be part of the problem or the solution. The Code of Conduct for United States Judges instructs that "a judge should practice civility by being patient, dignified, respectful, and courteous"[5] and hold court personnel to a similar standard of exemplary conduct. The authors tend to believe that judges embody good role models for professionalism and civility, but there are examples of judges participating in uncivil conduct, including using inappropriate language and tone, ridiculing parties and their counsel, and failing to recuse when they have close relationships with counsel or a party. Unfortunately, this type of behavior has an outsized impact in normalizing poor conduct. Canon 1 of the Code of Conduct explains that the reason judges are expected personally to uphold and enforce such high standards of conduct and civility is so that the integrity and independence of the judiciary may be preserved, while enhancing public confidence in the judiciary. As Chief Justice Burger said in an address to the American Law Institute, "Every judge must remember that no matter what the provocation, the judicial response must be a judicious response, and that no one more surely sets the tone and the pattern for courtroom conduct than the presider."[6]

A recent example of judicial incivility occurred when federal judge Stephen J. Murphy III, a Caucasian judge in the Eastern District of Michigan, stated at sentencing that the Black defendant "looks like a criminal to me." Judge Murphy claimed that his remarks were intended to refer to the defendant's conduct, not race, but this comment was found to have violated the defendant's right to due process, since a reasonable observer could construe it as indicative of a racial bias. The defendant's

---

5. U.S. Cts., Code of Conduct for United States Judges, Cannon 3(B)(4), https://www.uscourts.gov/administration-policies/judiciary-policies/ethics-policies/code-conduct-united-states-judges#:~:text=(4)%20A%20judge%20should%20practice,of%20harassment%20of%20court%20personnel (last visited Jan. 22, 2026).

6. Warren E. Burger, *The Necessity for Civility*, 1(1) Litigation 8–63 (1975), http://www.jstor.org/stable/29758176.

sentence and conviction were overturned by the Sixth Circuit and a new trial with a different judge was ordered. The Sixth Circuit noted that "Such remarks are wholly incompatible with the fair administration of justice."[7]

It is essential that judges adhere to the highest standards of conduct in their work, particularly in their public-facing roles, to demonstrate professionalism, fairness, and good judgment to create and preserve public confidence.

## Are Sanctions the Answer?

With incivility being so ubiquitous, it is worth considering whether sanctions should be implemented to punish inappropriate conduct. Discipline for unprofessional behavior can run the gamut of severity. A common refrain from judges is that they are reluctant to sanction rude, uncivil behavior out of justifiable concern that public sanctions can ruin a lawyer's career. But other options, such as a private reprimand, can serve the appropriate salutary impact, without ignoring improper conduct. A probated discipline would allow a lawyer to practice conditionally. An order to take educational programs would also fit the bill. A bar association could also require a lawyer to attend specific programs on ethics, mental health, substance abuse, and the like. A lawyer could be assigned a highly regarded mentor. And, in the most serious cases, a lawyer could be suspended or disbarred. Clearly, a range of possible options would be available to rehabilitate, educate, and discipline lawyers to combat the rampant incivility within our profession.

We should be prepared to endorse a wide range of potential disciplinary measures if incivility continues to threaten our profession. Judges play a key role. While refereeing disputes

---

7. United States v. Liggins, 76 F.4th 500 (6th Cir. 2024).

is tedious and it can be tempting to let a matter of incivility go, this approach excuses bad behavior. Uncivil behavior pays off when lawyers and judges involved take no action. Judges must intervene if appropriate, utilizing whatever disciplinary measures are appropriate for the formality and severity of the offense. Promoting civility continues to reflect a nuanced effort, because express calls for civility are often ignored.

In a framework that views civility as more than just a superficial nicety but as a genuine attitude, violations would prompt rehabilitative and, when necessary, punitive measures for deterrence. This approach is likely to foster constructive dialogue, allowing for the sharing of diverse opinions and difficult conversations in a civil manner.

## The Future of Civility: Everyone Has a Role to Play

Cultivating civility in the legal profession requires adopting a multifaceted approach in which law schools, attorneys, judges, and bar associations all participate in creating a future where civility is not just a social veneer but also a basic expression of a lawyer's character, and the legal field effectively self-regulates violations of these expectations. We deserve to have pride in our profession and to have the trust and admiration of the public. Working together to reduce virulent behavior and reorienting the focus of our advocacy to the merits of our clients' cases is a first step to achieving this worthy goal. Justice Sandra Day O'Connor, in an article in the Washington University Law Review in 1998, noted that civility brings more joy to practicing law, increases the effectiveness of doing so, and improves the public's regard for lawyers.

It can be easy to lose sight of our obligations and the oaths we have sworn as lawyers and judges and it is imperative that we never forget that our democracy depends on our fellow citizens having confidence in us and our work. Uncivil behavior reinforces the worst stereotypes of our profession and betrays our privilege to practice law. We owe it to ourselves, our colleagues, and the public to relentlessly pursue a universal, civil approach that champions the highest ideals of our profession.

# The Necessity of Professionalism in Litigation Today

*Tiffany Rowe*

> [L]awyers who know how to think but have not learned how to behave are [a] menace and a liability, not an asset, to the administration of justice.[1]
>
> — Chief Justice Warren Burger

The legal profession plays a vital role in ensuring the fair and efficient administration of justice, protecting individual rights, and serving the public good. However, in the realm of litigation, one must ask: Is professionalism still alive? Are lawyers still assets to the administration of justice, or is there such a decline in the professional conduct of litigators that they are now a hindrance? And if they are a hindrance, how can we restore professionalism not only to preserve the integrity of the legal system but also to serve the public better and ensure justice is delivered efficiently?

In a 1955 South Carolina Law Review article, Judge John J. Parker, former Judge of the U.S. Court of Appeals for the Fourth Circuit reminds us:

---

1. David A. Grenardo, *A Lesson In Civility*, Geo. J. Legal Ethics 135, 150 (2019) (quoting *Excerpts from the Chief Justice's Speech on the Need for Civility*, N.Y. Times, May 19, 1971, at 28).

> [T]he practice of the law is a profession—not a business or a skilled trade. While the elements of gain and service are present in both, the difference between a business and a profession is essentially this: the chief end of a trade or business is personal gain; the chief end of a profession is public service.[2]

Parker further writes, "This is the function of the lawyer, his reason for existence—not primarily to make money or to assist other men in their personal struggles or difficulties, but to give peace and order to society."[3] The practice of the profession is not limited to his client; "it involves three fundamental relationships: his relation to his client, his relation to the law and his relation to the community in which he lives. The standards of the profession grow out of these relationships."[4]

Striking this balance is particularly challenging for litigators. Litigation is by definition an adversarial process where opposing perceptions of a situation drive interaction between counsel for the parties. It is easy for clients' emotions to run high, and lawyers are also not immune to responding to emotion and layering the emotion onto the zeal that motivates advocacy at every step of the litigation process. For this reason, it is not left to the individual lawyer to decide whether to treat others involved in the judicial process in accordance with professionalism and ethics; codes of conduct and professionalism require lawyers to show respect and act with civility while interacting with everyone involved in the judicial process, as each person is indispensable to the proper functioning of an efficient judicial system and must be treated as such.

---

2. *Id.*

3. *Id.*

4. Will Sylianteng, *Is Professionalism and Civility in the Legal Profession Dead?*, THE LEGAL INTELLIGENCER (Sep. 8, 2022) (quoting John J. Parker, *A Profession Not a Skilled Trade*, 8 S.C.L.Q. 179 (Winter 1955)).

## Civility as a Core Aspect of the Profession

> Life is about manners and courtesies and things that make life a little bit less stressful and less hard to take. Life is hard enough as it is.[5]

Although it may seem counterintuitive, the best way to serve a client's needs is to maintain a professional character and reputation and to respect the character and reputation of others, which is why civility and professionalism are crucial components of our daily work as stewards of proper legal representation. Civility in this context refers to "the courteous and respectful behavior exhibited by legal professionals throughout their practice."[6]

Civility and mutual respect enhance communication and coordination for the benefit of the clients and the public, promoting trust among lawyers and leading to better, more efficient outcomes for individual clients. "Professionalism also ensures that lawyers can collaborate effectively, fostering a cooperative atmosphere where legal issues are addressed efficiently."[7]

Admittedly, there is a challenge because the legal system is built upon opposing parties making their case to an impartial judge or jury as they advocate for the clients' best, most just outcome—as to which each has a different perspective. Nonetheless, it is possible to have a passionate presentation of the case by both sides without personal attacks or disrespectful behavior. Disagreement with opposing counsel is unavoidable in litigation. But courtesy does not need to fall victim to

---

5. Jill Switzer, *Incivility and Rudeness in the Legal Profession*, Above the Law (Oct. 31, 2018), https://abovethelaw.com/2018/10/incivility-and-rudeness-in-the-legal-profession.

6. *The Importance of Civility in the Practice of Law*, Advocate Mag. (July 2023), https://www.advocatemagazine.com/article/2023-july/the-importance-of-civility-in-the-practice-of-law.

7. *Id.*

zealous advocacy. Those who are disrespectful or attacking risk alienating the judge or arbitrator as much as they risk offending the other party. Accordingly, the more we pursue a collegial discourse, the better suited we are to represent our clients and our profession in the courts and the eyes of the public.

## The Power of Professionalism

Although much of the focus in discussions of professionalism is on its effect on others, it is also a crucial means of mitigating the emotional toll for clients and is critical to a lawyer's own mental and emotional well-being. Professionalism "reduces stress levels among lawyers, allowing them to approach their work more effectively and efficiently."[8] Lowering the temperature in a heated dispute not only insulates clients from the bad behavior of other lawyers but minimizes its impact for ourselves.

Professionalism requires more from lawyers than "civil" behavior: It requires a commitment to competence, integrity, and ethical decision-making that recognizes that unprofessional conduct harms everyone—including bystanders, who lose trust in a system that seems filled with bullies, aggressive or untruthful lawyers who will do anything to "win" for a client.[9]

Because professionalism is an essential part of a lawyer's identity, and that identity doesn't turn off after hours, civility should be in mind when lawyers are on the sidelines of a kid's baseball game. Or in line at the grocery store. Or in rush hour traffic. Anonymity does not nullify the standards of civility that lawyers should adhere to.

---

8. *Id.*

9. Jeanne Huey, *The Power of Three: Civility, Professionalism, and Zealous Advocacy*, Ethics & Professionalism (Nov. 5, 2024), https://www.americanbar.org/groups/litigation/resources/newsletters/ethics-professionalism/power-three-civility-professionalism-zealous-advocacy/.

## The Importance of the Rules

The rules of professionalism and ethics that are issued by state bars, courts, and legal associations provide guidance on how to maintain professionalism and avoid unnecessary distractions from legal representation. There are many rules specifically aimed at litigation. For instance, the American Bar Association's Model Rules of Professional Conduct Rules 3.1 through 3.9 address the conduct of a lawyer as an advocate. ABA Model Rule 3.3 requires a lawyer to act with candor toward the tribunal and avoid knowingly making false statements, failing to disclose controlling legal authority, or knowingly offering false evidence.[10] Rule 3.4 places similar obligations on lawyers when interfacing with the opposing party and opposing counsel.[11]

A majority of state and county bar associations have also published professionalism codes. For example, the preamble to the Civility and Professionalism Guidelines of the U.S. District Court for the Central District of California highlights the essential role of professionalism and civility in the administration of justice:[12]

> Uncivil behavior does not constitute effective advocacy; rather, it serves to increase litigation costs and fails to advance the client's lawful interests. Perhaps just as importantly, this type of behavior causes the public to lose faith in the legal profession and its ability to

---

10. Model Rules of Pro. Conduct r. 3.3.

11. The rule articulates several unethical acts that may occur during discovery, in pretrial procedure, and at trial, some of which can lead to disciplinary action.

12. *Preamble*, United States District Court for the Central District of California, Civility and Professionalism Guidelines, https://www.cacd.uscourts.gov/attorneys/admissions/civility-and-professionalism-guidelines (last amended Jan. 10, 2020).

> benefit society. For these reasons, we find that civility and professionalism among advocates, between lawyer and client, and between bench and bar are essential to the administration of justice.[13]

Some states have done more. In 2004, the South Carolina Supreme Court took a proactive step to encourage civility by revising the oath that attorneys must take when joining the bar. The revised oath requires lawyers to commit to treating judges, court staff, opposing parties, and their counsel with civility, fairness, and integrity—specifically stating that this commitment applies not only during courtroom proceedings but also in all forms of communication, both written and spoken. The court also updated its disciplinary rules to provide that breaking this civility commitment could lead to disciplinary action. Following South Carolina's lead, the Supreme Court of Florida implemented a similar pledge in 2011, and California's Supreme Court did the same in 2014.[14]

This indicates a shift from a basic moral approach focused on avoiding deception toward a more holistic standard of honesty that also emphasizes mutual respect and civility.

## Civility Promotes Efficiency

Justice Sandra Day O'Connor was of the opinion that a lawyer's satisfaction with the practice of law and the effectiveness of the justice system is buoyed by good manners, discipline, and civil behavior.[15] In contrast, incivility escalates minor disputes,

---

13. *Id.*

14. Jayne R. Reardon, *Civility as the Core of Professionalism*, Bus. L. Today (Sep. 18, 2014), https://www.americanbar.org/groups/business_law/resources/business-law-today/2014-september/civility-as-the-core-of-professionalism.

15. Grenardo, *supra note 1*, at 138.

transforming routine procedural issues—such as ordinary discovery disagreements—into protracted and costly conflicts. It can also have more severe implications that are time-consuming and unpleasant for clients and courts. Indeed, a lack of civility affects more than the outcome of an individual case: Increased costs for an individual client, negative perceptions of the lawyer from others in the legal field, and an erosion of the public's perception of lawyers generally threaten the legal profession by degrading its reputable and honest foundations into nothing more than a capitalist business.[16]

For example, the absence of civility and professionalism of Attorney Robert L. McKenna III[17] cost a client a favorable verdict. McKenna was counsel for defendant, a gastroenterologist, in a medical malpractice suit alleging that the doctor negligently inserted a feeding tube into his patient that allegedly pierced the patient's colon, leading to an infection that resulted in his death. McKenna gloated after winning the case and made statements implying that the case was won *in spite* of the facts and calling into question the reliability of a death certificate issued by the county coroner's office. (The Orange County coroner's office confirmed that the injury and resulting infection was the cause of death.) The video of McKenna was posted on the firm's social media account. This spectacle of a victory lap led the plaintiff to file a motion for a new trial.[18] Plaintiff's motion pointed out that the gloating and bragging excluded any "mention [of] justice or righteousness or a

---

16. John J. Parker, *A Profession Not a Skilled Trade*, 8 S.C.L.Q. 179, 182 (1955).

17. Debra Cassens Weiss, *Backlash Follows Lawyer's Recorded Celebratory Comments About How He Won His Case*, ABA J. (June 7, 2022), https://www.abajournal.com/news/article/backlash-follows-lawyers-recorded-celebratory-comments-about-how-he-won-his-case.

18. Sylianteng, *supra* note 4.

search for the truth" and that it "implies that the truth does not matter—only winning matters."[19] The court granted a new trial.

## Professionalism Must Be Practiced—and Passed On

Experienced attorneys are responsible for ensuring that others in the profession adhere to professional standards, written and unwritten. Supervising attorneys and partners within a law firm must ensure that all lawyers at that firm conform to the Rules of Professional Conduct.[20] Often, the best way for a young lawyer to learn professionalism is to see it modeled by more experienced colleagues. There are movements to broaden law school instruction beyond the Model Rules of Professional Conduct to prepare young lawyers better to face a highly competitive, stressful, and demanding profession. Teaching law students how to conduct themselves in the face of hostility is as necessary as it is to teach the practice of law itself.

The Washington, DC, Bar publishes Voluntary Standards of Civility in Professional Conduct (Voluntary Standards),[21] which stress not only the obligations of lawyers but also the importance of teaching the Voluntary Standards to law students and new lawyers; they "should be incorporated as an integral component of the teaching of professionalism to law students and practicing lawyers alike." The Voluntary Standards emphasize that this responsibility falls not only to law schools but also "the District of Columbia Bar, the voluntary bar associations, law firms, government agencies, and other legal institutions in

19. *Id.*

20. Model Rules of Pro. Conduct r. 5.1.

21. *D.C. Bar Voluntary Standards of Civility in Professional Conduct*, DC Bar.org, https://www.dcbar.org/for-lawyers/legal-ethics/d-c-bar-voluntary-standards-of-civility-in-profess.

our community to teach and promote these standards as part of their continuing legal education programs."

One of the many reasons that teaching and modeling civility in the legal profession is so important is because law serves as "the life principles of society,"[22] and those principles are ever-changing as society evolves and focuses on improving diversity, inclusion, open-mindedness, and mutual respect. If these principles are not taught in law school and reiterated and modeled thereafter by supervisors, mentors, and colleagues, we will be held responsible for the public's perception of the entire judicial system.

## Conclusion

Media frequently portrays lawyers as self-serving and cutthroat bad guys, an image that, unfortunately, is not wholly undeserved. It is up to each of us, in our dealings with clients, with our colleagues, with our mentees, with the legal system, and with life, to demonstrate that advocacy, truth, and justice are the hallmarks of law and that the profession of law pursues them diligently—and civilly.

---

22. Parker, *supra* note 16.

# Professionalism in Negotiation: The Skill That Makes the Difference

*Jeanne M. Huey*

> Discourage litigation. Persuade your neighbors to compromise whenever you can. Point out to them how the nominal winner is often the real loser—in fees, expenses, and waste of time.[1]
>
> — Abraham Lincoln

Lawyers often see themselves as warriors in the courtroom and strategists in legal disputes. Still, our role as negotiators—the third hat we wear alongside advocate and advisor—is too frequently neglected or delegated to a hired mediator. This is a mistake. We cannot help our clients achieve their goals if we always stand in perfect opposition to the other parties in a lawsuit or transaction and are unprepared to advance our clients' interests through direct negotiation when the opportunity arises.

Our clients often believe a good lawyer is merely a fighter. They may mistake a show of belligerence and force for effective negotiation on their behalf. It is up to us, as lawyers, to explain the strategic value of negotiation done early and well:

---

1. Abraham Lincoln, *Notes for a Law Lecture*, *reprinted in* Collected Works of Abraham Lincoln, Vol. 2 (Roy P. Basler ed., 1953).

quicker resolution, lower costs, and greater control of the process. When we persuade our clients at the start of a matter that negotiation is one of many tools we use to help them, we allow ourselves to pursue multiple means of achieving their goals rather than being bound by their preconceptions about how we do our job.

Mediators can help—of course—but they're not a replacement for lawyer-driven negotiation. When attorneys defer too much to neutrals, they give up strategic control. The best resolutions often come from lawyers who are knowledgeable about the law, understand the case, and are prepared to lead the process themselves.

## Negotiation and the Rules

> Craft is the vice, not the spirit, of the profession. . . .
> Truth and integrity can do more in the profession
> than the subtlest and wiliest devices.[2]

The role of negotiation in legal ethics has evolved significantly over time, especially in how lawyers are expected to balance their duties to clients with broader principles of fairness and professionalism. The 1908 Canons of Professional Ethics emphasized the idea that lawyers should not simply follow their clients' demands, but should also be guided by their own moral compass and exhibit "candor and fairness" in dealing with other lawyers.[3]

---

2. James M. Altman, *Considering the A.B.A.'s 1908 Canons of Ethics*, 71 FORDHAM L. REV. 2395 (2003) (quoting Edward G. Ryan, p. 117).

3. *Id.* (Canon 15, p. 123; Canon 22, p. 124).

This notion was a precursor to modern ethics rules regarding negotiation: The Preamble to the current ABA Model Rules reminds us that a lawyer, as a negotiator, "seeks a result advantageous to the client but consistent with the requirements of honest dealings with others"[4] underscoring the value of honesty in negotiations.

Ambrose Bierce defined a lawyer as "one skilled in circumvention of the law."[5] It was not intended as a compliment. It still resonates because it captures a persistent problem in the legal profession: the confusion between technical rule-following and true professionalism.

There is no shortage of publications parsing the ethics rules and advising lawyers about negotiation tactics and strategies that skirt the line of a rule violation but do not cross it. However, negotiation, like everything else we do for our clients, isn't about clever maneuvers or subtle deception; as the quote above reminds us, trickery isn't a mark of professional skill—it is a betrayal of it.

Professionalism in negotiation means more than merely complying with the rules—the rules are the minimum standard, not the ultimate goal. When fully employed in all of its aspects, professionalism helps lawyers go beyond just finding legal loopholes—it provides the foundation for effective and competent negotiation. Professionalism requires honesty, integrity, and trust, and when lawyers lead with these values, the ethical boundaries regarding what can and cannot be done in negotiation are made clear.

---

4. Model Rules of Pro. Conduct, Preamble & Scope.
5. Ambrose Bierce, The Devil's Dictionary (c. 1911).

## Negotiation and Honesty

> Resolve to be honest at all events; and if in your own judgment you cannot be an honest lawyer, resolve to be honest without being a lawyer.[6]
>
> — Abraham Lincoln

The formal obligation of honesty is just one part of the larger obligation of professionalism in negotiation. Honesty in negotiation means presenting facts and intentions truthfully and clearly. It is the bedrock of a lawyer's credibility. Without it, any short-term advantage gained through deception is almost always outweighed by loss of trust and long-term reputational harm.

The words of 1906 may sound old-fashioned, but they are still valid today: "It is unprofessional and dishonorable to deal other than candidly with the facts."[7] Negotiation is all about creating a relationship between two parties. While that relationship may be formalized in an agreement, it requires a foundation of honesty to have any hope of success.

The ABA Model Rules of Professional Conduct, particularly Rule 4.1, underscore the importance of truthfulness in statements to others. Lawyers are prohibited from knowingly making false statements of material fact or law to third parties.[8] While certain statements in negotiation, such as price or value estimates or a party's intentions regarding settlement, are not considered material facts under the rules,[9] affirming falsehoods

6. Abraham Lincoln, *Notes for a Law Lecture*, *reprinted in* Collected Works of Abraham Lincoln, Vol. 2 (Roy P. Basler ed., 1953).

7. James M. Altman, *Considering the A.B.A.'s 1908 Canons of Ethics*, 71 Fordham L. Rev. 2395 (2003) (Canon 22, p. 124).

8. Model Rules of Pro. Conduct r. 4.1(a).

9. *Id.* r. 4.1 cmt. 2.

or omitting key facts can be material and, therefore, an ethical violation.[10]

However, knowingly misstating the existence of another offer or concealing facts that create a false impression during negotiation is not mere "puffery." It is deception—and it's almost certainly unethical. ABA Formal Opinion 06-439[11] confirms that while lawyers may offer optimistic predictions, they must not knowingly lie about material facts.

## Negotiation and Integrity

> A lawyer, without the most sterling integrity, may shine for a while with meteoric splendor; but his light will soon go out in blackness of darkness.[12]
>
> — George Sharswood

Popular culture has glamorized intimidation and threats between lawyers who fiercely advocate for their clients' interests. Still, effective negotiation is about discipline, not dominance, and discipline can be maintained only on a foundation of personal integrity. Integrity—the combination of honesty and discipline—is essential in negotiation to prevent the process from going off the rails.

Discipline requires preparation, which sharpens a lawyer's understanding of risk and potential outcomes and helps shape their legal and negotiation strategy. If all we know is what our client wants, we will have few tools other than bullying or

---

10. *Id.* r. 4.1 cmt. 1.

11. ABA Standing Committee on Ethics & Prof. Resp., Formal Op. 439 (2006).

12. George Sharswood, *An Essay on Professional Ethics* (5th ed. 1896) (Project Gutenberg eBook Released Aug. 20, 2007 [eBook #22359], p. 30)).

dishonesty to help achieve their goals. Preparing with negotiation in mind from the start of a representation leads to the kind of focused analysis that helps negotiations succeed.

For example, if we understand the opposing party's reasons for their position, we can more effectively evaluate the risks and costs involved for both parties. Going one step further—if we also understand the opposing lawyer's personality, we can accurately interpret their behavior and communicate with them more productively. When we prepare thoroughly in this way, we can engage constructively and with integrity, rather than wasting time with grandstanding and gamesmanship.

## Negotiation and Trust

> The most important thing in negotiation is trust.
> If you don't have that, everything else falls apart.[13]
>
> — Roger Fisher

Trust is the unseen leverage in negotiation that allows the process to progress. Others give it to you after you've shown consistent honesty and integrity. We all know from our reactions to dishonesty that it makes negotiation more difficult, so we should also understand that matching the opposing lawyer's dishonesty with our own will never benefit our client in the long run.

Trust must be earned—it cannot be conjured in the moment. And, once gained, it must be jealously guarded. Even one lapse—misleading opposing counsel, bluffing beyond credibility, or breaching a commitment—will diminish our ability to serve our clients effectively. Word will inevitably get around,

---

13. Roger Fisher & William Ury, Getting to Yes: Negotiating Agreement Without Giving In (3d ed. New York: Penguin Books, 2011).

and, for lawyers, reputation matters. Even in the most challenging negotiations, lawyers who build and maintain trust will find that they are able to advocate more effectively for their clients.

## Professionalism: The Skill

> So let us begin anew—remembering on both sides that civility is not a sign of weakness, and sincerity is always subject to proof. Let us never negotiate out of fear. But let us never fear to negotiate.[14]
>
> — John F. Kennedy

Professionalism in negotiation is the sum of a lawyer's conduct, character, and competence. When faithfully employed, it's what moves negotiation from posturing to possibility. For lawyers, it means having the ability and discipline to control the tone of conversations, avoid unnecessary hostility, and allow dialogue even when no one can agree on a single fact and tensions run high. Professionalism requires lawyers to separate strategy from ego and purpose from emotion. Every lawyer should see effective negotiation as a standard for professional excellence. This means teaching negotiation to law students not just as a simplified version of advocacy or a set of memorized strategies and theories aimed at avoiding a technical rule violation. Instead, it should be taught as a proactive effort necessary to promote our clients' interests that requires thorough preparation and the full use of our emotional and intellectual capacities.

---

14. *Inaugural Address of President John F. Kennedy* (Jan. 20, 1961), John F. Kennedy Presidential Library and Museum, https://www.jfklibrary.org/archives/other-resources/john-f-kennedy-speeches/inaugural-address-19610120.

The heart of effective negotiation is professionalism, not tactics. Honesty is the starting point. Integrity sustains it. Trust moves it forward. Professionalism ties them all together. Lawyers who lead with these values don't just resolve disputes and make good deals for their clients—they elevate the profession. Let's aim to be counted among them.

# Attorney as Counselor: The Hardest—and Most Rewarding—Role We Have

*Richard M. Hunt*

There are many ways to slice and dice a lawyer's various roles. The ABA Model Rules say we act as advisors, advocates, negotiators, and evaluators, but we really have only two jobs. We stand beside our clients against the world as advocates and sit opposite them, advising them about the world as counselors. Counselor is the more difficult of these jobs because it requires us to step outside the comfortable world of legal issues defined by a specific legal conflict and apply all our life experience and intellect to help our clients understand what they want and figure out whether the law provides the tools required to achieve that.

## Being a Counselor: More Than Knowing and Applying the Law

As advocates, our job is defined by an us versus them conflict. It may be a polite effort to find a win-win in a business deal or a bitter fight to keep someone out of jail (or put someone in jail), but the goal is usually clear: Use your legal skills to achieve your client's goal in this us versus them conflict. You serve your client, but the focus is on the conflict, and it defines the legal questions you must deal with. As a counselor, on the other hand, your focus is on the client. A client comes with a problem or a goal. They think they have a legal problem or that the instruments of the law will advance their goals. As counselors, we must first determine whether the client has a legal problem. We must step outside the law and the limits of our legal training to get a bigger picture of our client's situation so we can tell them if they've come to the right person. Does this partnership dispute require that the partners sue each other? Or can we, looking at the facts and having some experience with the expense and bitterness of litigation, help our client explore ways to resolve the situation that lies outside the narrow realm of legal remedies? The adage "if all you have is a hammer, everything looks like a nail" reminds us that as counselors, we must think about every tool that might help our client, not just the hammer we learned about in law school. Our best advice to a client may be that they don't need us at all.

Even in those "us versus them" situations where our client's immediate interest is obviously adverse to that of an opponent—as, for example, when the client is a defendant in a lawsuit—our role as a counselor requires that we consider and present alternative courses of action to our client. A client, offended and angry by the injustice of the claims against them, may wish to adopt an expensive, no-holds-barred litigation posture. The lawyer knows that eventually the client will tire of paying legal fees or recognize their actual risk and want to settle the case. As advocates, we are willing to fight, but as counselors, we must use our experience to help clients understand that despite their immediate desire to fight, an early settlement may be in their best interest. This may not be an easy conversation, and our self-interest can make it hard for us to recognize that the best course of action for our client is not the most profitable for us. Nonetheless, we are counselors, not torpedoes, and our duty of loyalty to our clients often means helping them find a way to spend less money on us and more on some alternative resolution to a dispute.

Using our experience to help our clients may also mean acting as an advisor on matters that are not, strictly speaking, legal. Lawyers often tell clients that a certain decision "is a business decision" outside the scope of their legal training. Stepping aside from giving nonlegal advice is the right thing to do when the lawyer has only knowledge of the law to offer. On the other hand, as lawyers gain experience, they inevitably gain knowledge about matters that are not strictly legal. The most valued lawyers in many business negotiations can advise on business and legal matters because they have more experience with the kind of transaction in question than their client. When we call ourselves "attorneys and counselors," we offer our clients all our knowledge and experience, not just our knowledge of the law. We must be careful to recognize the limits of our nonlegal knowledge, but we cannot pretend that we know nothing of the world beyond the law if we are to call ourselves counselors.

Finally, even the youngest and least experienced lawyer has something to offer as a counselor that falls outside the realm of giving strictly legal advice; that is, objectivity. Our clients' problems are not ours. Good advocacy requires commitment, but at the end of the day, our clients celebrate or suffer the outcome, not us. The battle is ours to fight, but our clients' to win or lose, and we can provide an objective view of the situation that is not available to our clients. No matter how passionately our client believes in their cause we, as counselors, may need to tell them that it is a lost cause. And, by the same token, when they are discouraged, we must, as counselors, make sure they understand the rewards to balance against the risks and costs of the fight. We are not just mirrors for our clients' changing desires and attitudes. We must be as willing to urge them forward as we are to hold them back if our advice is based on an objective analysis of their position.

## Being a Counselor: A Difficult Job

I've spoken of stepping outside the law to see the whole situation of which our client's specific legal problem may be only a part. I've spoken of having an objective view of that situation. Now, we must face the fact that this is far harder to do than to say; in fact, it is harder than any of the intellectual problems we encounter understanding or arguing the law. We practice law while mired in our own personal situation. We have families and friends, and we may be carrying some of their burdens. We have dreams and aspirations we hope the practice of law will fulfill. We have our own problems that may come from our personal lives or our professional relationships. Even if we are not suffering from a diagnosed mental disorder like depression, we all have our moods. Finally, we have clients who do not inspire much desire to help them. Clients come from the entire range of human behavior and are not always nice, honest, or pleasant to be around.

This is where professionalism enters our discussion. Discussions of professionalism often focus on how we treat opposing parties, opposing lawyers, and the court. Must I shake hands with an opposing lawyer who I know is dishonest or has misled the court? Should I delete the first ten drafts of the scorching email I planned to send to my opponent? But professionalism is not just about how we treat opponents and the court. Professionalism is also about how we treat our clients. Professionalism requires that we put aside our immediate feelings, wants, and desires to serve our clients, and professionalism requires that when we are working (you don't have to work 24/7), we devote all our energy to our clients' interests.

I have already mentioned one way we as counselors may have to work against our self-interest: the willing client with a fat wallet who wants to fight but shouldn't. There is, though, a different angle to consider. As lawyers, we have knowledge of the law and legal processes that are superior to those of our clients. The longer we practice, the more that knowledge is enhanced by experience. We like to give advice, and we like for our clients to take it. It makes us feel important and validates our years of training and hard work.

But as our confidence grows, it can become increasingly difficult to remember that our client's understanding of their self-interest may be based on things that would never occur to us. Early in my career, I advised a client that the amount of money they wanted to recover in a lawsuit against a tenant was too small to justify the cost of the litigation. What I did not know, but my client helpfully explained, was that for this apartment complex, allowing one tenant to get away without paying would encourage other tenants not to pay and create a far larger problem. The lawsuit cost was reasonable based on the cost of avoided future losses. I soon had the chance to show off my new knowledge by advising a different client that a lawsuit might be useful to set an example despite the cost. This client explained that failing to pay their bills had never been a problem for his customers. He thought I was promoting expensive litigation for my benefit and made it clear he wanted only a demand letter and whatever benefits that provided. Our desire to be respected and have clients follow our advice can lead us to forget that as counselors, we must have the humility to listen to our clients instead of just telling them what we think they need. As counselors, we can help our clients understand their self-interest, but we should not try to dictate what is in their self-interest.

Humility is challenging for most lawyers, including myself, but an even tougher job is rising above our situation to give our clients the best of ourselves. It is not easy to listen to a client, analyze their issues, help them identify their real goals, and figure out the best way to achieve those goals when you had an argument with your child at breakfast, spilled coffee in your lap at Starbucks, got an audit notice from the IRS, or were wounded by any of the other slings and arrows of outrageous fortune life hurls at us. Nonetheless, to be counselors, we must somehow shrug off life's daily setbacks and insults to keep a clear head and maintain an objective view of our clients and their problems. That may mean deciding today is not the day to meet a new client. But not working is usually not an option and the professionalism of being a counselor includes cultivating the mental toughness necessary to help our clients even when we feel like we need help ourselves.

## We Learned How to Be Counselors in Law School—Even If We Never Took a Class

Experience and age are important for effective work as a counselor, but the basic skills required are taught in every first-year class. Even if we never take a formal course in counseling, law school prepares us to be a counselor because we are trained to do what a counselor must do. The classic law school exam question requires reading a set of facts, identifying the issues and applying the law to resolve the issues. That's what a counselor does. Your client brings you a situation; you identify issues and look for their resolution. The only difference is that as counselors we do not limit ourselves to the facts presented by our client but instead ask questions and listen to see if other facts are relevant or helpful. We also do not limit our consideration of solutions to only those that can be found in the law. Instead of looking at every problem as a legal problem we ask the questions necessary to understand any larger problem in which the legal problem may be imbedded. Once we have identified the problem, we decide whether the problem is one best attacked with the tools the law provides and whether the client's self-interest is truly served by deploying those tools with the attendant expense. As a counselor, we use these skills continuously as a matter develops, and both we and the client gain more understanding of the situation. But no matter what the client or problem, the basic skill is the skill we are taught in law school: identify the relevant facts, identify the issues, and create a plan to resolve those issues in our client's favor. Experience helps, but every lawyer knows how to be a valuable—and valued—counselor if they are only willing to take an expansive view of their client's problems and possible solutions.

## Attorney as Counselor: The Hat You Always Wear

Lawyers are always counselors. Whether we are giving advice, fighting in court, or negotiating a business deal, we have a duty to help our clients understand the nature of their problems and how the legal tools at our disposal may (or may not) help them. It is the hardest work we do because it requires that we listen to our clients with humility and have the courage at times to say we can't help them even when we could use the money. At the same time, it is the most fulfilling work we do because we can be part of the solution for problems no purely legal tool or strategy can solve.

# Lawyers as Fiduciaries: Taking Accountability Seriously

*Susan Fortney*

For decades scholars and commentators have tackled the thorny and slippery concept of lawyer professionalism. Some wax eloquent in discussing the elevated role lawyers play in civil society and the law as one of the learned professions. Others focus more on the applied ethics issues that justify allowing lawyers to benefit from a state-enforced monopoly on the delivery of legal services. This chapter examines both angles in discussing how lawyers' special duties to clients differentiate lawyers from other professionals.

## Lawyers' Special Responsibilities as Fiduciaries

Beginning in medieval times lawyers, along with physicians and clergy, were recognized as members of the learned professions that required specialized knowledge and training to be used in discharging responsibilities to others. In each of these fields, persons served largely rely on the professionals' judgment and expertise because of the asymmetry between the information held by the professionals and others.

Although most professionals must abide by ethics codes and rules of conduct, lawyers exercise a great deal of autonomy in regulating themselves. As compared to other professions, lawyers as fiduciaries also stand in special positions of trust and confidence in fulfilling duties to clients. Clients entrust lawyers with their legal, financial, and personal affairs. In some cases, clients' lives are in their lawyers' hands. Unlike other professionals, lawyers also perform public responsibilities. As described by Professor Robert W. Gordon:

> Law is a service profession; but it is also a public profession. Lawyers are supposed to serve their clients faithfully and zealously; but they also are supposed to work, both on and off the job of representing clients, as counselors, citizens, reformers, community activists, and public servants, to maintain the integrity of the framework of laws, institutions, and procedures that constrain their clients' practices and their own—and not just to maintain that framework, but to help transform it so that it more nearly will approach the conditions of justice and civic community.[1]

Understanding lawyers' special positions and responsibilities to clients and the public helps distinguish how lawyers should approach self-regulation of the profession, as well as dealings with clients and others.

As a starting point, consider the formation of the attorney–client relationship. Prospective clients, regardless of their level of experience or sophistication, retain legal counsel to handle matters that laypeople are unable or unwilling to handle. Once hired, a lawyer assumes the role of fiduciary, "[a] person to whom another person's affairs are entrusted in circumstances that often make it difficult or undesirable for that other person to supervise closely the performance of the fiduciary."[2] Therefore, the Restatement of Law Governing Lawyers explains,

1. Robert W. Gordon, *Corporate Law Practice as a Public Calling*, 49 Md. L. Rev. 255, 255 (1990).

2. Restatement (Third) of Law Governing Lawyers § 16 cmt. b (2000).

"Assurances of the lawyer's competence, diligence, and loyalty are therefore vital."[3] In noting that a "fiduciary relationship creates the highest duty of loyalty known to the law, the Restatement (Third) of Torts: Liability for Economic Harm, simply states, "A fiduciary duty is, in general, a duty to act for the benefit of another on matters within the scope of the parties' relationship"[4] In explaining that lawyers are held to the highest standards of ethical dealings with their clients, court opinions often quote the words of Justice Benjamin Cardozo, who observed that that a fiduciary is held to "something stricter than the morals of the marketplace. Not honesty alone, but the punctilio of an honor the most sensitive, is then the standard of behavior."[5] Applying this standard, one Texas Supreme Court Justice emphasized that lawyers must conduct themselves with "inveterate honesty and loyalty, always keeping the client's best interest in mind."[6]

How do lawyers keep clients' best interests in mind? Professor Neil Hamilton, Holloran Professor of Law and co-director of the Holloran Center for Ethical Leadership in the Professions at St. Thomas School of Law, a leading figure in the professional identity movement, maintains that lawyers and law students must internalize a responsibility to put both the client's and the legal system's interests before the lawyer's self-interests.

---

3. *Id.*

4. Restatement (Third) of Torts: Liab. for Econ. Harm § 16 (2020).

5. Meinhard v. Salmon, 164 N.E. 545, 546 (1928).

6. Lopez v. Munoz, Hockema & Reed, L.L.P., 22 S.W. 3d 857, 866–67 (Tex. 2000) (Gonzales, J., concurring and dissenting).

## Recognizing the Concept of Financial Accountability

One important way of elevating client interests above lawyer self-interests is for lawyers to embrace the concept of financial accountability in their dealings with clients. In the context of lawyer–client relationships and lawyer misconduct, such accountability encompasses lawyers' recognition that they should maintain assets or insurance to compensate clients for losses they suffer due to attorney misconduct. In serving others, lawyers may make mistakes. When they do, lawyers fulfill their duties as fiduciaries by stepping up and being financially accountable to those who trust and rely on them.

In applying risk distribution principles, lawyers and their firms are the actors best positioned to avoid losses they cause and to obtain insurance to cover losses suffered by others.[7] Insurance costs could then be treated as part of the costs of practicing law and be factored into fees charged to clients.[8]

When attorney-fiduciaries do not carry insurance, injured persons may have no recourse because of the economics of legal malpractice cases. Professors Herbert M. Kritzer and Neil Vidmar discuss this problem in their book *When Lawyers Screw Up: Improving Access to Justice for Legal Malpractice Victims*.[9] Through interviews they learned that experienced legal malpractice lawyers almost never agree to handle malpractice

---

7. *See* Susan Saab Fortney, *Mandatory Legal Malpractice Insurance: Exposing Lawyers' Blind Spots*, 9 St. Mary's J. on Legal Malpractice & Ethics 190, 201 (2019) (citing Guido Calabresi, *Some Thoughts on Risk Distribution, and the Law of Torts*, 70 Yale L.J. 499, 500 (1961)).

8. *Id.*

9. Herbert M. Kritzer & Neil Vidmar, When Lawyers Screw Up: Improving Access to Justice for Legal Malpractice Victims (2018).

claims against uninsured attorneys.[10] This poses a particular risk for primarily individuals and small businesses when they hire solo and small firm attorneys who tend to be more likely to be uninsured than lawyers practicing in larger firms.[11] This effectively means that many consumers of legal services will not be able to retain counsel to pursue civil claims against uninsured attorneys, regardless of the extent or amount of their losses attributable to legal malpractice. Moreover, even when the prospective lawyer-defendants carry insurance, experienced plaintiffs' attorneys commonly decline representation unless the claim has significant value to justify handling a complex legal malpractice on a contingency fee basis. In their study, Professors Kritzer and Vidmar learned that the range of minimum thresholds for handling a claim on a contingency fee basis ranged from $100,000 to $5 million for others.[12] This also illustrates how the economics of legal malpractice cases often leave injured persons without a civil remedy.

When consumers of legal services do not have civil remedies, consider whether attorney disciplinary systems provide them recourse. Unfortunately, disciplinary regulators in the United States (U.S.) order restitution in only limited circumstances, such as situations when lawyers have wrongfully withheld or misused funds or property or when lawyers have not

---

10. *Id.* at 148.

11. *See, e.g.*, Attorney Registration and Disciplinary Commission of Illinois, 2023 Annual Report of the ARDC (2003) (reporting registration data revealing that 63.7 percent of solo practitioners reported that they carried malpractice insurance compared to 94.5 percent of lawyers in law firms with two to five lawyers).

12. Herbert M. Kritzer & Neil Vidmar, When Lawyers Screw Up: Improving Access to Justice for Legal Malpractice Victims 147–48 (2018).

earned their fees.[13] Despite the fact that the ABA Commission on Evaluation of Disciplinary Enforcement criticized this and other shortcomings of disciplinary systems in not providing relief to injured consumers of legal services, 30 years later the problem of an inadequate remedy persists.[14] This provides another illustration of how lawyers in the U.S. may not be accountable for their actions as fiduciaries and do not fulfill their fiduciary responsibilities of putting client interests above their own. At a minimum, fiduciaries should stand behind their work, and the legal system and profession should support initiatives to provide injured persons avenues and mechanisms for seeking redress.

## Insurance-Related Requirements That Promote Financial Accountability

Jurists, bar leaders, and lawyers who recognize that fiduciary and professional duties require financial responsibility can look to other countries for models on how regulators and bar associations promote financial accountability and public protection. In the U.S., only Idaho and Oregon require that lawyers in private practice maintain minimum levels of professional liability insurance or its equivalent. By comparison, most developed common law countries outside the U.S., as well as European civil law counties, require lawyers in private practice to carry

---

13. Susan Saab Fortney, *Keeping Lawyers' Houses Clean: Global Innovations to Advance Public Protection and the Integrity of the Legal Profession,* 33 Geo. J. Legal Ethics 891, 909–10 (2020) (citing A.L.R. survey of cases).

14. Raymond R. Trombadore, ABA, *Lawyer Regulation for a New Century: Report of the Commission on Evaluation of Disciplinary Enforcement*, Appendix C (Sep. 18, 2018), https://www.americanbar.org/groups/professional_responsibility/resources/report_archive/mckay_report/.

some form of malpractice insurance.[15] The following excerpt from an International Bar Association study paper outlines key reasons why other countries require insurance:

> The primary reason for mandatory insurance is widely cited as being in the name of public protection and the right to access to remedy. This is seen as protection for clients, not just lawyers. Clients of lawyers and victims of malpractice should have some basis for recovery of damages. Without mandatory insurance, in various cases, the lawyer may not have assets sufficient to satisfy a judgment. In creating a more comprehensive and reliable protection framework for the public and to ensure a healthy lawyer–client relationship, mandatory insurance requirements are viewed as helping to improve public confidence and the overall perception of the legal profession. This will also help to preserve the self-regulatory status of the legal profession as there is less requirement to implement public protection measures through legislative regulation of the profession.[16]

Lawyers from countries requiring legal malpractice insurance may be shocked to learn that most U.S. jurisdictions do not impose such a requirement.

Query why only two U.S. jurisdictions require legal malpractice insurance that is commonly mandated in counties

---

15. Leslie C. Levin, *The Politics of Lawyer Regulation: The Case of Malpractice Insurance,* 33 Geo. J. Legal Ethics, 969, 973 (2020).

16. Int'l Bar Ass'n, International Bar Association Principles on Professional Indemnity Insurance for the Legal Profession 10 (Nov. 3, 2022), https://www.ibanet.org/document?id=IBA-International-Principles-on-Professional-Indemnity-Insurance-for-the-Legal-Profession.

around the world. Case studies conducted by Professor Leslie C. Levin provide some answers. Professor Levin examined how six states (California, Idaho, Nevada, New Jersey, Texas, and Washington) handled the regulation of uninsured lawyers.[17] Based on her case studies, she identified a number of factors that seemingly explained states' handling of "public-regarding" laws related to uninsured attorneys. The first factor Professor Levin identified was the state bars' lack of willingness to support a proposed insurance-related requirement.[18] The experiences in the states where insurance-related requirements were not adopted reveals that state bar leadership, individual lawyers who opposed mandated insurance, and the jurists who agreed with them, apparently do not believe that lawyers, as fiduciaries, have professional duties to be financially accountable when their acts and omissions injure others.

## Regulatory Avenues Providing Alternative Remedies to Injured Persons

Similarly, jurists, regulators, and lawyers in the U.S. appear to be comfortable with disciplinary systems that provide limited restitution to persons harmed by lawyer misconduct. Looking abroad, governing bodies in other countries are increasingly creating avenues for injured persons to obtain restitution without having to file legal malpractice actions. Recognizing the challenges that countless persons face in seeking recovery through the courts, regulatory reforms in other countries now enable aggrieved persons to use administrative channels to

17. *Id.* at 993–1026.
18. *Id.* at 1026.

seek monetary redress for claims, including ones that otherwise would not support the pursuit of a legal malpractice claim.[19]

For example, in the United Kingdom, the office of Legal Ombudsman assists legal service providers and complainants to resolve disputes with speed and informality.[20] In addressing complaints, the Legal Ombudsman may direct the legal service provider to pay compensation and costs of up to 50,000 British pounds.[21] The Legal Ombudsman scheme provides a model for American jurisdictions considering dispute resolution approaches that may include the use of more restitution and monetary relief awards.

In the U.S., efforts to expand restitution and monetary awards through regulatory systems likely will face opposition from lawyers and the organized bar, similar to that expressed in response to mandatory insurance proposals.[22] This points to a fundamental disconnect between rhetoric and actions. Members of the legal profession often espouse commitments to the public good and commitment to clients. At the same time, many of the same lawyers oppose initiatives that promise to provide injured persons more protection and remedies. When pressed, these lawyers may acknowledge that they do not believe that they have professional responsibilities to be financially accountable for their errors and omissions.

19. Saab Fortney, *supra* note 13, at 912–14 (reviewing programs in the United Kingdom and Australia).

20. *Id.* at 912.

21. *Id.* at 913.

22. *See* Saab Fortney, *supra* note 7, at 213–24 (examining arguments asserted in opposition to requiring lawyers in private practice to maintain professional liability insurance).

## Inculcating the Professional Value of Accountability

As a legal educator and empirical researcher who studies legal ethics and legal profession issues, this perspective reflects how law schools and lawyer organizations have failed to inculcate and foster the professional value of accountability. Many students enter law school with preconceived notions of lawyer roles, often shaped by news stories and popular depictions of lawyers on television and in movies. Rather than challenging these images, legal educators may unknowingly reinforce these images by emphasizing the adversarial nature of the lawyering. Professors devote far less attention to examining the position of lawyers as trusted advisors with financial responsibilities to clients. As a result, too many law school graduates enter the profession without internalizing the professional value of responsibility.

From the standpoint of client and public protection the good news is that recent changes to law school accreditation standards now require more attention to professional identify formation. In 2022, the House of Delegates for the American Bar Association (ABA) added the following provision to ABA Accreditation Standard 303(b) that applies to accreditation of law schools: "[A] law school shall provide substantial opportunities to students for . . . (3) the development of professional identify."[23] To provide additional guidance, Interpretation 303-5 states: "Professional identity focuses on what it means

23. Neil Hamilton & Louis Bilionis, *Fostering Law Student Professional Identity in a Time of Instability and Strife*, Legal Evolution (Aug. 28, 2022), https://www.legalevolution.org/2022/08/fostering-law-student-professional-identity-in-a-time-of-instability-and-strife-326.

to be a lawyer and the special obligations lawyers have to their clients and society. The development of professional identity should involve an intentional exploration of the values, guiding principles, and well-being practices considered foundational to successful legal practice."[24]

The book *Law Student Professional Development and Formation: Bridging Law School, Student and Employer Goals* provides a framework, guiding principles, and practical suggestions for supporting professional identify formation.[25] In recommending that practice-like conditions best help students develop professional identity, one author discusses the value of simulations drawn from practice.[26] In my own teaching, I use such a simulation to give the students an opportunity to seriously reflect on the role of lawyer as an accountable fiduciary. Before the simulation, I assign an article in which a former bar president suggests that lawyers and the legal profession do not need public relations to change the negative image of lawyers held by some. Rather, the author urges, "We must remind ourselves from time to time that how we practice law daily, how we deal with our clients, how we serve our community—*these* are what determine how the public will view us. . . . Personal relations, not public relations, is our proper focus."[27] After the

---

24. American Bar Association, 2024–2025 Standards and Rules for Approval of Law Schools, Interpretation 303-5, https://www.americanbar.org/content/dam/aba/administrative/legal_education_and_admissions_to_the_bar/standards/2024-2025/2024-2025-standards-chapter-3.pdf.

25. Neil Hamilton & Louis Bilionis, Law Student Professional Development and Formation: Bridging Law School, Student and Employer Goals (2022).

26. Katherin T. Vukadin, *Outside the Ivory Tower; How Law Students Benefit When Their Professors Revisit Practice*, 102 Or. L. Rev. 313, 323 (2024).

27. Darrell Jordan, *Lawyer Bashing for Fun and Sport: Do Vicious Barbs Miss the Mark?*, 54 Tex. Bar J. 752, 754 (1991).

students read the article, they participate in a partner meeting in which a firm partner admits to other firm lawyers that the partner made a mistake that harmed a client. The firm lawyers and partner discuss whether they should settle the former client's claim or defend it on a "technical" legal basis. Debating whether to settle or fight the claim on legal grounds helps the students see that it is easy to talk about professional obligations, but harder to pay the price when the lawyers' own financial interests conflict with client interests.

Although law schools may use different approaches to meet the new ABA accreditation standard, persons who embrace the fiduciary role of lawyers should urge legal educators to devote serious attention to helping students appreciate the importance of being financially accountable for the quality of their work. Practitioners participating in the teaching and discussions would help make the exploration of professional identity realistic and meaningful. Jurists, legal employers, and bar leaders can also play an important role in socializing lawyers to understand and fulfill their financial responsibilities and obligations. By recognizing and embracing the role of accountable fiduciary, lawyers distinguish themselves from other professionals—making our actions speak louder than words.

# Fostering Civility as Good Lawyering and Good Loss Prevention[1]

*Lucian Pera*

A confession: I generally don't read articles about lawyer civility.

If you share my aversion, make an exception and see if you share my view that, by encouraging more civility in our practices and firms, we can advance our efforts to be better lawyers, to practice more safely, and to engage in better loss prevention.

## The Problem with Articles on This Subject

I avoid articles about lawyer civility for a few reasons.

First, too often they read like lectures from old lawyers lamenting the decline of the profession. As a young lawyer, I resented them; as an old lawyer, I have no interest in either being resented or lecturing to empty rooms. I don't believe the profession is in decline; there were no Good Old Days; and if I die before hearing another old guy decry the coming generation's lack of commitment to core values, I'll die happier.

Second, and perhaps more important, I believe in doing only things that matter and work. I believe lawyers are human;

---

1. An earlier version of this article was published in the Attorneys' Liability Assurance Society's *Loss Prevention Journal* (Winter 2023), under the title "Fostering Civility as Good Loss Prevention."

that humans learn the things that generate innately civil behavior (like empathy) from those they grow up with; and that it's very hard to teach or instill these things after someone becomes a lawyer. If your Mama didn't teach you to be civil, there's not much hope that a law firm or a court can.

Still, on the chance that either someone is listening or that I can add a practical reason to the allegedly noble ones supporting civil behavior, I offer these thoughts as an exercise in hope.

## What's Civil?

Let me pause to outline what I mean by civility.

I think of it as a mindset that, to matter, must show itself in many small ways every day. It is a code that requires we act with respect toward our clients, colleagues, opposing counsel, judges, everyone else involved in the legal process, and our legal institutions as a whole. To be clear, it's not only about how a lawyer treats opposing counsel or courts. No lawyer who is a professional toward opposing counsel and courts but treats her partners and employees as subhuman is worthy of respect, whether as a lawyer or a person.

In my view, civility is a necessary component of professionalism, or at least one facet of the professionalism that many of us revere. This mindset helps us remember the purposes of the law and lawyering, tied so closely to simultaneously serving both clients and the rule of law, whether inside the courtroom or negotiating a deal. It helps us recall that we have to serve values beyond any one client, or case, or deal, and beyond any one interaction with any one lawyer, client, or judge, and beyond our law firm and colleagues.

I locate civility in the aspect of professionalism that drives specific behaviors, large and small. Those include consenting to some extensions or continuances that don't prejudice our client (even when our client might not understand why), trying to schedule in ways respectful of opposing counsel or their clients' needs, and avoiding gratuitously responding to incivility in kind. They include finding artful ways to be both zealous *and* courteous as advocates, in deals and depositions. Haven't we all seen a great lawyer find a way to way to argue to a court the utter falsity of opposing counsel's argument—or even their factual statement—effectively, but without calling her a liar?

As to clients, I include occasionally ignoring a client's angry or unreasonable demands or instructions, at least until more rational conversations can be had. Or delaying emailing bad news to a client already in distress late on a Friday afternoon when a comforting conversation can accompany the news on Monday, and be just as timely.

In this same category have always been basic, Mama-inspired behaviors, like being on time (or early), whether for court, client meetings, or video calls with witnesses or opposing counsel.

## Is Civility Cultural?

While civil behavior by lawyers proceeds from the same kind of empathy as ordinary human civility, I've come to believe there's much more to it.

I've known a few lawyers who are perfect ladies or gentlemen in their practice, but who I have come to learn are perfect jerks to their spouses or children.[2] There are also some groups of lawyers—often in particular firms or practice groups or even whole areas of practice—who do, in fact, continually behave in uncivil (or highly civil) ways to one another, to clients, and to

2. By the way, the ABA Standards and Practices Department forbids me from using the correct technical lawyer term for "jerks." But please mentally substitute it.

courts. Culture in any human group is powerful, and civility can be cultural.

For example, in many communities, the bankruptcy bar is a different world—not perfect, but regular members of that bar in some places behave in a noticeably more civil manner toward each other. Perhaps it's because of the insular, repeat-player nature of their world, or perhaps because so much of what they do is more transactional than adversarial, even when they are in court. Whatever the reason, that standard of behavior can become a cultural norm, enforced by judges and lawyers.

Our local domestic relations bar is different. While some of the most civil and professional lawyers I know do this work, this portion of the bar here in Memphis has a reputation for markedly uncivil behavior amongst their own, in a way noticeably different from the bankruptcy bar and even from divorce lawyers in other Tennessee cities. I cannot explain this, but it's a cultural fact with which lawyers, courts, and clients must contend, often at real cost.

These experiences confirm for me that there is a cultural component of lawyer civility that may well be teachable. There are professional norms about how we behave toward one another, and toward clients and courts, that we do recognize, and can follow, and can enforce. That gives me hope for lawyer behavior, hope that it might be able to be changed, and improved.

So how might we exercise that hope? Can we—and should we—make that a priority in our practices and firms?

## Loss Prevention and Civility

The two law firms I have practiced with have both been members of the same large, old, and venerable mutual lawyer malpractice insurance company.

That mutual company insists that we each have designated loss prevention partners, responsible to the firm and our colleagues for not only claims and their defense but also for aggressively forward-leaning loss prevention work to educate and protect our lawyers. In fact, this company, more than any other, invented loss prevention in law firms and it has a very particular method that all of its loss prevention partners share in their work, and have done for generations now. I have served as one of my firms' loss prevention partners for more than 30 years, and I firmly believe in that method.

This method is founded on the sincere belief—I choose that word precisely—that members share that there is a way to establish, maintain, and continuously improve law firm loss prevention by mutual efforts, working within our firms, with the company, and with our fellow member firms. We learn from each other and spread that knowledge, and perhaps some wisdom as well.

Central to the method is a firm belief that good loss prevention proceeds from particular aspects of good culture within a law firm. As the modern business saying goes: Culture eats strategy for breakfast. We believe culture not only drives success in law firms, but that a certain kind of good culture is foundational to not only good lawyering but also safer lawyering and thus good loss prevention.

For example, we want everyone in the firm—from senior partners to new lawyers to paralegals to IT people—to understand the value of individual firm lawyers and others seeking help *before* a loss prevention crisis. This type of good culture promotes the open and inviting availability of expert help from loss prevention partners (and others) to address problems, and maybe even spot and head them off. And the willingness to seek such timely help has to rest on an avoidance of a blame-driven, scapegoat-seeking culture.

The kind of culture we want internally is fundamentally empathetic. It requires some form of institutional humility (even if lawyers are loath to admit it). And, yes, it requires civility.

If some part of civility is cultural, and this loss prevention method is aimed, at least in part, at shaping and improving our firms' culture, can we tangibly improve the culture of civility in our firm? Yes, we can.

A more important question: Should we? Yes, we should.

And it's hard for me to imagine that a culture of internal civility cannot also be harnessed to drive more civil behavior by a firm's lawyers aimed at the outside world.

## Why We Should Care

I don't need a psychologist or social scientist to offer me proof of the value of greater civility to us as lawyers, to our firms, to our clients, and to our staff.

Lawyers who practice in environments of greater civility among their firm colleagues, as well as with clients, other counsel, and courts, are fundamentally happier, and are able to handle the stress of life and practice better.

As a loss prevention partner, I'm confident that lawyers in a setting of greater civility are less prone to mistakes and poor judgment, and much more likely to surface issues earlier to my firm's loss prevention partners. I'm convinced that an environment where lawyers feel and practice greater civility contributes directly to a positive loss prevention culture.

Enhanced civility should tangibly lower some risks for all of us, and for our clients.

If you doubt this, recall the last time you dealt with your least favorite opposing counsel, or suffered through your most contentious deal. If you had been able to turn down the emotional temperature—perhaps not on substance, but just on routine interactions between parties and counsel—might that have affected the result? Or might it at least have reduced the emotional wear-and-tear on you, your team, and your clients?

I do realize that this is not a matter susceptible to proof, but I choose to believe the only reasonable answer is, Yes.

## Tit for Tat

More tangibly, how many of us can recall instances where uncivil behavior by one lawyer or party has called forth equally or more uncivil behavior in reply. Could that motion for sanctions have been headed off with a phone call, rather than have led to a contentious hearing?

Might allowing the empathetic element of professionalism to silence our lawyer lizard brain have ended a cycle of behavior that did nothing to solve the client's problems?

And we can all remember a client whose demand for scorched-earth tactics produced exactly the bad result we predicted. Who among us doesn't wish, once in a while, that we had done more to quench our client's lust for contentious behavior?

Setting aside lawyer and client mental health, don't we agree that, in some instances at least, encouraging civility in handling client matters can directly lead to lower fees and quicker results, just as we all believe that escalating incivility costs clients money and time?

## What Then Must We Do?

First, in our own individual practices, we should be more conscious and intentional in working toward civility and acting against incivility.

In my experience, behavior that is either uncivil or gives that appearance to others is sometimes the product of our too-immediate response in a world of always-on, relentlessly quick communications. I have no doubt whatsoever that taking the time to be conscious and intentional about the tenor and tone of our conduct, especially our communications, can allow us to practice civility more effectively. In my opinion, that's why God—or maybe Bill Gates?—invented the Drafts folder in Outlook.

When faced with the urge to respond quickly to an incendiary email, go ahead and pound out that immediate response if you like. (It might make you feel better.) But put it in Drafts; walk around your office; get a cup of coffee; and maybe sleep on it. If you are not in the habit of using your Drafts folder this way, try it consciously for a while. (For the mental health corollary to this as a drafting technique, Google "the value of the unsent letter.")

Along similar lines, each of us would do well, when we feel the fierce urgency of an angry email reply, to seek the counsel of others—our partner, our paralegal, our spouse—a two-minute conversation with someone whose judgment we trust can be even more valuable that an overnight rest in the Drafts folder for an intemperate email.

## Avoid Complaints; Give Praise

Second, almost every lawyer is a leader in some setting, however large or small.

We old lawyers need to stop hectoring others about civility, even privately. Instead, we should concentrate on deliberately modeling better behavior ourselves. Most of us learn best by seeing compelling examples by people we know and respect.

We all also need to quietly (or maybe loudly) encourage and praise acts of civility, however small, by those we come into contact with or simply observe.

When a colleague deftly defuses a client's angry outburst before it leads to a bad decision, comment on it to them—or maybe more importantly, to an associate or a partner. When you see a lawyer from another firm gently but effectively take apart an over-the-top sanctions request by opposing counsel while waiting for your own case to be heard, discuss it with your paralegal over lunch the next day. Being an evangelist for civility need not involve lectures about its great value. Remember that some of our most effective teachers have taught us vastly more in parables than sermons.

And lest I be unclear, the youngest, most junior lawyer or paralegal can do precisely the same things to promote civility. I, and many other older lawyers, have learned much from the (supposedly) small or off-hand comments of paralegals and associates. So, on the subject of civility, as on so many other topics, we do well to be our brothers' and sisters' keepers.

## One Last Thing

I counsel a lot of lawyers leaving firms. I counsel them on the rules, and the law, their fiduciary duties and all that, and I advise them to do their best to strictly comply with all those ethical and legal obligations.

I also tell them that, if they need a really tangible reason to hew to the straight and narrow in departing, it's this: Whether they realize it or not, everyone they know at their firm, in the legal community, and among clients is watching their and their firm's behavior toward each other in this awkward period. And both the departing lawyer and the departed firm Will Be Judged.

Lawyers, clients, judges, and others *all* know of the aspect of professionalism we think of as civility. No matter how much some clients will say they want the most aggressive, take-no-prisoners behavior from their lawyers, at the end of the day, they nevertheless know the value that immensely powerful, effective, and civil lawyers bring. And they know this value is fundamentally greater than that of allegedly effective lawyers who are jerks. It's good to be judged for your civility as a professional.

# Chapter 2

## Professional Identity and Responsibility

This chapter turns toward the parts of our work that sit beneath the surface—the pieces of ourselves we carry into every conversation, conflict, and long night at the office. It examines how we make sense of who we are as lawyers, how we respond when the pressure becomes too great, and how much it matters to view the people around us as more than just their roles in a case.

The adversarial system can stretch even the strongest among us, sometimes to a breaking point, and the stories in these pages remind us that none of us gets through this work alone. They show what it looks like when lawyers step in for one another, offer steadiness when someone is struggling, and create room for honesty and compassion in a profession that doesn't always encourage it.

# Legal Ethics, Professionalism, and the Road to Professional Identity

*Teresa J. Schmid*

> Professional identity focuses on what it means to be a lawyer and the special obligations lawyers have to their clients and society. The development of professional identity should involve an intentional exploration of the values, guiding principles, and well-being practices considered foundational to successful legal practice.[1]

## Professional Identity as Mission Statement

In its *Standards and Rules of Procedure for Approval of Law Schools*, the American Bar Association's Section of Legal Education and Admission to the Bar amended Standard 303 to require that law schools provide students with opportunities to develop a professional identity. Such opportunities invite reflection on an important question: Why did I choose law school? If the primary motivation is to make the highest salary in the workforce, the student may regret the choice. According

1. STANDARDS AND RULES OF PROCEDURE FOR APPROVAL OF LAW SCHOOLS, Standard 303, Interpretation 303-5 (AM. BAR ASS'N 2025), https://www.americanbar.org/content/dam/aba/administrative/legal_education_and_admissions_to_the_bar/standards/2025-2026/2025-2026-standards-and-rules-of-procedure-for-approval-of-law-schools.pdf.

to the ABA's 2023 Profile of the Legal Profession,[2] a study of the average industry wage by occupation,[3] on average lawyers make less than medical professionals such as surgeons, family medicine practitioners, and dentists. Furthermore, the practice of law is grueling and demands full mental, physical, and emotional commitment. "The law is a jealous mistress and requires long and constant courtship. This is not to be won by trifling favorites but by lavish homage."[4] Law is a profession, not a career; professional identity is its mission statement.

What exactly is a professional identity? It is the professional self-image that each lawyer adopts, consciously or unconsciously, as a personal brand. It is the lens through which the lawyer chooses to be seen. Standard 303, Interpretation 303-5, is remarkable for this important insight: A strong professional identity is one built on values (ethics), guiding principles (professionalism), and well-being (mindfulness and self-care.) It is the key to success in the practice of law. For litigators especially, a strong professional identity is a competitive advantage.

## The Core Values of Legal Ethics

Responsibilities, not privileges, define the role of lawyers in society:

> Lawyers play a vital role in the preservation of society. The fulfillment of this role requires an understanding by lawyers of their relationship to our legal system. The Rules of Professional Conduct, when properly applied, serve to define that relationship.[5]

---

2. *See ABA Profile of the Legal Profession*, Am. Bar Ass'n, https://www.americanbar.org/news/profile-legal-profession (last visited Jan. 7, 2026).

3. *Id.* (chapter on demographics).

4. Attributed to Supreme Court Justice Joseph Story (1775–1845).

5. Model Rules of Pro. Conduct, Preamble, ¶ 13.

Collectively, the Model Rules are expressions of the core values of the profession. There are as many formulations of core values as there are people who speak of them, yet the elements have remained constant over time. In 2008, past ABA President H. Thomas Wells defined the four core values as: access to justice, independence of the bar and the judiciary, diversity, and rule of law.[6] A lawyer with a strong professional identity embraces the core values and honors the rules by compliance or by legitimate challenge. Following are examples of how the Model Rules reflect the core values:

## Access to Justice

This core value is the lawyer's reason for being, which is to make the legal system accessible. Legal rights that cannot be effectively asserted are not rights. The Legal Services Corporation, a federal agency that advocates for legal aid, defines the gap between the need for civil legal assistance among low-income Americans and the resources available to meet that need as the "justice gap." The LSC defines basic civil legal needs as housing, education, healthcare, income, and safety. In its 2022 report on the justice gap, the Legal Services Corporation noted: "Low-income Americans do not get any or enough legal help for **92% of their substantial civil legal problems**."[7] This value is a commitment to bridge the justice gap. Related Model Rules include the sections on the Client-Lawyer Relationship, Rules 1.2 through 1.18; Counselor, Rules 2.1 through 2.4; Public Service,

---

6. *See* H. Thomas Wells, *Common Core Values*, 33(1) Bar Leader (Sep./Oct. 2008), https://www.americanbar.org/groups/bar-leadership/publications/bar_leader/2008_09/3301/corevalues/#:~:text=The%20profession%20we%20share%20with,a%20difference%20as%20a%20profession.

7. *See The Justice Gap Executive Summary*, Legal Servs. Corp., https://justicegap.lsc.gov/resource/executive-summary (last visited Jan. 7, 2026) (emphasis in the original).

Rules 6.1 through 6.5; Information About Legal Services, Rules 7.1 through 7.6; and Misconduct, Rule 8.4.

## Independence of the Bar and the Judiciary

This value refers to preserving the independence of the bar and judiciary by ensuring that their independent professional judgment is not compromised by outside influences or false or misleading information. The ABA's Division for Public Education notes that "Judicial independence means that judges are not subject to pressure and influence and are free to make impartial decisions based solely on fact and law."[8] It represents lawyers' duty of candor to the courts that prohibits false representations of law or fact. The duty extends to all lawyer-litigants, regardless of whether they initiate or defend against the legal action. Related Model Rules include the sections Advocate, Rules 3.1 through 3.9, and Maintaining the Integrity of the Profession, Rules 8.1 through 8.5.

## Diversity, Equity, and Inclusion

The diversity, equity, and inclusion (DEI) value represents an ideological commitment to equality and inclusion. It is a truism in the DEI community that what is not measured is not valued. The ABA's 2023 Profile of the Legal Profession reported that in 2023, fewer than half of all state bars and licensing agencies tracked race and ethnicity in the legal profession.[9] Ineffective monitoring can only yield suboptimal results; the Profile

8. *See* ABA Division for Public Education, American Bar Ass'n, https://www.americanbar.org/groups/public_education (last visited Jan. 7, 2026).

9. *See* Profile of the Legal Profession 2024, Am. Bar Ass'n, https://www.americanbar.org/news/profile-legal-profession/demographics (last visited Jan. 7, 2026).

also reported that, while the percentage of White lawyers in the profession declined from 88.7 percent in 2013 to 79 percent in 2023, they are still overrepresented as compared to the U.S. population, which is only 75.3 percent Caucasian. Rule 8.4(g) prohibits "harassment or discrimination on the basis of race, sex, religion, national origin, ethnicity, disability, age, sexual orientation, gender identity, marital status or socioeconomic status in conduct related to the practice of law." The rule inhibits intentional bias but does not address implicit bias. So long as the legal profession does not reflect the diversity of the community it serves, it is incapable of fully practicing this value.

## Rule of Law: The Keystone

> For the United Nations (UN) system, the rule of law is a principle of governance in which all persons, institutions and entities, public and private, including the State itself, are accountable to laws that are publicly promulgated, equally enforced and independently adjudicated, and which are consistent with international human rights norms and standards.[10]

The inverse of rule of law is chaos.

## Professionalism Today: Taking a Stand

Where the Model Rules provide minimum standards for lawyers' professional conduct, professionalism focuses on optimal conduct. Law students still in the process of forming a professional identity must consciously decide how their new

---

10. *See* What Is the Rule of Law, United Nations, https://www.un.org/ruleoflaw/what-is-the-rule-of-law (last visited Jan. 7, 2026).

legal personas will behave. In the spectrum of lawyer behavior between junk yard dog and Thurgood Marshall, where will they place themselves? There is a school of thought that confuses bad lawyer behavior with zealous advocacy. That notion is misguided. The fact is that lawyers who impede the legal process with obstructive conduct will find no favor with judges, juries, other lawyers, or the public.

The best and most professional advocacy can also invite retaliation. On March 3, 2025, ABA President Bill Bay released a statement entitled "The ABA Rejects Efforts to Undermine the Courts and the Legal Profession."[11] In it, President Bay protests retaliatory government actions against lawyers and courts who have, while discharging their professional duties, taken positions or issued opinions with which the government disagrees. How well lawyers and judicial officers respond to such attacks depends on the strength of their professional identities: Are they only servants of the law or its champions? In the end, professional identity is about taking a stand: being active, not passive, in living in the persona. For lawyers, the ultimate expression of a professional identity will always require courage.

---

11. *See* American Bar Association,The ABA Rejects Efforts to Undermine the Courts and the Legal Profession (Mar. 3, 2025), https://www.americanbar.org/news/abanews/aba-news-archives/2025/03/aba-rejects-efforts-to-undermine-courts-and-legal-profession.

# Professionalism Across Personality Barriers: The Key to Communication

*Paige L. Adamczyk*

Effective communication is the cornerstone of professionalism for lawyers. It is essential given the diverse personalities that lawyers engage with daily. When interactions falter or misunderstandings arise because of different communication styles and points of view, the journey toward resolution can become challenging and expensive for everyone involved. While all parties are invested in the outcome of each legal matter, as a lawyer, your success in navigating the complexities of a modern law practice largely depends on your ability to comprehend and bridge these differing perspectives.

## Personality Matters

Whether you are a litigator or transactional lawyer, whether you practice criminal law or spend your days drafting wills and estate plans, the success of your dealings with others relies on your ability to tailor communication to the unique personalities of clients, colleagues, and judges. For example, transactional lawyers need to manage and negotiate complex agreements. They need to understand when to push for a concession, when to concede, and when to table a discussion for later. Before the negotiation even begins, they need to fully understand their clients' objectives.

Litigators, on the other hand, benefit from adaptability in their communication approaches when interviewing potential clients, evaluating a client or witness's credibility, and dealing with a less than professional opposing counsel. For litigators, a thorough grasp of behavioral tendencies can enhance jury selection, shape arguments, and refine courtroom tactics. In short, awareness of personality dynamics provides lawyers with the ability to adjust their communication styles to suit their audience and effectively deliver their messages in any setting.

Most of us have heard of the personality-typing protocol—the Myers–Briggs Type Indicator (MBTI).[1] In fact, many people know their exact four-letter MBTI combination off the top of their head and can tell you what it means. However, a newer and somewhat lesser-known model, Shipley's Four Lenses™ (Four Lenses), is helping raise awareness of the benefits of personality typing for legal professionals seeking to improve their communication abilities regardless of their areas of practice.[2]

## Shipley's Four Lenses Overview

The Four Lenses groups individuals into four categories or "preferences," each identified by a color and each with unique traits or "lenses" through which they perceive the world and interact with others.

A *Green preference* typically applies to an analytical, logical, detail-focused individual who thrives on accuracy and evidence. They value factual, well-structured information and may focus more on tasks than relationships and emotions. Because a great deal of precision is required by the profession, lawyers often

1. Myers & Briggs Foundation, https://www.myersbriggs.org.

2. To learn about Shipley's Four Lenses™ Training, visit https://theshipleycompany.com/scfourlenses/fltraining.

have a strong green preference. Lawyers are trained to think in terms of "what they can prove"—an approach that inherently appeals to this personality type.

A *Gold preference* is most common in practical, task-oriented, and realistic individuals. These personalities enjoy clear hierarchies of authority, are meticulous, and are focused on achieving tangible results. Gold lawyers are often efficient and task-driven, excelling in project management, case organization, and meeting deadlines. They are focused on getting things done and are highly effective at it but may overlook the emotional aspects of client interactions.

Both "Golds" and "Greens" prefer straightforward, efficient communication and may be less concerned with theoretical or emotional considerations. A key difference between the two, though, is that while both color preferences value structure and "rules," a Gold will be inclined to honor a rule even if they disagree with the rule in principle and then seek to change the rule itself later and through the proper channels. By contrast, Greens may disregard existing structures/rules if they feel the restrictions do not make sense. While Greens like order, they evaluate everything through their logical framework and only comply with the existing structure when it makes sense to them.

An individual with a strong *Blue preference* is relationally oriented. They care deeply about others' feelings, demonstrate sensitivity and compassion, and may compromise on issues (at their own expense or detriment) to maintain a positive working atmosphere. "Blues" value harmony, empathy, and connection. Blue lawyers are typically supportive and cooperative, making them excellent in roles where personal relationships are essential. They excel in client counseling, mediation, and collaborative negotiations, where building rapport and maintaining harmony are priorities.

*Orange preferences* are usually creative, big-picture thinkers who enjoy innovation and strategy. These individuals are energetic, enthusiastic, and open to novel ideas. Due to their outgoing nature, this personality type is generally well liked. They are active, adaptable, and able to inspire; however, they may be less attentive to details or structure. Orange lawyers are often imaginative strategists, excelling at creating persuasive narratives and examining cases from unique angles. However, they may need support with detail-heavy or highly structured tasks.

Two of the Four Lenses, the *Green* and the *Gold* preferences, are structure-driven personalities. *Blue* preference depicts a relationally focused personality, and *Orange* preference describes an active, unbounded personality. The colors assigned do not mean anything in and of themselves. They could easily have been cat, dog, bird, and fish. What is meaningful is the characteristics of each color. It is important to note that most, if not all, individuals possess some of the colors in varying degrees. This model focuses on an individual's primary orientations and takes into consideration strong secondary characteristics as well.

## Witnesses and Clients Through the Four Lenses

Because Greens are typically unemotional in their decision-making, they make excellent witnesses. They are fact driven, which gives them credibility. This type of witness will not make statements without believing they have supportive evidence or facts to back them up. In depositions, they're likely to focus on what they clearly remember, which can be advantageous for accuracy, but they are not verbose so they may require encouragement to expand on the larger context of their knowledge.

Golds are similar in this respect. They are practical witnesses and will likely recall key facts; however, they may skip over details they view as unnecessary. They often must be encouraged to elaborate. They will respond well to straightforward questioning and may become frustrated with hypotheticals or abstract inquiries.

While both Greens and Golds could be excellent witnesses given their logical, factually driven nature, likeability can impact how jurors respond to a witness. Therefore, it may be necessary to encourage these kinds of witnesses to emote when possible and appropriate to enhance their relatability.

Unlike the practically oriented Greens and Golds, Blue witnesses are likely to focus on social dynamics and relationships rather than strict facts. They often recall events in terms of their impact on people and may need guidance to focus on objective details. They are inherently likable and relatable; however, their testimony may fall flat to a jury comprised mainly of individuals with Green and Gold preferences. To ensure that a Blue witness is effective, it is essential to help them focus on delivering information that is supported by the facts, not solely emotional conclusions, and to do so concisely.

Orange witnesses might recall events in a generalized or thematic way, sometimes inferring motives or focusing on overarching themes. They may require redirection to stick to specifics. They will typically captivate the jury, at least initially; however, they are also prone to "going rogue" and down rabbit holes if left unchecked. These are big personalities, so before putting an orange witness on the stand it is important to prepare them so that they can stay focused on the questions asked and give direct thorough answers rather than positing alternate theories.

As clients, both Greens and Golds like direct, concise communication. Additionally, both prefer to know what they are up against and to face it directly; setting realistic expectations with

Greens and Golds may be easier than with Blues and Oranges. Their reactions are typically measured, practical, and solution oriented. Greens may focus more on the evidence and process, while Golds may focus more on practicalities like cost, time, and outcome, but both clients are logical, practical, and not predisposed to extreme emotional reactions.

A key difference between the two personalities arises, however, when trying to direct a Green or Gold as to legal strategies. A Gold will typically defer to their lawyer's expertise, skill, and professional judgment, whereas a Green may be more inclined to challenge their lawyer's thinking.

Greens prioritize information, detail, and well-founded explanations. They are also procedurally and technically oriented by nature, so they may ask numerous questions, seeking clarity as to each step of the legal process. To communicate with Green clients, be prepared to provide support to validate your proposed strategy and legal theories.

Golds appreciate an efficient, no-nonsense approach. To communicate effectively with them, focus on the results and avoid sharing unnecessary details. Additionally, Golds value efficiency, so concentrate on providing straightforward, concise information and answers to avoid them growing impatient.

As clients, Blues appreciate empathy and reassurance. They want to connect with their lawyers, they value trust above all else, and they will go above and beyond for their legal team once that trust is established. They may be concerned with their case's potentially negative impact on relationships, particularly in emotionally charged cases like family law or employment issues. To communicate effectively with Blue clients, it is necessary to communicate with warmth, to show empathy, and to build trust. Using taxonomy focused on collaborative language and demonstrating a focus on preserving relationships is also helpful. Most importantly, whenever possible, use a positive tone. When setting expectations, do so sensitively and demonstrate an understanding of potential emotional consequences. Reassure them of the legal process and provide consistent updates to maintain rapport. Blues can process difficult information, but it should be delivered as gently as possible from a lawyer that they trust.

Orange clients are often naturally drawn to Orange lawyers. Orange clients may struggle with lawyers of any other color preference. As with Gold lawyers, they may struggle to communicate because they will not have patience for the very structured, practical approach. Where Golds value efficiency, that is not an Orange client's focus. Orange clients do not want to hear all the details that a Green lawyer will share and are likely to be impatient with the Blue lawyer's desire to connect and build a relationship. They are drawn to big-picture solutions, dynamic personalities, and innovative approaches. They are primarily concerned with the outcome of a case and are not typically interested in the details of the process. To communicate with Orange clients, highlight innovative solutions and focus on the bigger picture. Also, as Oranges are typically creative, use creativity to engage them and obtain their input whenever possible.

## The Four Lenses in Action

The Four Lenses can be a powerful tool to help lawyers navigate different personality types encountered in their practice. Understanding them can provide lawyers with a clear framework for adapting to communication barriers, especially in high-stakes interactions.

For example, consider the scenario of a transactional lawyer, Jane, representing an Orange client whose tech startup is in contract negotiations with a large corporation. The corporation is represented by a Gold opposing counsel. As a reminder, the

Orange client is focused on the big picture and the outcome but is not interested in the details. The Gold opposing counsel, by contrast, is consumed with the details and no agreement will be reached unless the details are addressed.

Immediately, there are some inherent conflicts in this scenario. Jane's client is excited about the potential of the partnership but is not focused on specific terms and does not want to be bothered with them. By contrast, opposing counsel is highly focused on the some very specific terms, like deadlines and cost controls. Obviously, Jane must get her client to consider the specific terms or the negotiation will fail.

Jane knows her client values big-picture solutions, so she can use that understanding to help her direct her client's focus towards the details. She can bring each contract term into her client's purview by framing it within the client's overall business strategy and pointing out how specific clauses will support the client's long-term goals.

Next, Jane must communicate with the Gold opposing counsel. For areas where Jane is seeking concessions, she should focus on presenting precise terms for each point of negotiation, and using data to support her client's requests, showing that the startup's goals align with achievable outcomes, which the Gold opposing counsel will appreciate.

By applying the lenses, Jane can help her client understand the importance of specific terms and persuade her client to focus on details for which they would not usually have patience. By understanding the mentality of opposing counsel, Jane understands in advance that she must provide data to support any sought-after concessions and focus on efficiency and practicality as key points. Jane can, therefore, simultaneously address the practical concerns of opposing counsel and maintain her client's interest because she is knowledgeable about the personality types and preferences involved in the negotiation.

## Overcoming Communication Barriers by Applying the Four Lenses

The need for understanding other personalities is most evident in conflicts when communication is challenging. To use this protocol to address common communication hurdles, consider each color preference and then deliver information in the manner most likely to be preferred by that personality.

**For Greens, be prepared to back up claims, strategies, and thought processes.** Also, it is crucial to avoid overload, whether information overload or emotional overload. Additionally, it is vital to consider that Greens need to understand the "why" of things. Focus on concise, fact-based communication and provide evidence to support key points you are trying to convey. Do not make an emotional appeal, as it is likely to fall on deaf ears. Do not waste time on your information delivery, as that will strike a Green preference as disorganized and they are likely to disengage. Present well-organized information and avoid being overly emotional or abstract.

**For Golds, efficiency is key.** Focus on results and be organized in your thoughts and communication. Adhere to existing structures and demonstrate respect for, or at least an understanding of, the process. Do not use unnecessary legalese or cloud the issues; use clear language and provide tangible, realistic outcomes. Avoid ambiguous statements, as that will try their patience, and always demonstrate respect for their time.

**For Blues, remember to always be patient and sensitive.** Information cannot be delivered in a harsh, direct manner but should be tempered. Criticisms must be delivered with a light hand and are best balanced by a compliment or acknowledgment of some sort. Prioritize trust and empathy, especially in challenging or high-stress cases, as this will help to minimize emotional hurdles.

**For Oranges, expect to be challenged and do not take it personally when you are.** Oranges may naturally be skeptical, but that can be overcome by aligning case details with big-picture goals. Oranges need room to explore ideas and creative strategies, but boundaries are particularly important to ensure efficiency and focus on the issues at hand. Oranges respond well to active communication, so walking with an Orange during difficult conversations can ease the discussion.

## Conclusion

The Shipley Four Lenses can be a powerful tool for lawyers, enabling them to navigate diverse personalities in their daily interactions. By tailoring communication to each lens, lawyers can build stronger, more trusting relationships, avoid miscommunications, and foster an atmosphere of respect and understanding. This not only improves outcomes in negotiations and legal proceedings but also demonstrates a commitment to professionalism through thoughtful and effective engagement with everyone they encounter in their practice.

# Balancing Humility and Confidence: Is It Possible?

*Tiffany Shimada and Abigail Stone*

"If you are humble nothing will touch you, neither praise nor disgrace, because you know what you are."

— Mother Theresa[1]

## What Is Humility?

Most people probably do not think of the word "humility" when listing desirable traits for lawyers to develop. Indeed, humility—which can sometimes evoke thoughts of timidity, low self-esteem, and shyness—does not seem to fit with the loud, confident persona often portrayed by lawyers on television and in the media. Some might even go so far as to say that humility and confidence cannot coexist in one's legal practice.

In this essay, we argue that humility and confidence *can* be balanced in one's legal career, and that achieving this balance can actually help lawyers achieve a more ethical, successful legal practice. However, we cannot succeed in our argument without first defining a key term—humility. In the spirit of Mother Theresa's quote, we will define humility as an accurate understanding and appreciation of one's standing, including one's

1. *Mother Teresa: No Greater Love*, p. 55, New World Library, 2002.

strengths and weaknesses. This definition of humility has been adopted not only by Mother Theresa but also by others in the fields of education and psychology.[2] This type of humility is not antithetical to confidence but can instead coexist with confidence; an accurate, full appreciation of one's own strengths and weaknesses, as well as the strengths and weaknesses of a case, client, and opposing counsel, can give a lawyer greater confidence in their practice.

## Balancing Confidence and Humility

An examination of the Model Rules of Professional Conduct with this definition of humility in mind reveals that the drafters of the Model Rules actually incorporated this balance of confidence and humility into many of the Model Rules. This is particularly evident in those rules involving an attorney's relationship with clients, the court, opposing counsel, and potential clients.

### *Rule 2.1—Advisor*

Model Rule 2.1 sets forth a lawyer's role as an advisor and specifically states that, when representing a client, a lawyer "shall exercise independent professional judgment and render candid advice."[3] Comment 1 to Model Rule 2.1 further elaborates that clients are entitled to "straightforward advice expressing the

---

2. *See, e.g.*, Vicki Zakrzewski, *How Humility Will Make You the Greatest Person Ever*, Greater Good Science Center (Jan. 12, 2016), https://greatergood.berkeley.edu/article/item/humility_will_make_you_greatest_person_ever; Anna Katharina Schaffner, *What Is Humility & Why Is It Important? (Incl. Examples)*, Positive Psychology (Aug. 27, 2020), https://positivepsychology.com/humility.

3. https://www.americanbar.org/groups/professional_responsibility/publications/model_rules_of_professional_conduct/rule_2_1_advisor/.

lawyer's honest assessment" of a case, and that, while a lawyer should endeavor "to sustain the client's morale and may put advice in as acceptable a form as honesty permits," a lawyer "should not be deterred from giving candid advice by the prospect that the advice will be unpalatable to the client."[4]

This guidance makes clear that, when advising a client, a lawyer needs to present advice in a confident manner that will sustain a client's morale. However, this confidence needs to be tempered with a strong dose of humility—namely, an accurate understanding of the client's standing and odds in the case. This rule also requires a lawyer to exercise humility by offering candid advice, even if such advice may not be what the client wants to hear. Ultimately, this balance of confidence and humility will lead clients to have more faith and trust in a lawyer's abilities because the clients know that the lawyer will be a zealous advocate for them, and also be truthful and realistic in their advice.

## *Rule 3.3—Candor Toward the Tribunal*

Model Rule 3.3 also sets forth a need for both confidence and humility in a lawyer's interaction with judges.[5] Model Rule 3.3 states that a lawyer must not knowingly (1) make a false statement of fact or law to the tribunal, or fail to correct such a statement, (2) fail to disclose to the tribunal a legal authority in the controlling jurisdiction that is directly adverse to the position of the client and not disclosed by opposing counsel, and (3) offer evidence that the lawyer knows to be false. Comment

---

4. https://www.americanbar.org/groups/professional_responsibility/publications/model_rules_of_professional_conduct/rule_2_1_advisor/comment_on_rule_2_1_advisor/.

5. https://www.americanbar.org/groups/professional_responsibility/publications/model_rules_of_professional_conduct/rule_3_3_candor_toward_the_tribunal/.

2 to Model Rule 3.3 further sets forth that "A lawyer acting as an advocate in an adjudicative proceeding has an obligation to present the client's case with persuasive force"—that is, with confidence. However, "[p]erformance of that duty while maintaining confidences of the client . . . is qualified by the advocate's duty of candor to the tribunal"—that is, the humility to give an accurate accounting of the law and facts to the court, even if that law or fact may not be favorable to the client.[6]

Here, again, this need for balance and confidence seems to be written into the Model Rules and comments themselves. A lawyer must be confident and prepared to effectively present a client's case with persuasive force and to give a true, accurate account of the facts and law. However, a lawyer must also have the humility to disclose potentially unfavorable binding legal authority if not disclosed by the other side. Achieving this balance of confidence and humility will allow a lawyer to gain credibility with the court and create a reputation of integrity and reliability before the tribunal.

## *Rule 3.4—Fairness to Opposing Party and Counsel*

Model Rule 3.4 states that a lawyer shall not, among other things, "unlawfully obstruct another party's access to evidence or unlawfully alter, destroy or conceal a document or other material having potential evidentiary value," or "falsify evidence, counsel or assist a witness to testify falsely, or offer an inducement to a witness that is prohibited by law."[7] It forbids a lawyer from engaging in tactics that obstruct or undermine the

6. https://www.americanbar.org/groups/professional_responsibility/publications/model_rules_of_professional_conduct/rule_3_3_candor_toward_the_tribunal/comment_on_rule_3_3/.

7. https://www.americanbar.org/groups/professional_responsibility/publications/model_rules_of_professional_conduct/rule_3_4_fairness_to_opposing_party_counsel/.

opposing party's access to evidence or ability to present their case effectively; this includes prohibitions against altering evidence, influencing witnesses improperly, or failing to comply with proper discovery requests.

In the context of this rule, exercising humility can give a lawyer greater confidence. Humility under these circumstances means adhering strictly to the rule, even if it means setting aside personal ambition or a client's demands for victory at all costs. This kind of humility provides the confidence that one's actions will withstand scrutiny, eliminating the risk of sanctions. More importantly, it fosters a reputation among other lawyers that one's word can be trusted, even in the heat of adversarial proceedings.

## *Rules 7.1 and 7.2—Advertising*

Model Rule 7.1[8] states that a lawyer must not make "a false or misleading communication about the lawyer or the lawyers services," which includes omitting necessary facts that might make the communication misleading and creating unjustified expectations of certain results.[9] Additionally, Model Rule 7.2 states that a lawyer must not state or imply that the lawyer is certified as a specialist in a particular field except under very specific circumstances involving certification by the relevant authorities in the jurisdiction where the lawyer is admitted to practice law.[10]

As these rules indicate, confidence and humility can play out uniquely in the context of a lawyer's advertising. In the

---

8. https://www.americanbar.org/groups/professional_responsibility/publications/model_rules_of_professional_conduct/rule_7_1_communication_concerning_a_lawyer_s_services/.

9. *See* Model Rules of Pro. Conduct r. 7.1 cmts. 2 and 3.

10. https://www.americanbar.org/groups/professional_responsibility/publications/model_rules_of_professional_conduct/rule_7_2_advertising/.

context of advertising to the public, the Model Rules allow us to market our skills to the public and share our credentials, skills, and achievements with confidence. However, the Model Rules also build in humility checks to temper any overconfidence that lawyers may tend toward when trying to gain new clients. Humility—having an accurate understanding of one's abilities and experience—helps a lawyer produce advertisements and communications that are truthful and contain all the necessary facts and information to prevent the communication from being misleading. This will allow lawyers to be confident in their public-facing persona and express their achievements and levels of expertise in compliance with the rules.

## *Rule 1.4—Communication*

Model Rule 1.4 requires lawyers to keep clients reasonably informed about the status of their legal matters.[11] Under Rule 1.4, the "status" of the client's case includes a requirement to disclose any material mistake made by the lawyer that is discovered during the representation.

ABA Formal Opinion 481 explains what is required under Model Rule 1.4 when a mistake is discovered.[12] In the Opinion, a mistake is defined as "material" if a disinterested lawyer would conclude that the mistake is reasonably likely to harm or prejudice the client or the mistake would reasonably cause the client to consider terminating the representation even if it does not lead to immediate harm.

This embodies the true test of a lawyer's humility and confidence: A lawyer must have the humility to recognize when a

11. https://www.americanbar.org/groups/professional_responsibility/publications/model_rules_of_professional_conduct/rule_1_4_communications/.

12. https://www.abajournal.com/files/Formal_Opinion_481_FINAL_formatted_04_16_2018(2).pdf.

mistake has been made, and the confidence and strength to disclose such a mistake to the client openly and honestly.

As Alexander Pope famously said: *To err is human; to forgive, divine.* All lawyers are human, and clients will typically forgive a lawyer's mistakes, provided the admission comes swiftly and fully, and with a plan for rectifying the mistake, where possible. It is those instances in which a lawyer refuses to exercise humility, and their mistakes are hidden and allowed to fester, that can ruin a case and client relationship. On the other hand, humbly admitting a mistake but confidently pressing forward to remedy the mistake can often salvage, and eventually even strengthen, a client relationship.

## Conclusion

The practice of law demands a delicate balance of confidence and humility to cultivate integrity and achieve success. Confidence empowers lawyers to advocate zealously for their clients, make decisive judgments, and navigate the complexities of the legal system with assurance. It is humility, however, that keeps them grounded, fostering a commitment to ethical standards, continuous learning, and the acknowledgment of their own limitations. By harmonizing these traits, lawyers not only uphold the principles of justice and fairness but also build a reputation for reliability and trustworthiness, paving the way for a distinguished and honorable career.

# What It Means to Be a Zealous Advocate

*Jon May*

There is a small but growing movement to remove any reference to zealous advocacy from ethical codes. Those objecting to this language cite its use by lawyers in disciplinary proceedings who are trying to justify unethical conduct. There is also an effort by some in academia to convince law students that zealous advocacy on behalf of certain businesses and industries is wrong and that they should dedicate themselves to the common good, even if that conflicts with the best interests of their clients.

I believe that both movements are wrong, that zealous advocacy is an ethic that lawyers must subscribe to, and that zealous advocacy advances the public welfare in ways that advocacy solely on behalf of causes does not.

The first part of this chapter discusses what it means to be a zealous advocate; the second part discusses what motivates lawyers to practice law the way that they do; and the third part discusses why zealous advocacy is an essential component of our system of justice.

## What Is a Zealous Advocate?

Examples of zealous advocacy are found throughout fiction and real life. In the movie *12 Angry Men*, 11 jurors voted to convict a young man of first-degree murder until Juror #8 convinced them that the evidence proved that the defendant was innocent.[1] In real life, Clarence Darrow epitomized the zealous advocate. Darrow is remembered for his defense of John Scopes, who was prosecuted for teaching the theory of evolution;[2] for saving the lives of Nathan Leopold and Richard Loeb, who had murdered 14-year-old Bobby Frank in their pursuit of committing the perfect crime;[3] and for his successful defense of 11 Black men in Detroit who were prosecuted for killing a White neighbor during a confrontation with a mob after one of the defendants, Henry Sweet, moved into a White neighborhood.[4]

Many people know that Darrow represented Leopold and Loeb and that he saved them from execution. But not everyone knows that Darrow pled these young men guilty and convinced Judge John Caverly to spare their lives at sentencing. Fewer still know that the sentencing proceedings lasted a month, that the state put on 80 witnesses, and that Darrow decided not to contest the state's evidence because nothing about the crime was in dispute, only why it happened.[5]

Darrow's defense was that Leopold and Loeb murdered Frank because they suffered from a diseased mind. In making his case to the court, the defense had to defeat the prosecution's effort to convince Judge Caverly that the court should

---

1. *12 Angry Men (1957 Film)*, Wikipedia, https://en.wikipedia.org/wiki/12_Angry_Men_(1957_film).

2. *The Clarence Darrow Digital Collection: The Scopes Trial (1925)*, Univ. of Minn., https://librarycollections.law.umn.edu/darrow/trials_details.php?id=7 (last visited Jan. 7, 2026).

3. *The Clarence Darrow Digital Collection: The Leopold & Loeb Trial*, Univ. of Minn., https://librarycollections.law.umn.edu/darrow/trials_details.php?id=1 (last visited Jan. 7, 2026).

4. *The Clarence Darrow Digital Collection: The Sweet Trials, Clarence Darrow and Race*, Univ. of Minn., https://librarycollections.law.umn.edu/darrow/trials_details.php?id=6 (last visited Jan. 7, 2026).

5. *The Leopold & Loeb Trial*, *supra* note 3.

exclude psychiatric testimony because Darrow had not raised an insanity defense. Darrow presented as modern a defense as any found in a courtroom today, calling to the stand two psychiatrists, an endocrinologist, and a neurologist.[6]

Darrow is also the archetypal example of zealous advocacy gone too far; Darrow was prosecuted twice for attempting to bribe two jurors while defending John and James McNamara, who were accused of bombing the Los Angeles Times in 1910. Darrow's first trial ended in a not guilty verdict, the second in a hung jury—eight to four for conviction.[7]

There is substantial evidence today that Darrow was guilty of attempting to bribe both jurors. In the first trial, Darrow did not quite admit his guilt but argued that if he had bribed the juror, he would have been justified. He argued that he was not being prosecuted because he attempted to bribe a juror, but because he was "a lover of the poor, a friend of the oppressed because I have stood by labor for all these years" and because the true criminals, the ones who had amassed their power through bribery, were the business groups arrayed against him.[8]

In the Leopold and Loeb case, Darrow was a zealous advocate, providing his clients with the most vigorous representation possible: making brilliant tactical decisions, presenting the best scientific evidence available, and arguing a defense of mental disease without raising the more difficult and often unsuccessful defense of insanity. But in the McNamara prosecution, Darrow acted as a zealot. Rather than risk a conviction and the certainty of execution, he chose bribery. And when he was

---

6. *Id. The Clarence Darrow Digital Collection: The Bribery Trials of Clarence Darrow*, Univ. of Minn., https://librarycollections.law.umn.edu/darrow/trials_details.php?id=17 (last visited Jan. 7, 2026).

7. *The Bribery Trials of Clarence Darrow*, *supra* note 6.

8. Geoffrey Cowan, The People v. Clarence Darrow: The Bribery Trial of America's Greatest Lawyer (1994).

prosecuted for bribery, Darrow presented a political defense: that he was being prosecuted because he had stood up for the poor, the oppressed, and labor against a business establishment bent on crushing him.

A federal circuit judge recently told me that our system of justice, civil and criminal, cannot work, and certainly cannot work well, unless there is a contest between advocates representing the interests of their clients with zeal.[9] But what does zeal mean? It is easy to see that Clarence Darrow provided zealous advocacy in defending Leopold and Loeb, but not when he defended the McNamara brothers. Our adversarial system of justice does not tolerate lawyers who violate rules of professional conduct or break the law in pursuit of an outcome. As the lawsuits to overturn the 2020 presidential election have shown, any lawyers who believe that their client's cause justifies filing lawsuits with no basis in fact will come to realize that there is a price to be paid for abusing the judicial system—a price that may cost them their freedom, their reputation, and the privilege of practicing law.

A federal district judge who was previously a state judge and before that a federal prosecutor said to me recently that the level of incivility between civil lawyers is at times disheartening, whereas dealings between defense attorneys and prosecutors are generally cordial.[10] He was referring to conduct that is far more often exhibited in civil litigation than in criminal, such as maliciously accusing opposing counsel of misconduct, engaging in obstructive behavior during depositions, or willfully disobeying court orders (the list goes on and on). Such conduct is not advocacy at all; it is sanctionable, and when uncovered, no one is fooled by the claim that counsel were justified in their actions by the obligation of zealous advocacy.

9. Interview March 2024.

10. *Id.*

Any discussion of what it means to be a zealous advocate should begin with an acknowledgment that, except for the District of Columbia and Massachusetts, no jurisdiction expressly requires that a lawyer be a zealous advocate on behalf of a client.[11]

The ABA Model Rules of Professional Conduct, which has been adopted in some form by every state, uses the words zeal, zealous, or zealous advocacy only in the preamble and in the comment to Rule 1.3, neither of which imposes a binding obligation on lawyers. Indeed, 13 states have had these words removed from their ethical rules. Florida rejected a proposal to remove the words zeal and zealous from Florida's Code of Professional Conduct.[12]

In criminal cases, lawyers and law professors have anchored the obligation of zealous advocacy in the right to counsel guaranteed by the Sixth Amendment and in the right to due process of law provided for by the Fifth and Fourteenth Amendments.[13] Although the Supreme Court has opined on what zealous advocacy means, the Court has set a low bar for the kind of representation defense counsel is constitutionally required to provide—a bar far lower than zealousness.

The Supreme Court discussed zealous advocacy in *McCoy v. Court of Appeals of Wisconsin*, observing:

> The attorney must . . . provide his or her client precisely the services that an affluent defendant could

---

11. Anita Bernstein, *The Zeal Shortage*, 34 Hofstra L. Rev., 1165, 1188 (2006), https://scholarlycommons.law.hofstra.edu/hlr/vol34/iss3/17.

12. Jim Ash, *Supreme Court Declines to Erase "Zealous Advocacy" from Bar Rules*, The Florida Bar News (Sep. 5, 2024), https://www.floridabar.org/the-florida-bar-news/supreme-court-declines-to-erase-zealous-advocacy-from-bar-rules.

13. David Luban & W. Bradley Wendel, *Philosophical Legal Ethics: An Affectionate History*, 30 Geo. J. of Legal Ethics 337 (2017).

> obtain from paid counsel . . . the attorney must be zealous and must resolve all doubts and ambiguous legal questions in favor of his or her client.[14]

However, the Court has not held that the Constitution requires that a defendant receive the assistance of a zealous advocate. In *Strickland v. Washington*, the Supreme Court held that the Sixth Amendment requires only that a defendant receive "effective assistance of counsel."[15] To establish that a defendant did not receive effective assistance of counsel, the defendant must demonstrate that counsel "made errors so serious that counsel was not functioning as 'counsel,'"[16] and that counsel's lapses rendered the trial so unfair as to "undermine confidence of the outcome."[17] What this means is that a lawyer need only be "reasonably effective," and that in considering a claim that defense counsel did not do all that counsel should have on behalf of a defendant, courts are to "indulge a strong presumption that counsel's conduct falls within the wide range of reasonable professional assistance."[18] To make it perfectly clear that the measure of professional competence was not to be defined by ethical provisions that might place a higher burden on counsel, such as one of zealousness, the Court stated that ABA standards and the like are merely "guides."[19]

Where a lawyer has failed to live up to their obligations under the very low standard of "effective assistance" there are consequences: a new trial for the defendant, potential sanctions against the lawyer by the bar, and in rare cases a malpractice

---

14. McCoy v. Court of Appeals of Wisconsin, 486 U.S. 429, 444 (1988).
15. Strickland v. Washington, 466 U.S. 668 (1984).
16. *Id.* at 687.
17. *Id.* at 694.
18. *Id.* at 689.
19. *Id.*

suit. Where a lawyer fails to provide zealous representation, however, the defendant has no remedy—because the law does not recognize an obligation to advocate zealously, even though it could make the difference between a not-guilty verdict and a life behind bars.

In civil practice as well, there is no requirement that an attorney provide zealous advocacy in the representation of a client. But, unlike criminal practice (except in rare cases), civil counsel face the very real threat of a malpractice suit if counsel are negligent in their representation. The threat of malpractice provides some impetus for counsel to provide careful, if not exactly zealous, representation.

## What Motivates Lawyers to Practice as They Do?

We do not think about being a zealous advocate when we file a lawsuit or make an opening statement to a jury. When we first meet with a client, and they tell us their story, and they ask us our advice on what to do, or tell us what they want to do, we may become emotionally involved in the wrong they have suffered. We may hear how they acted in self-defense, how they trusted a business partner or lost a child in an accident. The more time we spend with our clients and their families, and the more evidence we uncover that supports their claim, the more committed we become to righting the wrong or to making them as whole as possible.

This is also true of attorneys representing small businesses or large corporations. While companies are artificial entities, they embody the interests of employees and stockholders whose financial well-being depends on the success of the company. Lawyers working in-house or as outside counsel may justifiably feel anger when their employer is faced with litigation counsel believes is unjustified. They are no less committed to protecting the business than lawyers representing an individual, because in a very real way, they are representing people as well.

Or we may have no sympathy for the client at all. We may represent a company in a commercial dispute, and the rightness or wrongness of the cause may in some cases be completely irrelevant, to the extent we are motivated by a desire to win and by the money we will earn for our efforts. But we will be compensated whether we win or lose (unless it is a contingency case). In such cases, what causes us to be enthusiastic in our efforts is pride in our work, and, if we are litigators, an overwhelming desire to win and to be regarded by our peers and the public as the best (or most feared) trial lawyer around. This is equally true for lawyers who are not litigators but want to be known as the "go-to" lawyer for every aspect of practice, from administrative law to zoning.

We are also motivated by the client's expectations.

Civil and criminal clients may have different motivations, the former redress for alleged harm or insult or defeating liability for the alleged harm or insult; the latter the defendant's freedom, livelihood, and reputation. But lawyers generally believe that prospective clients are looking for a fighter, that clients want someone who will be just as angry as they are and will "fight like hell" for their cause. Thus, while some people are just jerks, much of the bad behavior we see in our practices is motivated by a drive to satisfy our clients' actual or perceived expectations.

Sometimes the task requires that we act aggressively. I once had to cross-examine a middle-aged woman who had accused my client, the president of a medical records review company, of instructing her physician employees what life expectancy determinations to issue for each policyholder. The witness was assuredly viewed positively by the jury after the government's direct was completed. But she had lied several times in the past, and as I took her through her lies, I became more confrontational, more accusatory, and by the time I became cruel, the jury didn't hold it against me; she had betrayed their initial trust and they were angry.

On other occasions, when a lawyer has an important government witness (often an expert) who can provide testimony that will support the defense, the lawyer might treat that witness with kid gloves. I once cross-examined the president of the New York Mercantile Exchange about hedging commodities. I was able to lay much of the foundation for my defense through his testimony. When he got off the stand, he walked up to me, held out his hand, and said he appreciated how much of a gentleman I had been. I was flabbergasted. And my client was none too happy by my failure to destroy this witness in cross (although his anger was somewhat assuaged when the jury came back with a hung verdict).

## Why Zealous Advocacy Is an Essential Component of Our System of Justice

If various motivations are driving us to do our best for our clients, why do we even need to consider whether there is an obligation to be zealous advocates, whatever the limitations of such advocacy are in a particular case?

Zealous advocacy requires more from us than just "doing our best." It is part of an ethic that is critical to our identity as members of a profession engaged in the practice of law, not just people engaged in a business. Admittedly, this runs counter to both public perception and the actions of some lawyers who only view their work in terms of the wealth it can generate. And that perception could become reality if we as individuals do not commit ourselves to a calling that is greater than just a means to generate income.

Zealous advocacy should have as powerful a hold on the practice of lawyering as the so-called Protestant Work Ethic has had on the exceptionally driven American workforce. It impels us to reach beyond our own perceived limitations even when we detest our clients, be they serial killers or corporate polluters. For those like myself who practice criminal law, the commitment to being zealous advocates is what keeps us from burning out even though 90+ percent of our clients are convicted and go to prison. It is what causes us to forge ahead when the only thing we can do is convince the judge to impose a lower sentence than that sought by the prosecutor.

Some believe that eliminating zeal from ethical codes will reduce ethical violations or lapses. As I have tried to show, it is not zealous advocacy that is responsible for lawyers engaging in improper conduct. Accordingly, the causes of misbehavior will not suddenly evaporate with the elimination of language from an ethical code. Moreover, when individual lawyers abuse the legal system, there exist remedies that judges and bar associations can employ to sanction their misconduct. Indeed, the lines that lawyers must not cross are clearly identified in all ethical codes.

For instance, the Model Rules specify the duties of: adhering to strict truthfulness and avoiding deception (Rule 3.3), using the legal forum and process for legitimate means (Rule 3.1), respecting the forum as an officer of the court (Rule 3.5), refraining from abetting fraud and misconduct (Rules 3.3(a)(2), 3.3(c), and 3.4(b)), refusing to engage in conspiracy or collusive conduct that benefits the lawyer or the client (Rules 3.3, 3.4, and 3.5), asserting non-frivolous claims or defenses (Rule 3.1), expediting litigation (Rule 3.2), being fair to opposing counsel and not making untruthful statements to third parties (Rules 3.4 and 4.1), refraining from using false and misleading evidence and misinformation (Rule 3.4), and showing candor to the tribunal (Rule 3.3(a)).

Where lawyers engage in practices that undermine the balance of power between parties, either through the filing of frivolous pleadings or demanding unnecessary depositions, or engaging in boorish behavior, these provisions provide ample grounds for discipline by bar associations.

Where these provisions have been inadequate to ensure that counsel acts within the bounds set by ethical rules, the demands of constitutional rights, or even the prevailing moral values, courts and legislatures have enacted rules and statutes to address abuses. For instance, when the practice of withholding exculpatory information from defense counsel in violation of the Supreme Court's decision in *Brady v. Maryland*[20] had become more common among some federal prosecutors, Congress enacted legislation to give the courts greater authority to sanction prosecutors who failed to follow the law.[21] The long-standing practice by some prosecutors to strike jurors based on race was eventually prohibited by the Supreme Court.[22] But that does not mean prosecutors suddenly became less zealous in their pursuit of justice.

Lawyers will occasionally confront hard questions that test their judgment in determining the best course of action. In 1966, Professor Monroe Freedman posited three such questions that he believed had to be resolved in favor of the defendant.

1. Is it ethical to discredit a truthful witness?
2. Is it proper to knowingly put a witness on the stand who will commit perjury?
3. May a lawyer provide a client with legal advice when the lawyer suspects the client may use that advice to commit perjury?

---

20. Brady v. Maryland, 373 U.S. 83 (1963).
21. Fed. R. Crim. P. 5(f).
22. Batson v. Kentucky, 476 U.S. 79 (1986).

(His answers so angered Chief Justice Warren Burger, that Burger sought to have Freedman disbarred.)

Fifty years later, Professor Todd Berger offered three more hard questions:

1. What is the ethically appropriate response when a victim of a crime who does not wish to pursue prosecution asks a criminal defense attorney, "So, what happens if I don't come to court?"
2. What should defense counsel say to a judge who directly asks counsel about incriminating information that is protected by attorney–client confidentiality when the judge can easily infer that defense counsel's refusal to answer such a question is an indication of the client's culpability?
3. Can defense counsel zealously advocate for an individual client if doing so would potentially anger a prosecutor who is likely to retaliate by punishing the attorney's other clients?

Professor Berger demonstrated that counsel can find the answer to these questions, or at least meaningful guidance, in the rules of ethics.[23] Zealous advocacy only comes into play when counsel must make a judgment call. In that case, the Supreme Court's decision in *McCoy* tells lawyers that, "the attorney must be zealous and must resolve all doubts and ambiguous legal questions in favor of his or her client."[24]

Some in academia argue that law students should be taught that the public good comes before the interests of the client.[25]

---

23. Todd A. Berger, *Professional Responsibility of the Criminal Defense Lawyer Reduz: The New Three Hardest Questions*, 7 St. Mary's L.J. Legal Malpractice & Ethics 96 (2017).

24. McCoy v. Court of Appeals of Wisconsin, 486 U.S. 429, 444 (1988).

25. Etienne C. Toussainte, *The Miseducation of Public Citizens*, 29 Geo. J. on Poverty L. & Pol'y 287 (Summer 2022).

Of course, the academics who espouse this philosophy believe that what is in the public interest is not subject to debate. Most of them have spent the greater part of their careers teaching and little time representing clients. A full discussion of their ideas is beyond the scope of this chapter, but I will make a few observations.

With rare exceptions, such as where a judge appoints a lawyer to represent an indigent defendant, a lawyer is never required to represent any particular individual or cause. If a law firm or public office orders a lawyer to represent a client in a matter that the lawyer cannot in good conscience handle, the lawyer can and should resign. In other words, the ethic of zealous advocacy suggests that if a lawyer cannot be a zealous advocate, he or she should not be an advocate at all.

Lawyers who believe that they should dedicate themselves to some public interest can represent parties in litigation they hope will change society. For example, those who believe that the administrative state has harmed small businesses and stifled competition can work with or for the U.S. Chamber of Commerce and file lawsuits to limit the reach of regulations; those who believe that school boards have violated the First Amendment rights of students by banning books from school libraries can assist the American Civil Liberties Union in filing lawsuits to overturn a school board's actions. Indeed, it is difficult to conceive of a mechanism that can bring more issues to the consciousness of the American public or more vividly illustrate the differences in values expressed by those issues than litigation instituted by zealous advocates.

This brings us to the final avenue available to lawyers who seek to change the status quo. Like any citizen, they can lobby for legislation that promotes their vision of the public good. And they can vote for those who share their vision.

Being a zealous advocate is something we do in part because of who we are but also because of what we aspire to be. It is a mindset that causes us to look for creative solutions to hurdles that everyone else accepts as just part of "how things are": to seek out others in the profession for consultation and advice (which most will freely give), to dedicate ourselves to the constant improvement of our minds—which stimulates creativity—and our bodies—which gives us the stamina we need when we are working till all hours preparing for the next day in court.

Not everyone, for sure, but the longer an attorney practices law, the more they rely on what has worked in the past and become less committed to finding new and innovative ways to prevail. Since over 90 percent of defendants in state and federal cases plead guilty, defense attorneys have fewer and fewer opportunities to go to trial, and they begin to lose their enthusiasm for their work. They fail to realize that there are ways to win a case despite losing, that zealous advocacy provides a way to limit the harm to a defendant and the family by reducing the sentence that the defendant otherwise would get had the lawyer settled for nothing more than competent representation.

Throughout this evolution, the one thing that stays the same is the client's expectation that the client is hiring a lawyer who will find a way to help them. Whether express or implied, lawyers agree to do just that. Based on that commitment, counsel is ethically obligated to provide the kind of representation the client has paid for. This is true whether it is enforced by the counts or rules or not.

One final caveat. Zealous advocacy is what we owe our clients. But zeal for life beyond the law is what we owe to ourselves; we need to ensure that our dedication to the practice of law does not come before our commitment to our families and our mental and physical well-being. While there are times when we must allot all of our time to a specific task, we cannot allow the law to define us or consume us. No one will remember our victories, but our children will remember our absences.

# Bullying in the Legal Profession: Why It Matters and What We Can Do About It[1]

*Roberta D. Liebenberg and Stephanie A. Scharf*

Many of us think of bullying as aggressive and hurtful conduct that takes place in a schoolyard—name-calling, threats, humiliation, insults, physical intimidation, and much more. But bullying also occurs in the legal profession, and adversely affects countless lawyers in their everyday practice of law. However, despite the prevalence of bullying, it is rarely discussed and has certainly not been effectively addressed.

As the profession has grown and become more diverse, new voices have begun to speak out about bullying and have emphasized that it is a serious problem that diminishes the practice of law. Bullying negatively affects a lawyer's day-to-day experiences, emotional well-being, and even physical health. It also limits an employer's ability to create strong teams, retain lawyers who do good work and in whom legal employers have made a substantial investment of time and money, and foster an inclusive culture that supports lawyers at all levels. Bullying has

1. This essay is based on extensive research about bullying in the legal profession in Illinois, which was designed, conducted, and reported by the authors. *See* Stephanie Scharf & Roberta Liebenberg, *Bullying in the Legal Profession: A Study of Illinois Lawyers' Experiences and Recommendations for Change*, Illinois Supreme Court Comm'n on Professionalism (2024).

become an all-too-frequent experience, leading to an overarching question: What can we in the profession do about it?

It was our honor to have conducted, for the first time in the U.S., a large systematic study of bullying in the law, shining a much-needed spotlight on this pervasive problem.[2] This unique research, using survey data obtained from more than 6,000 Illinois lawyers, found that one in four lawyers had experienced bullying within the past year, and often multiple times in a year. Our report provides detailed findings about who is bullied, where bullying takes place, the significant consequences of bullying to its victims, and data-based recommended policies and best practices to ameliorate this problem. The thousands of lawyers who participated in our survey include lawyers in many different practice areas, and with widely varying employers, locales, and demographic characteristics. Thus, our research results are useful to understand the extent and impact of bullying in the legal profession not just in Illinois, but in other states as well.

## What Behaviors Constitute Bullying?

Our report defined bullying as inappropriate behavior intended to intimidate, humiliate, or control the actions of another person, including verbal, nonverbal, or physical acts.[3] In essence, bullying is more than incivility or being rude, overzealous, or disrespectful. It typically results from an inherent imbalance of power between the bully and the victim.

---

2. *Id.*

3. *Id.* at 20.

## Who Gets Bullied?

Although bullying affects lawyers from all backgrounds, we found that bullying disproportionately impacts female attorneys, attorneys with disabilities, attorneys of color, LGBTQ+ attorneys, and younger attorneys between 25 and 35.[4]

We both served as chairs of the ABA Commission on Women in the Profession, and were disappointed to find that 38 percent of female lawyers reported being bullied at work in the last year, compared to only 15 percent of male lawyers. Equally concerning was that 40 percent of the women lawyers surveyed experienced verbal bullying, such as negative comments and innuendoes, insults, off-color and sexist jokes, or even threats related to their gender, compared to just 17 percent of men.[5]

Not surprisingly, young lawyers were most likely to have experienced bullying, and 39 percent of lawyers aged 25 to 35 reported being bullied in the past year. Often this conduct results from more senior lawyers believing that bullying is simply a normal "rite of passage" that young lawyers must endure during their careers. The business and time pressures and highly competitive nature of the legal profession also contribute to this problem.

## Who Are the Bullies?

Lawyers reported being bullied by others within their organizations, especially by those who hold more powerful positions (31 percent), and also by persons outside their organizations

4. *Id.* at 27–36.
5. *Id.* at 28.

(33 percent). We also found that 14 percent of lawyers said they were most recently bullied by a judge.[6] The types of bullying experienced by lawyers who were bullied strongly parallel the bullying behavior described by those who said that they had bullied others at work.[7]

## What Are the Consequences of Bullying?

Bullying has a significant impact on the emotional well-being of lawyers: 54 percent of bullied lawyers reported anxiety, loss of self-confidence, and other negative feelings; 39 percent felt less productive at work; and 20 percent experienced a decline in physical health.[8]

Workplace bullying impacts employers as well, with 18 percent of lawyers reporting that they had left a job practicing law because of bullying, and 9 percent of survey respondents said they are currently looking for a new job or would leave their job because of workplace bullying.[9] Without effective leadership and appropriate anti-bullying standards, policies, and procedures, employers are more likely to lose women lawyers, LGBTQ+ lawyers, lawyers of color, lawyers with a disability, and younger lawyers because of bullying.

## What Types of Workplace Policies and Practices Offer Solutions?

Although almost every legal employer has policies forbidding sexual harassment and discrimination based on gender, race, national origin, and sexual orientation, bullying generally falls

6. *Id.* at 36.
7. *Id.* at 26.
8. *Id.* at 52.
9. *Id.* at 53.

outside the ambit of those policies. Therefore, it is imperative for employers to understand the extent of bullying in their organizations and to take strong steps to address that conduct.

Our research clearly shows that the specific policies and practices outlined as follows can substantially decrease bullying in the workplace, if not eliminate it.

*First*, there must be a clear message from leaders that bullying will not be tolerated. Employers should implement formal, written anti-bullying policies in all workplaces where lawyers practice.[10] Such policies should encourage the reporting of bullying, ensure confidentiality, prevent retaliation, and include sufficient sanctions to hold those who engage in such conduct accountable and deter future wrongdoing. Policies should also include annual training, confidentiality requirements, and anti-retaliation measures for lawyers who report bullying.[11]

*Second*, courts need to adopt and enforce anti-bullying standards for courtroom and litigation activities. Law schools can also play an important role in raising awareness and providing educational resources about the prevalence of bullying in the legal profession.[12]

*Third*, bar associations should likewise provide education about bullying and implement mentoring programs and other types of support for those who experience bullying. We especially value the types of anti-bullying discussions that can take place effectively and safely in well-structured bar programs.[13]

*Fourth*, and equally important, there are steps that individuals can take if they experience bullying. This is not to suggest that solutions are only at the individual level. But when an employer or court or other setting does not provide adequate

10. *Id.* at 62–64.
11. *Id.* at 65–66.
12. *Id.* at 66–68.
13. *Id.* at 68–69.

relief, individuals should be prepared to respond in ways that feel right for them and the situation, as detailed further in the report.[14]

In sum, our report provides groundbreaking empirical confirmation that bullying is widespread in the legal profession and is harming the careers and well-being of far too many lawyers. We believe that each member of the legal profession has a responsibility to eliminate bullying and create supportive workplace cultures that promote collegiality, civility, and respect. We hope that our report will serve as a wake-up call that bullying cannot continue to be swept under the rug. Rather, concrete steps can and must be taken for the benefit of individual lawyers, employers, and the betterment of the legal profession.

14. *Id.* at 69–70.

# We Are Each Other's Keepers

*Erica Grigg*

Fourteen years ago, I attempted to take my own life. I knew at that time that I desperately needed mental health assistance; anxiety, depression, and suicidal thoughts were a daily occurrence in my life as a litigator, but I did not seek help for two reasons.

First, I was in the throes of a severe substance use disorder. Alcohol was my drug of choice, the only tool I could depend on to change how I felt quickly enough to keep me moving through pressing deadline after pressing deadline. I also could not fall asleep at night without it. I was terrified that if I came forward and shared what was going on inside my head and my heart, all of you would tell me that I had to stop drinking. The thought of losing my lifeline and abandoning the only strategy I had to alleviate my symptoms seemed impossible. So, I did not say a word to anyone.

Second, as a female in litigation, I was fighting various stigma surrounding women practicing in our profession—stigma such as (1) women are overly emotional, (2) women do not have the constitution for litigation, and (3) women are unstable. I believed if I disclosed the deteriorating state of my mental health to anyone in the legal profession, my career in litigation would be over before it had even started.

## My History

My mental health challenges did not begin when I started practicing law. I had been battling what I now know is major depressive disorder since childhood. There was always this hamster in a wheel constantly running in my head. This hamster was not always a bad thing. It was the source of my persistence and determination. Unfortunately, this hamster was also the source of a maladaptive narrative that I bought hook, line, and sinker. That narrative was that I was unworthy, undeserving, and unlovable and that if anyone truly knew the real me, they would never accept me. What is so interesting about this narrative is that it did not align with my life experience. I was at the top of my class in school; I had a ton of friends and a very supportive family.

Despite all the evidence to the contrary, my depression controlled the messaging I believed. Abusive drinking began for me in high school. Neither a depression nor substance use diagnosis prevented me from achieving personal happiness or impressive academic accomplishments in college. Once I started law school, however, my untreated disorders mushroomed. I became physically addicted to alcohol. I had to drink to sleep at night, and many mornings, I had to drink to calm my hand tremors before I left for class. These symptoms continued to progress and intensify as I became licensed and employed by a law firm as a personal injury litigator.

Then I started to lie to my employer about meeting deadlines—I was missing them right and left. My schedule looked like a shell game. I was constantly moving, canceling, and rescheduling professional commitments based on whether I was sober, which was never, or if I was hungover, which was always. I stopped returning client phone calls. I was terrified because I knew that if I called a client, their questions about their case would only remind me I was not doing the job they had entrusted me to do.

## Rock Bottom

Six months before my suicide attempt, I prayed for God to take me in my sleep. I knew grievances were coming. I had let down the law firm that took a chance on hiring a young lawyer with no experience. I was throwing away the education my parents had made immeasurable sacrifices for me to attain. But, mostly, I was failing the clients who had come to me hoping and expecting to be helped through the most critical crisis of their lives.

Two weeks before my suicide attempt, while driving the winding, undulating canyons of the Texas Hill Country's backroads, I thought to myself: "All I'd have to do to end it all would be drive off one of these roads into one of these canyons." Several days after having that thought, on Mother's Day, that is exactly what I did. And I lived.

My actions were a shock to my parents. My actions were a shock to my closest friends. My actions were a shock to my coworkers. The secrets of my mental health torment and addiction to alcohol were now out in the open. On the advice of my psychiatrist and parents, I entered treatment with a dual diagnosis of substance use disorder and major depressive disorder.

## A Way Through

A few days into treatment, a lawyer friend called me and suggested that I call the Texas Lawyers' Assistance Program (TLAP) for support. I vaguely remembered a TLAP representative speaking at my law school orientation a decade prior but did not recall precisely what TLAP's purpose was. I had no idea how to navigate whatever future was in store for me as a lawyer after treatment, and out of desperation, I called them. That call saved my life.

By calling TLAP, I availed myself of a service most state bar lawyers' assistance programs (LAPs) offer, and that made all the difference for me: peer support. Most lawyers' assistance programs have a host of lawyer volunteers who are in remission from mental health challenges and/or recovery from substance use challenges and who are trained and willing to help professional colleagues wade through whatever challenges they may be experiencing.

TLAP paired me with a female lawyer who had been exactly where I was at that moment. She had gone through the same struggles and came out on the other side with a thriving practice and life full of joy and hope. Because of her own experience with mental health challenges, I felt comfortable sharing my own story with her. Because she was a fellow lawyer, she had a level of credibility with me like no one else. When my treatment therapist said, "You will be ok, your career is not over," I thought, "You have skin in the game. You have to say that." When my parents said, "You will be ok, your career is not over," I thought, "You love me; you have to say that." But, when my TLAP peer told me, "You will be ok; your career is not over," I believed her. After all, she had lived my experience and triumphed. For the first time in decades, this peer relationship enabled me to believe there was a light at the end of the tunnel.

I share my story not for sympathy or shock value. I share my story to illustrate how imperative it is that lawyers look out for, encourage, and support one another. Nothing moved the needle more for me in terms of getting help, staying in treatment, and continuing my mental health and sobriety journeys than the support and aid of fellow lawyers. Hearing other lawyers share their struggles and solutions was a lifeline. I finally realized I was not alone. I felt understood—a realization that drastically altered the direction of my life.

## The Problem—and Solution

As we enter a new era where mental health is more openly discussed in careers ranging from public school teachers to Olympic athletes, lawyers have an opportunity to continue reforming our professional culture to encourage the same kind of dialogue. Most of us by now are familiar with the grim statistics about mental health and substance use among lawyers. A 2022 study revealed that 77 percent of lawyers had experienced what they described as "burnout," 42 percent reported hazardous or unhealthy substance use, 26 percent reported that they suffered from anxiety, 21 percent reported being depressed, and 7 percent reported having had suicidal thoughts.[15] Our profession is at a critical crossroads where, if we are to thrive, we must be willing to take action and help one other get help when needed.

Fostering a culture of mutual support and understanding around mental health in the legal profession is essential to creating a healthier and more sustainable work environment for all lawyers. Whether through peer-to-peer sharing of mental health experiences, recognizing when a colleague is struggling and intervening, or leading by example in prioritizing well-being, these actions contribute to a professional culture that supports lawyers and combats the stigma surrounding mental health.

---

15. The study was authored by researchers at NORC at the University of Chicago in partnership with Lawyers Concerned for Lawyers (LCL), Massachusetts; https://www.norc.org/content/dam/norc-org/pdfs/NORC_MA%20Lawyer%20Well-Being%20Report_Final_2023_2_1.pdf.

There is no one better suited to recognize—and speak up—when another lawyer may be struggling than a fellow lawyer. This should be obvious when you consider that as lawyers, we have a common bond because our identities are deeply tied to our profession; lawyers tend to listen to other lawyers, especially those in leadership roles,[16] and our demanding work hours usually mean that we spend more time with other lawyers than with friends or family The practical effect of spending so much time together is that we may be the first person to witness changes to another lawyer's behaviors and habits—and to do so even before their loved ones or medical providers.

The importance of our shared profession and what it means to each of us to be a lawyer cannot be understated. Many times, as a professional counselor, I have worked with struggling lawyers who had lost their marriages, relationships with their children, and their homes. Yet, they remained unwilling to get help until their law license was at risk. For many struggling lawyers, it was not until another lawyer pointed out that their privilege to practice law could be revoked that the lawyer needing help would seek it. In numerous cases where pleading from spouses, parents, and children to get help failed, it was the prompting or recommendation from a fellow lawyer that ultimately encouraged a suffering lawyer to enroll in treatment.

## Peer-to-Peer Sharing

One of the most powerful tools for helping colleagues who may be struggling is peer-to-peer sharing. Research supports the relationship between balanced mental health and feeling

16. Adam J. Hampton, Amanda N. Fisher Boyd & Susan Sprecher, *You're Like Me and I Like You: Mediators of the Similarity-liking Link Assessed Before and After a Getting-Acquainted Social Interaction*, 36(7) J. Soc. & Pers. Relationships (July 30, 2018).

known, recognized, and understood. Studies show that when people feel misunderstood or as if others don't truly know them, it can lead to depression and loneliness.[17] These same studies show that when people feel isolated from others, it can manifest into suicidal action and ideation. As lawyers, these concepts are exacerbated by being in a profession where we are pressured to strive for perfection at all times, and our worth is judged by our performance.

On the other hand, feeling understood, recognized, and known by our lawyer colleagues fosters feelings of belonging to a greater community—something bigger than ourselves. Recognition of a colleague is more than saying "good job" when someone succeeds; it's about acknowledging hard work and being supportive. This kind of acknowledgment creates a sense of belonging, which can lead to a deeper sense of purpose, value, and empowerment. My own experience with lawyer peer assistance supports this data. Once I began talking to a professional colleague about my mental health struggles, I began to feel supported and empowered to make decisions about my future health, career, and personal life.

## Lawyer-to-Lawyer Intervention

Another effective strategy for helping other lawyers in crisis is through an intervention. Our proximity to each other presents unique opportunities for intervening when it is clear that a colleague is struggling. Is someone who is usually timely with deadlines suddenly missing them? Is a colleague with reliable work attendance now repeatedly calling in sick? These and

17. Leon F. Seltzer, *Feeling Understood—Even More Important Than Feeling Loved?*, Psych. Today (June 28, 2017), https://www.psychologytoday.com/us/blog/evolution-of-the-self/201706/feeling-understood-even-more-important-than-feeling-loved.

other such behavioral changes can indicate that a lawyer may be struggling. Trust your instincts and ask them how they are doing and if they are okay. If you are unsure how to have a conversation about well-being with a colleague do not hesitate to call your lawyers' assistance program. Lawyers' assistance programs have qualified professionals available who can help you walk through how to approach a colleague and undertake a mental health status check.

## Leading by Example

Mentoring has long been established as an excellent way for lawyers to learn from one another and it plays a crucial role in promoting wellness and mental health. Lawyers often look to each other for guidance, especially less experienced lawyers toward their more seasoned colleagues. In this context, mentoring can set a powerful example for prioritizing both professional success and personal well-being.

Years ago, when I was the director of the Texas lawyer assistance program, many of the calls I took were from associate lawyers working for firms of various sizes. Two things were especially interesting about those calls. First, associate lawyers often shared that their firms had some form of employee wellness policy. However, these policies provided little comfort, as few (if any) firm leaders took advantage of them. This lack of utilization created the perception that taking advantage of such policies was a sign of weakness. Second, associate lawyers often revealed that, despite their firm offering counseling through an employee assistance program (EAP) via health insurance, they were not comfortable using that service. They feared their firm would somehow discover they were seeking mental health support.

Even today, in my role as a private counselor, these same issues still come up in therapy sessions with lawyers who are my clients. Many work for firms with well-meaning employee wellness policies, but they will not take advantage of them because "no one else is." In this scenario, lawyers are presented with yet another opportunity to look out for one another. This can be done by leading by example—especially those of us in a leadership role in the firm—and by engaging in our own wellness practices.

As I learned firsthand, it is imperative that lawyers look out for each other. Another lawyer's willingness to open up about their own mental health challenges and support me as I navigated the fallout from mine saved my life and career. The path is simple and straightforward: When we start asking one another if we are okay, we disrupt the negative stigma surrounding mental health in our professional culture. By initiating conversations about well-being between colleagues, we seize a crucial opportunity to cultivate a healthier profession. And when we lead by example—by taking care of ourselves and seeking help and advice when we need it—we improve our own lives and create an environment where other lawyers feel empowered to do the same. By fostering a culture of support, empathy, and self-care, we not only protect careers but preserve families and save lives.

For more guidance on implementing these strategies individually or firm-wide, your state lawyers' assistance program is an excellent resource.

# Why Treating Opposing Counsel with Kindness Is the Right Choice

*Emil J. Ali*

As a legal ethics attorney, I interact with a diverse range of lawyers—from seasoned litigators to young, eager associates. Sometimes, I speak to them at their worst, when they are facing discipline. Other times I work with them when they are excited to take on a new matter or they are working to craft a new engagement letter—the happier times. I also have the privilege of working with aspiring lawyers as a legal ethics professor. Still, one area adjacent to legal ethics and the disciplinary rules that has shaped my approach to legal practice, and that I emphasize to my clients and students, is the importance of civility and, specifically, kindness. The adage "Treat others as you would want to be treated" is particularly relevant when dealing with opposing counsel in the adversarial world of law. Incivility is not just "bad manners," it is an obstruction to justice itself. It directly undermines the interests of clients by delaying cases and inflating costs. Lawyers are entrusted with their clients' resources, and when they engage in uncooperative or disrespectful conduct, they breach their client's trust and fail in their duty to act in the client's best interest.

I like to quote a California appeals court case that summarizes this point succinctly:

> Civility is not about etiquette. This is not a matter of bad manners. Incivility slows things down, it costs

> people money—money they were counting on their lawyers to help them save. And it contravenes the Legislature's directive that "all parties shall cooperate in bringing the action to trial."[1]
>
> Incivility is the adult equivalent of schoolyard bullying and we will not keep looking the other way when attorneys practice like this. They will be called out and immortalized in the California Appellate Reports.[2]

## Excellent Lawyers Are Civil

Most would agree that when attorneys treat each other with respect, they are more likely to engage in constructive dialogue, negotiate in good faith, and resolve disputes amicably. This can save time, reduce costs, and minimize stress for both clients and attorneys—something that every competent lawyer should strive to do. However, the legal profession is full of highly complex individuals, many with boisterous and even aggressive personalities. When combined with high stakes, tight deadlines, and intense pressure from clients, whether in a transactional or litigation setting, the result is often rude and confrontational behavior. However, I've found that even in the face of such conduct, a respectful and cooperative approach to opposing counsel can yield significant benefits, both professionally and personally.

My mother would always tell me that if someone was mean to you, you should be extra nice back to them. As a child, I hated the idea of being nice to someone who was not nice. However, as a lawyer, I see that treating opposing counsel how you wish to be treated (even in the face of their own incivility or

1. Cal. Code Civ. P. § 583.130.

2. Masimo Corp. v. The Vanderpool Law Firm, Inc., 101 Cal. App. 5th 902, 911, 320 Cal. Rptr. 3d 704, 712–13 (2024).

rudeness) fosters a more productive and efficient legal process. Not only can a respectful approach enhance your reputation as a fair and reasonable lawyer and build positive relationships with opposing counsel, but it can also help avoid the embarrassment or harm from sanctions or disciplinary issues.

Even more helpful is that being respectful can convince an otherwise upset opposing counsel to cool off or take a breather. It can also work to create a clean record of your civility in communications and highlight the bad behavior you have endured from the other side. In the *Masimo* case, this is exactly what happened:

> Evidently Vanderpool's principal attorney, Douglas Vanderpool, did not get the memo. We have quoted above from the condescending e-mail he sent to Masimo's counsel, Robert Ellison, expressing the firm's refusal to meet and confer. After being served with the moving papers for the motion to compel, Douglas Vanderpool began an e-mail to Ellison with the subject line "You are joking right?" The body of the e-mail continued in the same vein: "In 30 years of practice this may be the stupidest thing I've ever seen. Robert is this really why you went to law school? Quit sending us paper. [Y]ou know we are out of the case so just knock it off and get a life. Otherwise we're going to be requesting sanctions against your firm for even bothering us with this nonsense."[3]

Douglas Vanderpool made good on his threat to ask for sanctions against Masimo and its counsel, a request the trial court denied. Although he went into great detail about his 31-year career as an advocate and arbitrator, he badly missed

3. *Id.*

the mark of excellence articulated in *Karton v. Ari Design & Construction, Inc.*:

> [E]xcellent lawyers are civil.[4]

The *Masimo* case offers a striking example of how civility can not only be a mark of professionalism but also a strategic advantage in legal practice. The court's decision highlights a profound truth: While one attorney, Vanderpool, sought to wield rudeness and intimidation to gain leverage—going so far as to threaten sanctions—the other attorney, Ellison, stood firm with professionalism and courtesy. Instead of the desired sanctions against his opposing counsel, Vanderpool's own behavior became the subject of judicial scrutiny as the judge called him out, pointing to his conduct as a stark contrast to what is expected of attorneys.

The lesson is simple: Incivility may not only fail to yield the desired result, but it can also backfire, leaving an indelible mark on your reputation and in the legal record for all to see. By focusing on kindness and the golden rule as a key component of civility toward opposing counsel, lawyers not only protect their own reputation but also diffuse tension, create opportunities for resolution, and avoid the negative—and usually expensive—consequences of escalating conflict. In the long run, respect and kindness form the most prudent approach, regardless of the behavior of opposing counsel.

---

4. *Karton v. Ari Design & Constr.,* Inc. 61 Cal. App. 5th 734, 747 (2021), https://www.resolvingdiscoverydisputes.com/wp-content/uploads/sites/95/2022/06/Karton-v.-Ari-Design-Construction-Inc.-2021-61-Cal.App_.5th-734-747.pdf.

# The Adversary System: A Cautionary Tale for Lawyers and Their Well-Being

*Kathleen Havener*

In 1976, reviewing a book by Monroe Freeman, William Kunstler wrote that the adversary system "has been universally extolled as the most efficient nonscientific method of isolating the truth of any matter in dispute."[1]

Fifteen years later, in my law school ethics class taught by Judge John T. Noonan of the U.S. Court of Appeals for the Ninth Circuit, Judge Noonan echoed that opinion. As a third-year law student, I thought I understood what both Judge Noonan and Mr. Kunstler were saying: that like the often-misquoted line attributed to Winston Churchill on democracy, they believed that the adversary system is the best we've got. Three cheers for the adversary system.

I confess I was puzzled by an underlying message I believed the Judge was trying to deliver, but not expressly: He had reservations about whether the system was good for lawyers.

Three decades hence, I know that I did not then fully understand Judge Noonan's message. He certainly believed that the adversary system was the best we've got, but, more importantly, he was warning us that the nature of the adversary

1. William M. Kunstler, *Lawyers' Ethics in an Adversary System. By Monroe H. Freedman*, 4(3) Hofstra L. Rev. 895 (1976).

system could lead to abuse. He suggested that, as practicing lawyers, we needed to be on guard. I believe now that Judge Noonan wanted us to learn three critical lessons:

> Number one, govern your own behavior such that you never elevate zeal above civility.
>
> Number two, take care that you don't allow yourself to be victimized by opposing counsel, clients, and even judges who violate number one.
>
> Number three, we are responsible for our own conduct. No exceptions. No excuses.

To perceive Mr. Kunstler's point too, one must dig a little deeper. Mr. Kunstler described litigators as "high-pressure salespersons vociferously pushing their unseen wares on confused shoppers. What emerges so often is rarely truth but that which one side or the other seeks to palm off as truth."[2] Perhaps the most reviled occupation is that of a used car salesman, but Mr. Kunstler's description of litigators isn't too far off a precisely perfect description of our jobs. And despite 30 plus years of litigating, that's not a job I want, nor one—I hope—that I've ever performed.

Finally, there is yet another form of abuse that does not involve the adversary system but rather results from the simple fact of working as colleagues in close proximity over long periods of time in situations where there is a severe power imbalance. Lawyers can fall into patterns of bullying their colleagues, while others begin to suffer abuse and can't figure out how to escape it without sacrificing their careers.

---

2. *Id.* at 895.

## What's Going On?

Bloomberg's 2024 Attorney Well-Being Report: The Divide Between Health & the Legal Industry[3] released the following statistics about factors contributing to mental health among practicing lawyers:

- 56% reported disrupted sleep.
- 55% experienced anxiety.
- 44% reported lower energy/concentration.
- 37% experienced worsened mood.
- 30% experienced physical health issues.
- 29% reported depression.
- 25% reported issues in their personal relationships.
- 18% reported increased or decreased food consumption.
- 14% reported increased alcohol use and/or drug abuse.

## Why These Appalling Statistics?

Some answers may be simple. We put in long hours. Our work takes place in an unavoidable pressure cooker environment in which the stakes for our clients can be monstrously high while our time is too limited. No matter how hard we try, the results of our labor are unpredictable. We are routinely required to manage conflict and high-stress situations—often when there is no end in sight and no guarantee of success. We have the same everyday difficulties as nonlawyers—from serious financial difficulties, domestic differences, illness, childcare, and aging family members to simply managing a household—planning

3. https://pro.bloomberglaw.com/insights/litigation/2024-well-being-report/.

healthy meals, welcoming a new baby, supervising homework, and finding multiple pairs of mittens every morning. I know. It can be crazy making.

These explanations, however, do not account for why lawyers suffer mental health disorders at such a higher rate than people in other professions. For example, in contrast to lawyers, 28 percent of physicians (compared to 56 percent of lawyers) suffer from depression and 24 percent (compared to 55 percent of lawyers) live with anxiety.

Consider the nature of litigators' work. Too few of us acknowledge that legal advocacy is tough. It's gritty. Without doubt it is intellectually challenging, but it is emotionally, psychologically, and physically taxing as well. And that's not only true for the litigants and criminal defendants. It's true for the advocates as well.

Litigators' work is intense, stressful, even combative. We are constantly promoting our clients' position in a black-and-white win-or-lose environment. We are ever vigilant about our responsibility to protect our clients' interests. Is it any wonder that we have mental health challenges that practitioners in other professions do not seem to have to such an extent?

The website of the North Carolina Lawyers' Assistance Program provides a somewhat frightening perspective on the adversary system:

> As a lawyer, you are like a brain surgeon. Imagine the patient is laid out on the table in front of you. It is your job to operate and save his life. You are bringing all of your training, knowledge and skills to bear to try to save the patient's life. Now imagine that you have another doctor standing on the other side of the table—equally skilled, equally trained—and his primary goal is to kill

> the patient that you are trying to save. Now imagine you have 10 to 12 of these patients a day. And now imagine that after you have saved these patients' lives (and sacrificed time with your own family to do it), the patients are all complaining about your fee and refusing to pay.[4]

In addition to the adversarial nature of our work, many litigators report that the constant attentiveness to their clients' concerns leaves them emotionally drained, making it more difficult to interact appropriately in their personal lives. We feel helpless and inadequate. Lawyers who represent trauma victims, like family or personal injury lawyers, can experience secondary trauma. We experience what is sometimes called "compassion fatigue." It's a more severe form of burnout that occurs when we continuously absorb our clients' suffering. This can lead to emotional exhaustion and social isolation.

## But Wait—It Gets Worse

It's no secret that lawyers live with aggressive, bullying behavior from opposing counsel, judges, clients, and colleagues that can lead to symptoms of post-traumatic stress disorder. Personal attacks, threats, harassment, and even sexual violence can leave lasting emotional scars, resulting in hypervigilance, flashbacks, and emotional detachment. A wide-reaching study released in 2024 by the Illinois Supreme Court Commission on Professionalism,[5] conducted by Stephanie A. Scharf and

---

4. https://www.nclap.org/.

5. https://civility.wpenginepowered.com/wp-content/uploads/2024/10/2Civility_BullyingReport_Full_FN.pdf.

Roberta D. Liebenberg, found that at least 10 percent of Illinois lawyers have quit at least one job as a result of bullying. What a profound waste of time, training, and treasure.

It is beyond doubt that women lawyers suffer more. Although record numbers of women are graduating from law school—this year there are more women than men in law school—and there are an ever-increasing number of women judges and women in leadership positions, females in every sector of the legal profession continue to encounter unfair treatment. A 2018 survey of more than 7,000 women in the profession revealed that at least half had been bullied in connection with their employment. A third reported that they had been sexually harassed in the workplace.

My personal opinion is that almost every single woman lawyer experiences sexual harassment or worse at some point in her career. Although I witnessed it more times than I care to remember as a young lawyer, I did not experience sexual harassment myself until later in my career. When it occurred, it involved a remark made by another individual in a professional setting.

Because others were present, the comment was delivered quietly. The content was so disturbing that it caused an immediate physical reaction, and I had to step outside into the night.

The person who made the comment was someone I interacted with regularly and trusted. The experience changed our relationship immediately and permanently. My reaction was intense and disorienting. I was humiliated, revolted, and afraid.

As is common with such incidents, there was a power-differential between us. Because of that, it was necessary for me to continue engaging with them in professional settings. At the time, I did not feel I had a meaningful choice in the matter. Nevertheless, in the days and weeks following the incident, my distress was so enormous that I literally "lost time"—a symptom common to many trauma victims. And there was a period that continued for many years after the incident during which my personal commitments to my family and friends—even ones I looked forward to and would have enjoyed—were missed or neglected as I simply tried to move forward day by day.

No, I did not report the incident to anyone. I had significant family obligations and the potential harm to my career if I spoke up made it difficult if not impossible for me to do so. I tried to manage the impact on my own. I did not weep when the incident occurred. But I have cried gallons of tears in the years since.

It's also true—and critical to note—that smart, capable, productive women too often operate in a bubble of our own illusions. We believe our work is appreciated because it's good and on point and useful to our superiors. But woe betide us if, in a subordinate position, we begin to believe we actually matter in the context of our professional lives. If—in my mother's words—we get "too big for our britches."

The impacts of sexual harassment and sexual violence against female attorneys can be severe. We are caught off guard, frightened, humiliated, and worried for years—sometimes forever—after the incident(s). We feel not only victimized, unsafe, and belittled, even dirty, but also confused, hurt, and (almost always accurately) powerless. Our concentration and workplace performance suffer.

Astonishingly, disrespect of women does not cease when they become judges. A 2017 study by the Pritzker School of Law at Northwestern University found that female justices on the U.S. Supreme Court are interrupted—by counsel and by their male counterparts—three times more often than male justices.

## Discrimination and Harassment Under the Ethical Rules

As an aside, I cannot fail to point out that certain behavior that crosses the line—especially ill-treatment of subordinates—is not just boorish. Rule 9.1 of the District of Columbia Rules of Professional Conduct provides:

> A lawyer shall not discriminate against any individual in conditions of employment because of the individual's race, color, religion, national origin, sex, age, marital status, sexual orientation, family responsibility, or physical handicap.

Many other jurisdictions have similar provisions. Although its adoption by the various state supreme courts and mandatory bar associations has been resisted and remains controversial, Rule 8.4(g) of the ABA's Model Rules of Professional Conduct states that:

> [i]t is professional conduct for a lawyer to . . . engage in conduct that the lawyer knows or reasonably should know is harassment or discrimination on the basis of race, sex, religion, national origin, ethnicity, disability, age, sexual orientation, gender identity, marital status or socioeconomic status in conduct related to the practice of law.

It certainly feels that nothing we have been able to do thus far to address the problems of discrimination and harassment in the legal profession has been able to put a dent in the bullying behavior of some of our colleagues. I cannot help but think that if victims and witnesses began lodging ethical complaints and a few attorneys were disciplined in their jurisdictions, it might improve the situation.

## *Noli Illegitimi Carborundum*—and Your Ethical Responsibilities Are Yours

I have focused thus far on the many reasons why—as lawyers—our mental hygiene may be a bit less than pristine. The hardships imposed on us by the behavior of our clients, colleagues, superiors, judges, and neutrals, along with the everyday stresses we face along with everyone who isn't a lawyer, can get to be a lot to deal with. Note that the conduct I've described is certainly unethical at best and may be illegal—none of it should be tolerated or overlooked. But neither should it distract you from your duties.

We are lawyers, not police officers. We swore an oath upon admission to the bar, an oath that in almost every state and the District of Columbia includes a promise to exhibit the demeanor appropriate for an attorney. It is stated more definitively in some versions of the oath.

One of the first rules in every code of professional conduct in the United States is that a lawyer shall provide competent representation to a client. "Competent representation requires the legal knowledge, skill, thoroughness, and preparation reasonably necessary for the representation."[6]

It should go without saying that none of us can represent a client competently if, regardless of the reason, we are drunk, drug-impaired, severely depressed, overwhelmed by anxiety, suicidal, too sick, suffering from acute post-traumatic stress, distracted, in cognitive decline, or in any way less than our usual (if not our best) selves.

No matter how rough the seas we're trying to steer through, we cannot allow ourselves to be brought so low that we fail to honor our ethical responsibilities. And the duty to persevere

---

6. *See* DC Rule 1.1.

in upholding our ethical obligations is ours and ours alone. Indeed, there are times when our duty to the profession means reporting another attorney's impairment to the appropriate authority. But we cannot lose focus on our duties to our clients when our personal lives are disrupted.

Of course, we are going to face crises that we haven't foreseen. Encourage friendly relationships—and maintain them yourself—between your own staff and the employees of opposing counsel, court clerks' offices, judges' chambers, judicial law clerks, and even your own firm's hierarchy if that's necessary because of your firm's size. People who know each other—even casually—can smooth the path for having continuances granted when you cannot possibly keep a commitment at court.

Keep up to date with CLEs. It's so much easier to make time for an hour-long CLE at lunchtime than to find yourself needing an entire year's worth with only a couple of weeks until the deadline.

Participate in bar events. Including social ones. Even unwavering introverts can handle conversations with one or two people at a time, and it's a way to make friends who may be kindred spirits who will become good friends and supporters.

Know your bar's ethical rules. Know them at least as well as you know your rules of procedure. You ought to be able to cite them at least as well. Period.

My principal message is this: Your ethical duties are not diminished by bad moods or difficulties along your path. And while you can call on others for support, only you can ensure that you're fulfilling your responsibilities. Ask for help when you need it. That's your responsibility too.

# Chapter 3

## Serving Justice, Shaping the Future

This chapter turns our attention to what it means to serve justice in ways that reach beyond the limits of our own dockets. It reflects on the choices lawyers make when they offer their time, their talent, and their care to people who may have no one else to turn to. It highlights how the profession becomes stronger when we widen the path for those who have been left out and make room for voices that have struggled to be heard.

These essays remind us that our influence doesn't stop at the courthouse steps or boardroom door; it lives in the habits we model, the opportunities we open for others, and the communities we choose to build within our firms and schools.

# Pro Bono Work: The Benefits Outweigh the Costs

*Mary Gately and Lauren Grinder*

## Introduction

Engaging in pro bono work can help deepen relationships with clients who are also willing to devote their time to such charitable efforts, and it can enhance your personal and your firm's reputation in the profession and legal marketplace. Though the "business case" for pro bono has many laudable benefits, those benefits alone need not be the only motivating factors for choosing to help those who have unmet legal needs and cannot afford to pay for a lawyer's services. Not only does pro bono work profoundly impact the clients that receive these services, it also can provide important professional development opportunities, and it allows lawyers to connect with and build relationships in the communities in which we live and work.

Individuals with legal needs who can secure legal help achieve outcomes that are markedly different from similarly situated pro se parties. In the context of support of the Legal Services Corporation, the late Justice Antonin Scalia posed the following rhetorical question: "Can there be justice if it is not equal, can there be a just society when some do not have justice?" He went on to answer this question as follows: "Equality, equal treatment is perhaps the most fundamental element of justice. . . . And in today's law ridden society, denial of access to professional legal assistance is denial of equal justice."[1] The tremendous impact that having a lawyer has on pro bono clients is arguably the most important reason we should do pro bono work. These legal services are outcome determinative for most clients. Pro bono legal services can be the difference between deportation or staying in the United States, losing housing or retaining a much-needed apartment, or losing a child or retaining custody of that child.

Lawyers who do pro bono work are also profoundly impacted by the work in a way that is hard to measure. You will often hear that pro bono work is the most rewarding work a lawyer can do. One reason is because of the satisfaction that the lawyer gains from achieving an outcome that is so consequential for the client. But there are other tangible and intangible benefits to the lawyer in doing this work. It allows lawyers to pick a project that may further embed them in their local community or in an international project of interest. The lawyers develop relationships with those they help and local leaders and court officials. For some, it provides the ability to gain legal experience that might not come as quickly in private practice.

We have learned the benefits of pro bono work firsthand. The purpose of this essay is to offer our perspectives on the benefits of doing pro bono work at different career stages.

## Pro Bono Is a Career-Long Commitment: A Partner's Perspective

When you consider the consequential benefits, the cost of contributing time to pro bono work that might otherwise be devoted to other work pales in comparison. The benefits of

---

1. *Chairman Levi: Statement on the Death of Justice Antonin Scalia*, Legal Servs. Corp. (Feb. 14, 2016), https://www.lsc.gov/press-release/chairman-levi-statement-death-justice-antonin-scalia.

doing pro bono work have led me over the course of my career to always make time to provide pro bono services as an essential part of my practice. It is really not a benefit cost ratio but a win/win ratio. The clients benefit from our work on their behalf, and I benefit from the relationships with the clients, the satisfaction of knowing that I have had an impact for those clients, and from the mentorship and training of other lawyers who helped me with pro bono cases and those that I now get to mentor and train.

## *Positive Change*

The variety of benefits that come from pro bono work is something that I have experienced my entire legal career. For me, it started as an associate when the then-managing partner of our Washington, DC, office asked me to work on a pro bono sexual harassment lawsuit against the DC Department of Corrections on behalf of female correctional officers and other employees that were retaliated against for supporting the female officers. For an entire year of my career, I worked tirelessly on this case, taking over a dozen depositions, attending a six-week jury trial in federal court, presenting one of the named representative's cases at trial, and cross-examining an expert at trial. Not only did the jury return a verdict in favor of the class, but when the case eventually settled, I assisted with the damages phase for numerous other class claimants and was able to assist in the provision of sexual harassment training as part of the negotiated relief. I was privileged to get to know the many clients who endured terrible acts of sexual harassment and had the courage to stand up and demand change, and I also was part of a team that obtained relief that resulted in a cultural shift in which sexual harassment of any kind was not tolerated. In addition, I was able to gain valuable legal skills that helped make me the lawyer I am today. Simply put, a win/win calculus for the women in the class and for me.

## *International Reach*

Over time, I have taken on numerous pro bono cases, including international cases through our firm's nonprofit affiliate, New Perimeter, dedicated to providing long-term pro bono services to promote access to justice, sound legal institutions, social and economic development, and women's advancement. For example, I worked in Kosovo on a U.S. Agency for International Development project that facilitated women and other minorities with becoming members of the Kosovo bar, something that had been difficult for them to do in light of societal pressures. One of the young women that I met in that project is now the youngest female member of the Kosovo Supreme Court. It is the impact on individuals that makes the work so rewarding.

## *Local Impact*

Currently, I am serving as the outside pro bono litigation director of the DC Affordable Law Firm (DCALF), an access to justice organization that provides fellowships to recent legal graduates of Georgetown Law School and the University of the District of Columbia Law School. In exchange for receiving an LLM in advocacy from Georgetown, the fellows work for DCALF and represent clients in our local community that are in desperate need of legal assistance in family law, immigration, and probate work. DCALF clients are modest income DC residents who do not qualify for traditional sources of free civil legal services and cannot afford standard representation. I often co-counsel with DCALF to represent the clients, conducting cross-examinations of witnesses and experts. In other cases, I mentor the fellows so that they can take on that work. I provide strategic advice and supervise their written and oral work. After doing this for the last six years, I am embedded in the community of wonderful people who help the residents of the District of Columbia with numerous issues, and I now have a cadre of young lawyers who are passionate about their public interest work that have fanned out across the city and beyond, continuing to help those with pressing legal needs. Again, I am the one that has benefited from working so closely with the clients who have the courage to assert their legal rights and with the fellows who constantly push me to be creative and unwavering in our support of our clients.

## Benefits Beyond a Bonus: An Associate's Perspective

For associates, the cost-benefit analysis is different. The cost is largely the same; it is time. It is hours that otherwise may be devoted to billable work, business development, rest, or time with family and friends. But the benefit is more quantifiable for associates when firms encourage pro bono work by requiring a certain number of pro bono hours before an associate can be bonus eligible. This is an effective tool for motivating associates to carve out time for pro bono work, but associates should be wary of just checking the box without appreciating the significance of pro bono work to themselves and their clients. A couple of years ago, I took on a pro bono case and met a client who shifted my focus to other more significant benefits of pro bono work that far outweigh the cost. Connection, perspective, and confidence are among those benefits that transcend an annual performance evaluation.

### *Connection*

This shift in focus began when I took on a guardianship case through a local legal aid organization. I reached out to them because I was looking for pro bono time. But what I got was a loving father who needed help navigating the legal system so that he could get his adult son the right therapies and medical care. I had many things in common with this family. I grew up in a neighboring town and went to the same high school as my client's son. My mother taught at a school near where this family lived. And, like my own family when I was growing up, there were no lawyers in the family. There was not anyone who had the resources and knowledge to jump through all the legal hoops necessary to take care of a loved one who was not equipped to take care of himself. But now I had those resources through my law license and firm, and I had that knowledge with support from the local legal aid organization. I was able to help obtain the guardianship after making the necessary evidentiary showing at a hearing. Through doing this work, I connected not only with an inspiring family but with the community where I grew up. I reflected on where I came from and the incredible privilege it is to have a law license. This privilege is amplified in a state like mine where in most counties there is less than one attorney per 1,000 residents, and where around 17 percent of people live at or below the poverty level. But wherever you live and practice, pro bono work is an important way to stay connected to your community and to serve your neighbors. Without these connections, we are more prone to lose sight of the good we can do and the positive change we can make because of our profession.

## *Perspective*

This brings me to perspective. It is easy for associates to get in a rut, especially in the earlier years of learning how to practice law before they see how all the pieces fit together experience outcomes that demonstrate the importance of their daily work. Pro bono work provides perspective and an opportunity to do something different. Someone needs an attorney's skills and knowledge to obtain something they need to improve their life, whether it is a record sealed from decades past so that they can get a good job or whether it is a divorce from an abusive spouse. What a privilege it is to be equipped to help others achieve their goals and move forward. It is crucial to step outside your daily practice and use your skills for pro bono work. Not only is it your ethical responsibility, but the perspective you gain while helping others will make you a better person and a better lawyer. Intentionally balancing your practice with pro bono work can make your career more satisfying.

### *Confidence*

Finally, experience yields confidence, but for associates in private practice, hands-on experience can be hard to obtain. For litigators, it may be years before they argue a motion, take a deposition, examine a witness at a hearing or trial, or deal directly with clients. But doing pro bono work will get you on your feet. If you want to try cases, pro bono work can get you in the courtroom in front of a jury. But even if the pro bono work could not be more different from your daily work, you are practicing skills like communicating clearly with clients and gaining important experiences like solving unexpected problems. In the end, your pro bono clients' successes are a source of confidence that will be invaluable as you grow and develop as a lawyer.

## Conclusion

Wherever you are in your career, make pro bono work an intentional part of your practice. The myriad number of benefits outweigh any costs. And the pro bono work you take on is up to you. You can intentionally choose pro bono work that balances out your own practice with causes that interest and move you. You can help advance the justice system outside the United

States or make an impact in your own local community. You can help individuals meet their goals or conduct research for organizations who advocate for important policy change. Whatever pro bono work you choose, you will never regret donating your time and expertise to those in need.

# Hugs and Tears: A Pro Bono Manifesto

*John M. Barkett*

In my legal career of nearly 50 years, I have been involved in matters involving not just millions but also billions of dollars. So, why is it that the cases that stand out in my memory are pro bono cases? Two stories will explain why.

Some time ago, I received a telephone call just before Thanksgiving.

Female Caller: "Mr. Barkett?"

Me: "Yes. This is Mr. Barkett."

Caller: "I need a free mediator."

Me: "Why do you need a free mediator?"

Caller: "I have been sued by the Department of Education. I had a student loan."

Me: "Which you have not paid?"

Caller: "That's what the complaint says. I thought I had paid it, but the loan was taken out 20 years ago. I have lost my job. I moved in with my mother. And I no longer have any records. I cannot afford a lawyer. So I am representing myself. The judge has ordered mediation. And I have to find a free mediator because I have no money to pay a mediator."

Me: "May I just ask you how you got my name?"

Caller: "I looked up the list of approved mediators on the Court's website. I called everyone whose name began with an 'A.' Everyone turned me down. So I started on the list of names that began with a 'B.' That's how I got your name."

Me: "Okay. I will serve as a free mediator. But tell the lawyer for the Department of Education that I can only do it on the Monday before Christmas."

Christmas fell on a Saturday that year. I thought that the holiday spirit might enhance the likelihood of a resolution that would improve the plight of this alleged debtor.

We held the mediation on the Monday before Christmas. The complaint in the matter explained that the defendant had borrowed $4,000 in 1990. Based on interest and attorneys' fees, the amount due had ballooned to over $12,000. The "debtor" was a lovely, very bright woman who had a run of bad luck. The case resolved for $6,200, as noted in the publicly filed settlement documents. She had to pay $10 per month until she found a job and then the repayment amount would go up. She gave me a big hug when the mediation was over for serving as "free" mediator, even as she wondered how she would ever pay off this debt.

I had a generous friend and client who I had told about the case. He asked me to let him know what happened.

On Tuesday of Christmas week, I mailed a letter to my pro bono mediation party attaching copies of the documents filed with the court. This is what I said in the letter:

> I passed along the consent judgment to my friend, whom I refer to as Santa Claus. I am enclosing a copy of a cashier's check that was sent today (Tuesday) to the U.S. Department of Justice in the amount of $6,205.00 to pay off the judgment.
>
> You are now free of this debt. The only thing that my friend asked in return is that you always remember the needy in your prayers and in your actions.

She received the letter on Christmas Eve. I still get goosebumps when I recall her crying on the telephone thanking me. I told her that I did not deserve the thanks; I just happened to know a generous friend. The real thanks go to all of those mediators whose names began with an "A" that turned her down. And then she cried some more.

Tears: The compensation for pro bono work.

More recently, I received a call from a tenant who rented property that my family owned. She had been served with garnishment papers relating to the alleged failure to pay a credit card debt. The tenant cleaned houses for a living. She was a hard worker who barely made ends meet every month and had built up a very small savings account. She was forlorn and scared.

I stopped by to look at the papers. I told her I would represent her. She spontaneously hugged me.

A hug: My engagement agreement.

I had never handled a garnishment before, but I read the statute and realized that the debt collector/lawyer had only served my client with some of the papers that were required to be served. The remaining papers arrived a few days later. This was not a mistake. It was intentional, designed to try to confuse the garnishee so that a statutory deadline would pass and the garnishee could not contest the garnishment. Without a lawyer, she would have lost her savings.

In Florida, a head of household cannot be garnished. I filed the appropriate affidavit and attended the garnishment hearing that was noticed by the debt collector/lawyer. That lawyer never appeared. I asked the court to dismiss the writ of garnishment. Instead, the court called the debt collector lawyer to find out why he did not appear. He said that they dismissed their case after receiving the affidavit, but never bothered to inform me or cancel the hearing. Case won.

I delivered the good news personally. The worry of losing her only savings had created such an emotional peak, she instantly began to sob, and sob, and sob some more.

Tears: Compensation for pro bono work.

Yes, I know that I was just doing what I promised to do when I took the oath of admission to the Florida Bar: "I will never reject, from any consideration personal to myself, the cause of the defenseless or oppressed, or delay anyone's cause for lucre or malice. So help me God."

And yes, I know that Rule 6.1 of the Model Rules of Professional Conduct provides that, "Every lawyer has a professional responsibility to provide legal services to those unable to pay."

But the satisfaction of knowing that I kept my oath or complied with the ethics rules is not what I think about when I do pro bono work. It is the hugs and the tears. I cannot get out of mind the crying voice on the telephone or the sobbing client on the apartment steps.

If you do pro bono work, you know what I mean.

If you do not, you should start. Immediately. Hugs and tears await.

# Service and Solidarity: Strengthening Professional Ties in the Legal Field

*Rebecca Howlett and Cynthia Sharp*

"A rising tide lifts all boats."

— John F. Kennedy

The day-to-day practice of law can be pressure-filled and extremely stressful, which explains why members of our profession are at higher risk than the general population to suffer from mental health concerns. Indeed, studies consistently show higher rates of anxiety, secondary trauma, substance use disorders, and even suicide among lawyers. While it may not be possible to entirely eliminate these difficulties, we can help reduce them by fostering positive connections and collegiality in our profession.

The co-authors of this chapter believe that we have intrinsic obligations toward one another and to the profession that can be fulfilled, in part, by consciously establishing supportive interactions and relationships with our fellow lawyers. While law firms and other legal entities have the duty to create healthy work environments, our focus here is primarily on actions that individuals can take to build a healthier work culture now and for future generations to come.

## Cultivating Supportive Legal Environments

Reframing how we orient ourselves to colleagues (and even our adversaries) is a foundational step to implementing sustainable, positive change that promotes healthy professional relationships and legal work environments. Instead of strictly paying attention to our own agendas (our default), lawyers can choose to take active steps to build collegial, supportive communities that uplift us all.

Indeed, fostering supportive legal environments and institutions can help keep attorneys in compliance with our professional ethics obligations, like duty of competence, by insulating us from the ill effects of toxic stress and vicarious trauma. According to leading trauma expert, Dr. Bessel Van Der Kolk, "Study after study shows that having a good support network constitutes the single most powerful protection against becoming traumatized."[1]

Ultimately, fostering a legal culture that prioritizes holistic well-being and inclusion will lead to a happier, healthier, and more effective legal profession for all involved. Despite the rise of incivility and lack of empathy, attorneys want to be better and do better.

Significantly, well-being has emerged as a leading consideration for legal professionals when considering employment. According to the 2023 Law Firm Culture Survey, 85 percent of Gen Z/Millennial attorneys cite well-being and work–life balance as their top priority. Notably, younger generations also heavily prioritize diversity and inclusion, with 70 percent

---

1. Bessel A. Van der Kolk, *The Body Keeps the Score: Brain, Mind, and Body in the Healing of Trauma* 212 (Penguin, 2014).

seeking work environments that actively cultivate equity and inclusion.

Senior attorneys and decision-makers will be key driving forces to actively retool our legal institutions and processes to ensure they are meeting (and exceeding) lawyers' evolving priorities around what support they need to thrive as legal advocates and human beings. For example, legal decision-makers are encouraged to prioritize implicit or unconscious bias trainings, which can empower us with the requisite awareness and targeted tools to facilitate positive, healthy (and ethical!) interactions with each other and ourselves.

## Ethical Obligations to Each Other and the Profession

Notably, an attorney's duty to uphold ethical standards potentially includes an obligation to address and support our colleagues who may be impaired by mental health challenges, substance use disorders, or age-related issues. In the ideal world, we could identify and offer assistance to another before ethical infractions are committed. Unfortunately, this is not always possible because the colleague may be effective in concealing issues or may even refuse our help.

Many are unaware that Model Rule of Professional Conduct 1.16(a)(2) requires an attorney to withdraw from representation if "the lawyer's physical or mental condition materially impairs the lawyer's ability to represent the client."[2] However, lawyers suffering from depression, anxiety, severe stress, or other mental impairments may not be in a position to identify their own declining mental health.

2. https://www.americanbar.org/groups/professional_responsibility/publications/model_rules_of_professional_conduct/rule_1_16_declining_or_terminating_representation/.

In such a circumstance, that attorney's colleagues may be responsible for taking action, since Model Rule 8.3(a) mandates that "A lawyer who knows that another lawyer has committed a violation of the Rules of Professional Conduct that raises a substantial question as to that lawyer's honesty, trustworthiness or fitness as a lawyer in other respects, shall inform the appropriate professional authority."[3]

This duty is elaborated upon in ABA Formal Opinion 03-431 (2003), which requires "a lawyer who believes that another lawyer's mental condition materially impairs her ability to represent clients, and who knows that that lawyer continues to do so" to report that lawyer's violation of Model Rule 1.16(a)(2).[4] Furthermore, ABA Formal Opinion 03-429 (2003) discusses reporting requirements with respect to a lawyer with an impairment within your own firm.[5] NC State Bar 2013 Formal Ethics Opinion 8 examines the obligations of supervising attorneys and colleagues in the event that another firm lawyer may be impaired, laying out ten different scenarios that could occur in the legal setting and recommends the appropriate course of action for each. We suggest that readers review each of these opinions for a deeper understanding.

In short, firm partners and supervising lawyers must ensure compliance with professional conduct rules, report serious violations, and protect clients. Associates are required to report concerns to senior lawyers within the firm and seek guidance if ignored. The North Carolina opinion emphasizes that impairment due to substance abuse or mental illness triggers the

---

3. https://www.americanbar.org/groups/professional_responsibility/publications/model_rules_of_professional_conduct/rule_8_3_reporting_professional_misconduct/.

4. https://inns.innsofcourt.org/media/97942/11-20-14%20-%202%20Lawyers%20Duty.pdf.

5. https://inns.innsofcourt.org/media/97921/11-20-14%20-%203%20Obligations.pdf.

same obligations. Additionally, informing clients and involving the Lawyer Assistance Program are crucial steps in managing impairment.

## Empathy (or Lack Thereof) and Lawyer Well-Being

As a profession, we must ensure we are not unduly sowing the seeds of our own destruction, including preserving a state of play that we know is harmful to our health. Like a perfect storm, the inherently adversarial nature of our profession, outmoded ideas of effective advocacy, and common personality traits leave lawyers particularly prone to perpetuating a professional culture that contributes to burnout, mental health concerns, and lack of empathy for others and ourselves.

How we treat each other has profound effects on individual well-being, as well as the health of the legal community as a whole. According to Vermont Bar Counsel Michael Kennedy, "A lack of civility is contributing to an increase in the stress and burnout that impacts lawyers' well-being and wellness. We need to be better."[6] Indeed, one in four female attorneys and one in five attorneys under 40 are considering leaving the profession entirely because of the strain on their mental health and well-being.[7]

Many lawyers seem to have forgotten (or apparently never learned!) the Golden Rule, to treat others the way we want to

---

6. Rebecca Howlett & Cynthia Sharp, *Improving Attorney Civility with Mindfulness*, 10(8) GPSolo eReport (Mar. 2021), https://www.legalburnout.com/post/improving-attorney-civility-with-mindfulness.

7. Justin Anker & Patrick R. Krill, *Stress, Drink, Leave: An Examination of Gender-Specific Risk Factors for Mental Health Problems and Attrition Among Licensed Attorneys*, *16*(5) PLOS One (May 12, 2021), https://doi.org/10.1371/journal.pone.0250563.

be treated. Incivility in the profession manifests as an inherent lack of respect for others, which can be overt or subtle and can even take on the dynamic of a bullying or abusive relationship. Notably, incivility is not limited to interactions with opposing counsel but is far-reaching and extends to dealings with judges and even our own colleagues and staff.

One story of "strategic incivility" that particularly shocked us involved an attorney recovering from the birth of a son born four weeks prematurely. While still recovering in the hospital, Miranda H. received word that opposing counsel was threatening to subpoena her to a deposition. The reason? The requested leave of absence she had filed with the court did not technically start for two more weeks.

By way of reminder, our duty of zealous advocacy under the professional rules of ethics does not support the misguided sentiment that a "good" attorney is ruthless and wholly without compassion. Indeed, comment 1 of Model Rule 1.3 states: "The lawyer's duty to act with reasonable diligence does not require the use of offensive tactics or preclude the treating of all persons involved in the legal process with courtesy and respect."[8] As the saying goes, you catch a lot more flies with honey than vinegar.

So why is this incivility happening? Is the competitive, adversarial nature of our profession driving this trend, or are lawyers simply wired this way? Unlike any other profession, the majority of lawyers possess several unique personality trait outliers, including low levels of sociability or emotional vulnerability, empathy, and resilience. Conversely, attorneys tend to score high on skepticism, urgency, abstract thinking, and autonomy—don't tell us what to do.

---

8. https://www.americanbar.org/groups/professional_responsibility/publications/model_rules_of_professional_conduct/rule_1_3_diligence/comment_on_rule_1_3/.

By our nature, lawyers may have to consciously work harder than the general population to flex our empathy skills. According to data on lawyer psychology, attorneys typically demonstrate low cognitive empathy (41 percent), meaning they have a natural inclination *not* to pay attention to others' experiences or seek to understand others' point of view, feelings, or behavior. According to leading lawyer personality expert, Dr. Larry Richard, empathy amongst attorneys has been steadily declining over the years, with Millennial attorneys' empathy scores skewing even lower (38 percent).[9]

On the whole, lawyers would be well-served to seek out and implement targeted strategies to increase our ability to actively tune in to signs of distress or impairment amongst our colleagues, as well as to act with collegiality and compassion.

## Strengthening Bonds Through Professional Associations

> "No man is an island entire of itself; every man is a piece of the continent, a part of the main."
>
> —John Donne

Belonging to and participating in a professional association in person is one of the most effective ways for a lawyer to intermingle with other legal professionals, find a sense of community, and have opportunities for professional growth and development. Co-author Cynthia Sharp was active in her state and local bar association for close to 30 years while in practice

9. *The Legal Mindset Corner: Exploring the Psychology of Lawyer Behavior*, Answering Legal, Inc. (May 30, 2024), https://www.youtube.com/watch?v=ZC6V4Gq-YlQ.

and has been active at the national level in the American Bar Association for the past 13 years.

By taking full advantage of networking opportunities and attending as well as teaching association-sponsored CLEs, Cindy formed relationships with mentors as well as mentees and built many long-term friendships—both personal and professional. According to Cindy, "When I had an issue that I wanted to bounce off of another attorney, I always had someone to call who could at least point me in the right direction. A side benefit was that I built connections with potential referral sources."

Alongside the rise in incivility among lawyers is a decline in participation in professional associations. One of the most commonly cited reasons is that many lawyers now prefer to save time by taking advantage of online resources and virtual networking opportunities. To be clear, the authors heartily endorse online relationships, especially since that is how we met and ultimately built The Legal Burnout Solution. In addition to cultivating online connections, however, there are a number of advantages to building in-person relationships. Indeed, the commitment to meeting up with others IRL (in real life) can be well worth the effort.

A key benefit derived from face-to-face contact is the promotion of civility among colleagues. Connecting on a personal level allows even adversaries to gain at least a glimpse of each other's humanity. Subsequent interactions are then more likely to be civil since it is more difficult for most people to be rude to those with whom they have shared personal communication.

We hope that we have inspired even a few readers to become active in a local, state, or national professional association. Not only will individual attorneys benefit personally and professionally, but the profession as a whole will be strengthened through enhanced community and civility.

## Professionalism and (In)Civility

> "So let us begin anew; remembering on both sides that civility is not a sign of weakness, and sincerity is always subject to proof."
>
> —John F. Kennedy

Despite decades-old efforts to promote professionalism in the legal field (see the American Bar Association's 1995 recommendations encouraging bar associations to adopt aspirational standards of civility and courtesy) the issue of incivility continues unabated overall and appears to be worsening.[10] In response to the increase in lawyer incivility, the bars of most states as well as many local bars have adopted codes or guidelines of civility. Readers interested in reviewing various professionalism codes adopted throughout the U.S. can refer to a compilation put together by the American Bar Association.[11]

Not everyone is in favor of enacting civility codes, however, claiming that the rules may be applied unevenly and that free speech may be chilled. David L. Hudson Jr.'s excellent article *Lawyer Speech Triggers Both Civility and Constitutional Concerns* discusses this point of view.[12] We also recommend the article for its comprehensive legal and ethical analysis of professionalism and civility in the legal setting.

---

10. Seth Rosner, *Report with Recommendation to the House of Delegates*, ABA Standing Committee on Professionalism (Aug. 1995).

11. *Professionalism Codes*, Am. Bar Ass'n, https://www.americanbar.org/groups/professional_responsibility/resources/professionalism/professionalism_codes (last updated Mar. 2017).

12. David L. Hudson, Jr., *Lawyer Speech Triggers Both Civility and Constitutional Concerns*, A.B.A. J. (Sep. 1, 2019), abajournal.com/magazine/article/lawyer-speech-triggers-both-civility-and-constitutional-concerns.

As an aside, if an attorney's improper conduct warrants a complaint, the applicability or impact of all ethical rules must be considered. Attorney Karen Wachs of Springfield, New Jersey, cautions, "Attorneys, at least those in New Jersey, have to be very careful about 'complaining' about unprofessional or uncivil behavior due to the ethical risk of directly or indirectly divulging client confidential information and/or legal strategy even if done anonymously."[13]

The authors are in favor of articulating specific rules of professionalism and civility as a way of establishing formal boundaries. Even with specific rules in place, many will continue to act out their baser instincts through bullying—and most of those likely will continue to get away with it. With that said, we have hope and believe that all people are capable of evolving—if they would only stop and take a look at themselves. Those familiar with our work will not be surprised that one solution we suggest is to adopt a mindfulness practice as outlined next.

## Mindfulness Strategies to Forge Conscious Connection

> "Between stimulus and response there is a space. In that space is our power to choose our response. In our response lies our growth and our freedom."
>
> — Viktor Frankl

Only when we recognize the root cause of an issue can we identify effective solutions. This is why we promote mindfulness as a foundational strategy to improve our relationships with

---

13. Howlett & Sharp, *supra* note 2.

colleagues and consciously build legal work environments that safeguard our health and well-being. For example, consistently practicing mindfulness can strengthen our ability to communicate with courtesy and respect even in the face of challenging situations and interpersonal interactions.

Proactively learning and implementing healthy coping skills can help us effectively manage the ill effects of uncivil interactions and avoid perpetuating discourteous behavior. Through mindfulness meditation, we can increase our awareness of stress triggers—and the accompanying thoughts and feelings that arise—which, in turn, can reduce impulsive reactivity to these stressors.

We've all been there—getting an email that we perceive as rude or passive-aggressive, "seeing red," and immediately firing back a heated response that only adds fuel to the fire. When we practice mindfulness, we create and hold space to objectively observe our experiences, which helps us slow down and make conscious decisions rooted in awareness. Take the rude email scenario: An attorney who regularly practices mindful meditation will likely be better able to recognize how the discourteous email affected her, move past those negative emotions, and respond civilly, rather than instantly reacting in anger or frustration in the heat of the moment.

Increasing our mindfulness creates a powerful positive feedback loop, lowering our perceived stress levels, expanding our empathy, and increasing our overall sense of well-being, happiness, and life satisfaction. Further, the positive effects of mindful meditation are cumulative, meaning the more you practice it, the more you can maximize its benefits.

When beginning a mindfulness practice, keep an open mind and remember that there is no singular "right" way to meditate. We encourage you to experiment, have fun, and find a practice that resonates with you personally and that will help you form sustainable, healthy habits. Following are a few practical ways to integrate mindfulness into your everyday life and law practice:

### *Breathwork*

Our breath is the most foundational mindfulness tool at our disposal. Taking slow, deep breaths for even 30 seconds to a minute can turn off our "fight or flight" response and kick on our relaxation response. Particularly in moments of stress or anxiety, bring awareness to your breath. There are countless "pranayamas" to explore—*prana* meaning breath of life or vital energy and *yama* meaning control in Sanskrit. For example, take three long breaths in through the nose and out through the mouth focusing on making your exhales longer than your inhales. Check out legalburnout.com for several breathwork tutorials, including box breathing, alternate nostril breathing, and cleansing breath.

### *Movement*

Studies show that incorporating small movements into our daily routine can have immediate and long-lasting positive benefits on our mood, as well as protect us from developing mental health concerns, such as depression. Seek to incorporate simple, restorative movements throughout your workday, especially to relieve physical tension or the stress of challenging interpersonal interactions. Set regular reminders to get up from your desk and walk around, stretch, or give yourself a quick massage to your ears, neck, shoulders, hands, and so on.

### *Gratitude*

On average, we experience approximately 60,000 thoughts every day—critically, 80 percent of our thoughts are negative, and 95 percent are repetitive. By practicing gratitude, we can train our brains to adopt a more positive state of mind. Begin and end each day by reflecting on and/or writing down three things that you're grateful or thankful for in general or something that went well that day. Strive to identify new or different things to be thankful for each time.

Remind yourself that cultivating mindfulness is a skill set that takes time, dedication, and consistency to develop. Especially if you don't have much prior experience working with contemplative practices, initial attempts to practice mindful awareness of your thoughts, feelings, and bodily sensations may be challenging or even feel uncomfortable. Be gentle with yourself, have compassion, and stick with it!

If you are interested in learning more simple strategies to promote stress resilience, we have compiled a Mindfulness Resource Guide to get you started. Email us at cindy@legalburnout.com, and we will forward it to you.

## Moving Forward

Taking steps to create and nurture service and solidarity is a duty that we owe each other and the profession as a whole. We urge each of you to consider what shifts you can make in behaviors and attitudes that will help improve the culture of our profession as well as the lives of our colleagues. By working together, we can build a supportive community so that all can thrive.

# Re-Regulation of Law: A Professionalism Mandate

*Jayne R. Reardon*

## Introduction

The legal profession exists to provide legal services to laypeople. And as a profession, we are bound by ethical rules contained in rules of professional conduct (rules adopted by state supreme courts and principles of professionalism that are less prescriptive). The rules establish who can deliver legal services and how they can be delivered. Animating the rules are principles of professionalism that provide that lawyers have an obligation to extend services to those who may not be able to afford legal help—or even know that the law may provide a solution to their problems.

Unfortunately, data consistently shows that most Americans do not receive the legal services they need. That may be about to change—finally.

It has become apparent, particularly since the advent of generative AI-based large language models such as ChatGPT, that technology-based solutions may help fill this gap between those who need legal services and those who receive them. In response, many state supreme courts have adopted or are considering regulatory changes to their rules that would allow technology-based solutions and people other than licensed lawyers to deliver legal services.

These initiatives are laudatory. They exemplify professionalism aimed at furthering the public interest that our self-regulated profession demands.

This essay will discuss first, the source of attorney regulations and the professionalism principles that animate those regulations; second, the success metric of the legal profession in delivering services to the public; third, the nexus between attorney regulations and the access of the public to legal services; and finally, regulatory models of reform that are unfolding in multiple states to encourage the profession to better serve the public interest.

## Professionalism Is the Touchstone of Attorney Regulations

As members of the legal profession, lawyers have ethical obligations governing how they serve clients, the legal system, and the public good. While the rules delineate how lawyers *must* behave, the professionalism concepts outlined in the preamble to the Model Rules of Professional Conduct animate how lawyers *should* behave and practice.

The preamble outlines lawyers' "special responsibility for the quality of justice" (Preamble [1]), charging them with seeking "improvement of the law, access to the legal system, the administration of justice and the quality of service rendered by the legal profession" as well as urging them to use their time, resources, and civic influence to ensure equal access to our justice system for those who cannot afford or secure adequate legal counsel (Preamble [6]). Moreover, the preamble delineates lawyers' responsibility to "help the bar regulate itself in the public interest" (Preamble [6]).

In terms of regulating the legal profession, the preamble explains the need for self-governance, noting the close relationship between the legal profession and the "processes of government and law enforcement," and the goal of maintaining "the legal profession's independence from government domination" (Preamble [11]).

Moreover, Preamble [12] states that lawyers are responsible for self-regulating to serve the public interest, not their own:

> It is important to note that this relative autonomy carries with it special responsibilities of self-government. *The profession has a responsibility to assure that its regulations are conceived in the public interest and not in furtherance of parochial or self-interested concerns of the bar. . . .* Neglect of these responsibilities compromises the independence of the profession and the public interest which it serves. (Emphasis added.)

Given the focus on the public interest, questions should arise as we analyze the rules. Specifically, are the rules conceived in the public interest? Or are they in furtherance of parochial or self-interested concerns of the bar? Could the rules be operating, in fact, to inhibit the public's access to legal services?

## The Landscape of Public Access to Legal Services

The public—presumably Americans writ large—has an interest in protecting and asserting its legal rights. Those rights are created and influenced by an increasing volume and complexity of laws, regulations, treaties, and ordinances that are developed, interpreted, and protected by lawyers. It stands to reason, therefore, that attorney regulations "conceived in the public interest" would be drafted to facilitate the ability of the community at large to access quality legal services.

How is the public faring in obtaining legal services? The public is increasingly shut out or opting out of acquiring help for legal problems. According to the Legal Services Corporation's

2022 Justice Gap Report,[1] low-income Americans do not get any or enough legal help for 92 percent of their substantial civil legal problems, which are commonly consumer issues, healthcare, housing, and debt. These figures are even more damning than the 2017 Justice Gap Report,[2] which showed that more than 86 percent of low-income Americans received inadequate or no assistance when facing critical legal issues.

However, low-income Americans are not the only ones not getting their legal needs met. Middle-income Americans, according to various state surveys of civil legal needs, struggle to access legal services as well. For example, North Carolina's 2021 Report "In Pursuit of Justice: An Assessment of the Civil Legal Needs of North Carolina" found that middle-income Americans at 200 percent to 400 percent of the federal poverty level are unable to access legal services, as they do not qualify for legal aid but also cannot afford to pay a private lawyer.

The distribution of lawyers across our country is uneven. The American Bar Association's annual Profile of the Legal Profession reports for the last several years contain data that show the number of lawyers nationwide has grown, but the rate of growth has slowed. In addition, in 2024, 28 percent of the lawyers were located in New York and California, and the number of legal deserts (defined as a county with fewer than one lawyer per 1,000 people) numbered over 1,300. In my home state of Illinois, one-third of the 102 counties lack practicing attorneys, 13 counties have fewer than five practicing attorneys for the whole county.

American's access to affordable legal services does not fare well as compared to the rest of the world. The World Justice

1. https://justicegap.lsc.gov/the-report/.

2. https://www.lsc.gov/our-impact/publications/other-publications-and-reports/2017-annual-report-justice-gap.

Project's 2024 Rule of Law Index[3] ranks the U.S. as 107 out of 142 countries in the factor of the ability of people to access and afford civil justice.

This factor measures "the accessibility and affordability of civil courts, including whether people are aware of available remedies, can access and afford legal advice and representation, and can access the court system without incurring unreasonable fees, encountering unreasonable procedural hurdles, or experiencing physical or linguistic barriers."

Having a special responsibility for the quality of justice, lawyers should question why the U.S. ranks so low and whether the way legal services are regulated is contributing.

## The Nexus Between Regulation and the Public's Access to Legal Services

Our rules govern the relationship between attorneys and their clients, and they emphasize the protection of existing clients. But regulating to protect existing clients is a much narrower focus than regulating in "the public interest." The rules do not *require* lawyers to provide services to those beyond their current clients. However, such an exhortation is clearly referenced in the preamble to the rules, including the encouragement of pro bono service.

Another point of concern is that the Model Rules of Professional Conduct or their state counterparts have not had a significant overhaul in decades, so do not account for how technology and globalization have drastically transformed the industry and the lives and interests of the public.

The observation of ethicist Deborah L. Rhode from 25 years ago unfortunately rings true still today. Rhode wrote that

3. https://worldjusticeproject.org/rule-of-law-index/global/2024.

"the public's interest has played too little part in determining professional responsibilities. Too much regulation of lawyers has been designed by and for lawyers."[4]

But how exactly does attorney regulation relate to the United States' access to justice problem? The truth is that we are not sure. But data shows that our profession is currently failing the public, despite the fact that legal services have previously been provided to vast swaths of the American population economically and at scale. However, access to these services was shut down, ostensibly because they violated unauthorized practice of law (UPL) rules.[5] We also know that technology companies have attempted to provide legal information and services to needy consumers in innovative ways, but they were prosecuted and shuttered for violating UPL statutes and laws.[6]

It is important to note that defining UPL as "whatever lawyers historically have done" or "anything that affects someone's legal rights," as is typical in UPL statutes, is untenable when generative AI tools are performing tasks previously handled exclusively by lawyers, including taking the bar exam and receiving higher scores than most humans in minutes.

Therefore, lawyers have an obligation to consider if the way legal services are regulated is contributing to the access to justice gap.

---

4. Deborah L. Rhode, *In the Interests of Justice: Reforming the Legal Profession* (2000).

5. *See, e.g.*, Nora Freeman Engstrom & James Stone, *Auto Clubs and the Lost Origins of the Access-to-Justice Crisis*, 134(1) Yale L.J. (Oct. 2024).

6. *See, e.g.*, The Florida Bar v. TIKD Servs. LLC & Christopher Riley, Individually and as Founder of TIKD, No. SC 18-149; Unauthorized Practice of Law Comm. v. Parsons Tech., Inc., No. Civ.A.3:97CV-2859H (N.D. Tex. Jan. 22, 1999).

## Re-Regulation in the States

In the United States, lawyer regulation has been reactive. State bar counsel investigate complaints against lawyers and state supreme courts discipline those lawyers found to have violated ethical rules. However, regulation of the legal profession involves more than disciplining errant attorneys; it is the regulation of an economic market. And regulating the market in the public interest requires consideration of the entire market and the public interest.

Some state supreme courts have taken this responsibility to heart, promulgating new regulations around who can provide legal services and how they can be provided. These reforms focus on key traditional restrictions in the Model Rules and state counterparts: (1) the broad ban on UPL that prohibits (and may criminalize) people from offering legal services unless licensed by the state supreme court, or (2) the ban on fee-sharing between lawyers and nonlawyers expressed in Rule 5.4, which prohibits lawyers who offer the public legal services from partnering with, taking investment from, or being employed by nonlawyers.

Many state supreme courts have adopted different models of reforming these regulations, reflecting professionalism in action. These different approaches also exemplify states functioning as laboratories of democracy.

The regulatory changes fall into three broad categories: (1) authorizing professionals who do not have a JD (i.e., "nonlawyers") to deliver some limited legal services, (2) licensing entities containing both lawyers and other professionals engaged in providing legal services, and (3) establishing regulatory sandboxes.

These approaches overlap, but each is described in the following sections.

## *Model I: Authorizing Professionals Without a JD to Deliver Limited Legal Services*

While only licensed lawyers have historically been authorized to deliver legal services, paralegals have worked under the supervision of lawyers for decades. The idea that people who are not licensed lawyers can successfully be trained to provide some legal services to consumers is hardly a stretch.

Examples already exist in the federal civil justice system, which authorizes people who are not lawyers to provide representation in social security, veterans' benefits, tax, patent, and other administrative proceedings.

Currently, two primary models of authorizing lay advocates are unfolding in multiple states. They are (1) paraprofessionals, who provide legal services to consumers directly, and (2) community justice workers, who provide legal services to low-income individuals under the supervision of legal aid lawyers.

Iterating on the paralegal concept, states have been licensing a new category of legal professionals who are trained to deliver targeted services to people who would otherwise not access legal services. Given titles such as "allied legal professionals," "legal practitioners," or "limited legal practitioners," each individual must complete educational and examination requirements.

As of this writing, nine states have implemented programs that authorize individuals other than licensed lawyers to provide limited legal services directly to consumers. They include Arizona, Colorado, Delaware, Hawaii, Minnesota, New Hampshire, Oregon, Utah, and Washington (program sunset for future applicants).

In addition to specific education, experience, and examination requirements, the programs define and limit the scope of the paraprofessional's practice. The most common substantive areas are family law, housing, and debt.

Some states allow paraprofessionals to represent clients in depositions, mediations, or settlement conferences, while others restrict their activities to document review and preparation.[7]

Several other states are actively considering paraprofessional programs, including Indiana, Michigan, New Mexico, North Carolina, and Texas.

In addition to paraprofessionals, states are also exploring community justice workers. Community justice workers generally must be supervised by a legal aid attorney and serve clients at or below a certain income level.

Alaska pioneered this approach. Rather than issuing a new license, the Alaska Supreme Court instituted a waiver of the UPL provision for nonlawyers trained and supervised by the Alaska Legal Services Corporation. Nicole Nelson implemented this program in rural Alaska when she was the executive director of the Alaska Legal Services Corporation. The community justice worker approach piloted in Alaska is premised on research that shows many people do not recognize that their problem has a legal solution. Therefore, justice workers were recruited from those holding trusted roles in the community (such as health aides, faith leaders, and librarians), and then trained them using on-demand virtual programs providing legal-specific training in a clearly defined scope of practice.

Now as the CEO of Frontline Justice, Nelson is replicating the Alaska program nationwide. As of January 27, 2026, according to the Frontline Justice website [https://www.frontlinejustice.org/about#team] 14 states and the District of Columbia have authorized or proposed CJW programs and 20 are actively developing them.

---

7. See "Allied Legal Professionals: A National Framework for Program Growth" and other reports on the Institute for the Advancement of the American Legal System's website.

Similar programs have been launched in Arizona and Utah through Innovation for Justice (i4J), affiliated with law schools in both states. The i4J model trains law and graduate students to deliver legal services and trains nonlawyers to provide limited legal advice through roles in community-based organizations. Like the Frontline Justice program, the legal training consists of online and self-paced 60- to 80-hour courses.

Texas considered adopting both of these models of new service providers. The Texas Supreme Court issued preliminary approval to allow both licensed legal paraprofessionals and licensed court-access assistants. However, the anticipated effective date has been stayed.

In a related development, Illinois announced a pilot project in September 2024 to train librarians at 18 public libraries across the state as court navigators, focusing on divorce and child custody, domestic violence, debt, housing, wills and estates, and consumer debt issues. The program is a collaboration among the Illinois Supreme Court, the Illinois Secretary of State, and the Chicago Bar Foundation.

These regulatory approaches are new, and data is being gathered. It is quite possible, even likely, that lay community-based advocates may be able to connect with Americans in a way that lawyers currently do not. These individuals, who are vetted, trained, and accountable, are helping their communities understand there may be a legal solution to their problems—and deliver it.

A resulting benefit may be a more educated public that is knowledgeable about the law and individuals' rights, and is confident in our legal system.

## *Model II: Authorizing Entity Regulation*

In addition to issuing new regulations for individuals to deliver services, states are also exploring entity regulation to improve access to justice. Many states have implemented or are considering frameworks that regulate a firm or entity containing lawyers and other professionals working alongside lawyers to deliver legal services.

Entity regulation gets at the core of challenges related to how lawyers have been allowed to organize themselves to deliver legal services.

For many decades, the District of Columbia was the only jurisdiction to allow lawyers to form partnerships with nonlawyers, and that only in limited circumstances. More recently, however, Rule 5.4's proscriptions against fee-sharing between lawyers and nonlawyers were suspended in Utah and eliminated in Arizona, resulting in novel business structures that operate under strict guidelines. This initiative is also under a pilot program in Washington state.

Utah's "regulatory sandbox," which was approved in 2020, allows technology platforms and other business entities to experiment with legal service structures that are not traditionally allowed under the rules.

In addition, in 2021, the Arizona Supreme Court issued rules allowing an alternative business structure (ABS; defined as an entity that includes nonlawyers who have an economic interest or decision-making authority in the entity) to employ or engage lawyers to provide legal services under certain conditions, including licensure of the entity and a licensed Arizona lawyer designated to supervise the ethical compliance of legal practice. As of this writing, 117 ABSs have been authorized to deliver legal services in Arizona.

Several entities have been authorized to operate in both Utah and Arizona, and many target those who have not traditionally sought legal services.

For example, Rasa Legal's AI-driven software allows Utah and Arizona residents with criminal histories to discover in minutes if their records are eligible for expungement and, if so, guides them through the process. Other technology-driven solutions include a company that allows users to determine if they have a personal injury claim after a slip-and-fall or other accident and a platform that allows consumers to connect with lawyers to handle traffic tickets.

Washington state also has put in place entity regulation as a pilot project. In December 2024, the Washington Supreme Court issued an order adopting the Washington State Bar Association and Practice of Law Board's recommendation for a pilot project offering an exception from existing rules to allow lawyers and nonlawyers and/or technology solutions within the same entity. The rationale of the pilot framework is to protect the public while gathering data and information to allow the court to make an informed decision regarding whether to implement entity regulation.

In the court's detailed order allowing the pilot program and addressing application and monitoring procedures, the court stated:

> This Court has determined that while serving important public protection purposes, these court rules and statutes [including Washington's Rule 5.4] serve as barriers to the exploration, and data-driven testing, of legal regulatory reforms that would permit entities to provide legal and law-related services to consumers in Washington, whether or not the provision of those services would constitute the practice of law[.][8]

The pilot proposal opens the door to technology companies or other applicants who may not be licensed lawyers but believe they can provide services to benefit the public. The pilot's goal would be to determine (before any permanent rule

---

8. https://www.courts.wa.gov/content/publicUpload/Supreme%20Court%20Orders/Order%2025700-B-721.pdf?utm_source=chatgpt.com.

reform is implemented) whether entity regulation will increase the public's access to affordable and reliable legal services without creating risks to consumer harm. The pilot is set to run for ten years after the first entity is approved.

## *Model III: Establishing Regulatory Sandboxes*

Another way to explore potential regulatory reforms before implementing them is through a "regulatory sandbox," which allows the testing of innovative products, services, or models in a controlled setting with light regulatory requirements. This approach, which is common in finance and technology, allows data to be collected and examined before instituting permanent regulations. The pilot entity regulation approach of the Washington Supreme Court, discussed earlier, demonstrates elements of this approach.

### *Utah*

Unlike Washington's sandbox, which is focused on the entity model, Utah established a sandbox with more open requirements. The Utah Supreme Court established the first legal regulatory sandbox in the United States in 2020, noting its desire to "harness the power of entrepreneurship, capital, and machine learning in the legal arena."[9] Utah's sandbox was more wide-ranging. The court's Office of Legal Services Innovation (Innovation Office) allows new legal service models that would otherwise violate Model Rule 5.4, 5.5, or other unauthorized practice of law rules. Entities in the sandbox can be authorized by the Innovation Office to provide legal services by people other than lawyers, by software, or by entities that are not owned or controlled by lawyers.

9. Utah Supreme Court Standing Order 15 (Aug. 31, 2020).

Approved entities range from community justice workers to a legal services company offering estate planning through software, lay assistants, and lawyers. They also included for a while Rocket Lawyer, a large legal technology company that provides automated legal document services and also hires and partners with lawyers to offer legal assistance and advice.

The Innovation Office uses a "risk-based" regulatory framework to assess legal service entities. Entities are identified and evaluated by their innovation level (essentially the level of involvement by attorneys) and categories of potential consumer harm. The entities must report data on whether and to what extent consumers are harmed, defined as whether a consumer (1) achieves an inaccurate or inappropriate legal result, (2) fails to exercise legal rights through ignorance or bad advice, or (3) purchases an unnecessary or inappropriate legal service. The regular activity reports, which are published by the Innovation Office, show sandbox entities are providing services across a range of legal areas with very low incidences of measured consumer harm.

In September 2024, based on four years of operations, the Utah Supreme Court made changes to the pilot, narrowing the scope of acceptable entities to those that demonstrate the most potential to narrow the access to justice gap for underserved Utahns. Noting that many ABS entities had no meaningful presence in the Utah market and the number and variety of entities in the sandbox posed challenges for data collection and analysis, the court modified the requirement of innovation to require a Utah nexus. The court explained in its September 5, 2024, policy order that "Only applications that present an innovative service model with the potential to expand access to legal services in Utah should be submitted for Court approval.

The impact on Utah consumers must be substantial relative to the entity's overall reach."[10]

It is a feature of sandbox programs that they iterate in response to generated data. The experiences of the first adopters, such as Utah, should help inform the actions of other state supreme courts.

### *Minnesota*

In June 2024, the Minnesota State Bar Association adopted a report and recommendations from a working group on AI that posited a through-line between regulation and the justice gap.

The report, "Implications of Large Language Models (LLMs) on the Unauthorized Practice of Law (UPL) and Access to Justice," notes the tremendous potential of large language models to change legal practice and provide legal information and services to Americans. It also emphasizes the need to ensure new technologies are safe.

The working group recommended a risk-based regulatory framework and the creation of both a permanent AI Committee and an Access to Justice Legal Sandbox, which would provide a controlled environment for organizations to use LLMs without fear of UPL prosecution.

The report cautioned against regulations permitting only licensed attorneys to use generative AI for legal purposes, stating, "The rich will continue to hire lawyers, who will continue using the best LLM-backed tools. The poor—who lack

10. https://utahinnovationoffice.org/wp-content/uploads/2024/10/Letter-to-the-Legal-Services-Innovation-Committee-9.5.24.pdf?utm_source=chatgpt.com.

representation, needing those LLM-backed tools the most—will be denied them." As of this writing, the AI Committee has been formed and will begin to consider the parameters of a sandbox focused on solutions that cn provide help to underserved populations.

### *Indiana*

In April 2024, the Indiana Supreme Court created a Commission on Indiana's Legal Future, charging it with exploring options to address Indiana's lawyer shortage and asking the Commission to present findings and recommendations to the court. The Commission formed work groups addressing business and licensure models, incentivizing rural practice, and technology applications.

The Commission's Innovation Committee released an interim report in July 2024 with 27 recommendations, including establishing a regulatory sandbox. Following a public comment period, the court acted on some of the recommendations without waiting for the final report. The Innovation Committee's final report, issued in July 2025 includes a regulatory sandbox recommendation.[11]

## Conclusion

These innovative approaches to lawyer regulation represent scaleable models that may begin to reverse the access to legal services crisis. They upend traditional regulation, which attempts to ensure competent and ethical legal services by prescribing who can provide them.

---

11. https://www.in.gov/courts/admin/files/innovation-regulatory-reform-report.pdf.

Each model is proactive and predicated on the collection and analysis of data on actual consumer impact. They are certainly experimental, but they are consistent with our professional responsibilities to pursue regulation in the public interest. They should be studied, iterated, and adopted.

The state supreme courts described earlier are acting in furtherance of our collective responsibility to regulate the profession "in the public interest" to make a reality of the *raison d'etre* of our profession: that justice be accessible to all.

# Uniformity, Inequity, and Exclusion? The Ethical Lawyer's Response to Current Times

*Allegra Lawrence-Hardy and Michelle McClafferty*

## Preliminary Address

Since the outset of the legal profession, lawyers have served at the intersection of law and equity—domains once distinct, now largely merged in modern jurisprudence. This convergence mirrors a deeper truth at the heart of legal practice: that justice and fairness are not opposing forces, but complementary ideals, both essential to the lawyer's purpose. To that end, lawyers are not merely technicians of rules or advocates for private interests, but stewards of the legal system's moral and ethical legitimacy.

Throughout history, the legal profession has honored those who sacrifice personal gain to serve the underprivileged and underrepresented, stemming from a belief that the law must serve all, not just the powerful. Indeed, landmark cases like *Gideon v. Wainwright*, which guaranteed legal counsel to indigent defendants, and *Brown v. Board of Education*, which dismantled the legal framework of segregation, are cherished not only for their legal holdings but also for the values they enshrine. They remind us that the true measure of the profession lies in its commitment to those otherwise marginalized and sidelined in our legal system. While we may be rethinking what we call this commitment, it must continue to live in the fiber of the profession if law is to retain its credibility and effectiveness as a vehicle for equity.

## History of a Movement

Like any movement, the DEI movement is not driven by its moniker; it is driven by the values that animate it, including a commitment to build a more just and equitable society for all. With that perspective, it is indisputable that the movement did not begin with—and cannot be reduced to—unconscious bias training, affinity groups, or even affirmative action. Instead, the movement hearkens back to the Reconstruction Era, when we decided as a nation that our Black and brown neighbors were entitled to the same rights promised by the Constitution to free White men, including the fundamental right to vote and the protection of due process. The movement brought us women's suffrage, the Civil Rights Act, the Age Discrimination in Employment Act, the Americans with Disabilities Act, servicemember rights, the LGBTQ+ movement, and more.

For some time, DEI manifested as adding a woman or person of color to the team. Slowly but critically, the circle of inclusion has broadened. Over time, DEI became about more than who was allowed in the door—it grew to address who had a seat at the table of power. We began to acknowledge and confront socioeconomic barriers to progress, the burdens faced by working parents, the unique opportunities that come from neurodiversity, and the bridges for generational gaps. And yet, despite our progress, disparity often still predominates where parity and understanding should.

The ABA has reported that "the legal profession remains one of the least diverse of any profession."[1] While that statement was made nearly seven years ago, more current data reflects little change. According to Law360 Pulse's annual Women in Law Report, many firms remain "behind the curve when it comes to improving opportunities for women, and progress remains extremely slow."[2] In reporting its 2024 Diversity Scorecard, the American Lawyer indicated, "Law firms also have work to do if they aim to approach proportional representation with the broader U.S. population, which, according to 2020 U.S. Census data, contains 12% African Americans and 19% Hispanics."[3] And according to the 2023 Report on Diversity in U.S. Law Firms by the National Association for Law Placement (NALP), women represent only about 40 percent of all lawyers in firms, with women of color making up an even smaller percentage—approximately 11 percent.[4]

The ongoing challenges of diversity in the legal field are reflected in employee perceptions and experiences. According to a 2023 survey by Above the Law and Major, Lindsey & Africa, "71% of respondents of color believe that law firm culture is inherently biased against diverse attorneys" and

---

1. Allison Laffey & Allison Ng, *Diversity and Inclusion in the Law: Challenges and Initiatives*, Am. Bar Ass'n (May 2, 2018), https://www.americanbar.org/groups/litigation/resources/newsletters/jiop/diversity-inclusion-law-challenges-initiatives.

2. *The 2024 Women In Law Report*, Law360 (Aug. 2024), https://www.law360.com/articles/1867375/the-2024-women-in-law-report.

3. Dan Roe, *Slow But Steady: Law Firm Diversity Gains Continued in 2023*, ALM, Law.com (June 25, 2024, 10:01 AM), https://www.law.com/americanlawyer/2024/06/25/slow-but-steady-law-firm-diversity-gains-continued-in-2023.

4. 2023 Report on Diversity in U.S. Law Firms, NALP (Jan. 2024), https://www.nalp.org/uploads/Research/2023NALPReportonDiversityFinal.pdf.

"[a]lmost 35% of attorneys of color do not believe their firm is dedicated to the training and development of minority attorneys, and less than half say their firm treats people of color and non-minority attorneys equally when it comes to staffing."[5] Perceptions that their firms do not adequately foster inclusivity can create a cycle of disengagement, where talented individuals from diverse backgrounds feel marginalized and are less likely to remain within the organization.

Accordingly, many law firms are not achieving meaningful progress toward an inclusive workplace; instead, they view inclusion initiatives as peripheral rather than integral to law firms' operational success. This persistent lag by the legal profession underscores the need for a foundational commitment to cultural change under which fostering a genuinely inclusive environment is not merely a best practice. Rather, it is a strategic necessity that can directly influence a firm's competitive advantage. And more fundamentally, it is the moral and ethical way to practice law.

## A Lawyer's Dual Role

Notwithstanding the many hats we wear as legal practitioners, at the heart of our work, we fill two equally consequential roles: trusted advisor and zealous advocate.[6] Both demand a persistent commitment to inclusivity.

A lawyer's role as advisor extends beyond the provision of legal counsel; it necessitates a holistic understanding of a client's circumstances, including the client's unique cultural,

5. Vera Djordjevich, *Most Lawyers Believe a Diverse and Inclusive Workforce Should Be a Priority*, Above the Law (May 18, 2023, 11:47 AM), https://abovethelaw.com/2023/05/most-lawyers-believe-a-diverse-and-inclusive-workforce-should-be-a-priority.

6. Model Code of Pro. Resp., Preamble [2] (ABA 1983).

social, and personal background. Effective counseling hinges on the ability to build trust and rapport, which can be achieved only when clients feel respected and understood. By actively listening and validating clients' experiences, lawyers can provide tailored guidance that respects their clients' values and perspectives. Inclusive counseling practices enable lawyers to identify potential biases or barriers that may affect their clients' legal interests. And by prioritizing inclusivity in their counseling practices, lawyers can ensure that all clients receive the comprehensive support they need and deserve, ultimately fostering a more equitable and respectful attorney–client relationship.

As advocates, we also must embrace inclusivity to represent our clients effectively. Zealous advocacy requires a deep understanding of the varied experiences and challenges faced by individuals from different backgrounds. An inclusive approach allows lawyers to craft compelling narratives that resonate with judges and juries. Advocating for inclusive practices within the legal system enhances the quality of representation, ensures every client has a fair chance in the legal process, and contributes to broader societal change.

## Inclusion as a Cornerstone of Legal Ethics

The American Bar Association's Model Rules of Professional Conduct provides a framework for understanding inclusivity as an ethical imperative. Beginning with the preamble to the rules, we are charged with being "representative of clients, an officer of the legal system and a public citizen having special responsibility for the quality of justice."[7] The preamble requires members of the legal profession to "seek . . . access to the legal system," and "devote professional time and resources and use

7. *Id.* at Preamble [1].

civic influence to ensure equal access to our system of justice for all[.]"[8] The selection of these charges for the preamble makes clear the core values and principles that should be applied to our construction of the rules that follow, establishing a foundation for our ethical behavior and decision-making.

Proceeding directly from the preamble, the ABA's first model rule builds the critical role inclusivity must play in the construction of a lawyer's ethical duties. Model Rule 1.1, Competence, emphasizes the duty of lawyers to provide competent representation to all clients, a responsibility that necessitates an understanding of the diverse backgrounds and needs of those clients. Model Rule 1.1 inherently includes the cultural competence that develops from a commitment to understand the diverse backgrounds and needs of clients. Lawyers are ethically bound to stay informed about the cultural contexts and challenges their clients face, which necessitates an inclusive approach to client interactions.

The ethical imperative of inclusivity further manifests in Model Rule 8.4, which governs attorney misconduct. This rule prohibits lawyers from engaging in conduct that reflects adversely on their honesty, trustworthiness, or fitness to practice law, including actions motivated by discrimination or bias based on race, gender, ethnicity, or other protected characteristics. By emphasizing the need for ethical behavior free from bias, Model Rule 8.4 mandates that lawyers foster an inclusive environment both within their firms and in their dealings with clients and the community.

Beyond the Model Rules, ABA Resolution 113, passed in 2016, represents the ABA's significant commitment to promoting diversity and inclusion within the legal profession. This resolution recognizes that a diverse legal workforce enhances

8. *Id.* at Preamble [6].

the quality of legal services, fosters innovation, and strengthens the justice system. It urges law firms, legal organizations, and bar associations to take concrete steps to create and maintain inclusive environments that reflect the diversity of the communities they serve. The resolution calls for the adoption of best practices in recruitment, retention, and promotion of diverse individuals, emphasizing the need for accountability at all levels of an organization. It also encourages the establishment of mentorship and sponsorship programs that support the professional development of underrepresented groups. Moreover, the resolution reinforces the notion that inclusion is essential not only for ethical practice but also for fulfilling the profession's duty to promote justice and equity.

In the face of the onslaught of executive action in the first quarter of 2025 and beyond, the ABA reaffirmed its commitment to eliminating bias and enhancing diversity by passing another resolution on April 3, 2025. Therein, the ABA recommits to its goals of promoting full and equal participation within the legal profession and the justice system.

By adhering to these rules and resolutions, lawyers not only comply with ethical standards but also actively promote a culture of inclusivity within the profession, ensuring that diverse voices are heard and valued in the pursuit of justice.

## The Business Case for Inclusion

Inclusivity within the legal profession is not merely an ethical imperative; it also enhances client service in profound ways. Clients increasingly expect their legal representatives to reflect the diversity of the communities they serve. When firms prioritize inclusivity, they gain access to a broader range of perspectives and experiences, enabling them to understand better and address the unique needs of their clients. A diverse team is better equipped to navigate cultural nuances, foster stronger client relationships, and develop tailored legal strategies that resonate more effectively. Cognitively diverse teams foster innovation by encouraging different viewpoints and problem-solving approaches, which can lead to more creative and effective legal solutions. Diversity within legal institutions fosters a culture of accountability and helps to prevent "groupthink," a phenomenon where the desire for group cohesion leads to poor outcomes as members prioritize consensus. All in, diversity and inclusion lead to higher client satisfaction and can result in increased client loyalty and referrals, ultimately driving business success. Conversely, failing to embrace inclusivity can result in an environment that perpetuates bias, leading to unjust outcomes for clients and potential reputational harm for legal practitioners.

The impact of diversity on firm performance is well-documented. A 2019 McKinsey & Company report found that "companies in the top quartile for gender diversity on executive teams were 25 percent more likely to have above-average profitability than companies in the fourth quartile[.]"[9] Deloitte has reported similar findings, indicating that "research . . . shows that teams that operate in an inclusive culture outperform their peers by a staggering 80 percent."[10] A Harvard Business Review survey found that "companies with above-average total diversity . . . had both 19 percent points higher innovation revenues[.]"[11] This data reinforces the idea

---

9. Diversity Wins: How Inclusion Matters, McKinsey & Co. (May 19, 2020), https://www.mckinsey.com/featured-insights/diversity-and-inclusion/diversity-wins-how-inclusion-matters#.

10. *Becoming Irresistible: A New Model for Employee Engagement*, Deloitte Insights, Issue 16 (Jan. 17, 2015), https://www2.deloitte.com/us/en/insights/deloitte-review/issue-16/employee-engagement-strategies.html/#endnote-sup-42.

11. Rocio Lorenzo & Martin Reeves, *How and Where Diversity Drives Financial Performance*, Harvard Bus. Rev. (Jan. 30, 2018), https://hbr.org/2018/01/how-and-where-diversity-drives-financial-performance.

that diversity is not just about representation; it actively contributes to higher performance levels. It also suggests that diverse teams enhance creativity and problem-solving and drive better financial outcomes. In the legal profession, where creative problem-solving is crucial, these insights suggest that diverse teams are better positioned to generate innovative legal strategies and solutions.

Beyond client service, inclusion brings tangible benefits to the workplace. Inclusivity is closely linked to employee satisfaction and retention.[12] When team members feel valued and respected, they are more likely to be engaged and committed to their work, leading to lower turnover rates and a more positive organizational culture. Ultimately, embracing inclusivity is not just about fulfilling obligations: It is a strategic advantage that cultivates a dynamic, resilient, and high-performing legal practice.

Inclusion also serves as a safeguard against ethical violations and malpractice claims. A lack of diversity in legal teams can lead to blind spots that compromise the quality of representation and client relations. Inclusive legal practices may be more adept at identifying and mitigating risks associated with cultural misunderstandings or biases that could jeopardize a case or crisis counseling. By fostering a diverse and inclusive work environment, law firms can both enhance their ethical standing and improve their overall effectiveness in serving clients. In this way, inclusion is not merely a peripheral concern. It is an integral aspect of ethical practice that reinforces the legal profession's commitment to justice and equity.

---

12. *See* McKinsey & Co., *supra* note 9.

## Obstacles in the Pursuit of Inclusion

Obstacles arise when we take a one-size-fits-all approach to inclusion when, in reality, individuals from various backgrounds may experience differing levels of marginalization and barriers to belonging. One-dimensional approaches fail to address the unique challenges faced by various groups within the legal profession.

On a logistical level, firms and organizations often struggle with the data collection and analysis needed to assess their inclusion efforts effectively. Without clear metrics and a comprehensive understanding of the current landscape, organizations may find it difficult to identify areas for improvement, leading to stagnation and a lack of genuine progress in fostering an inclusive environment.

## Actioning Inclusivity

As noble an idea as inclusivity may be, its power manifests when we put it into practice, not when we simply revere it as an aspiration or unactioned element of our values system. As leaders in our firms, companies, communities, and even around the dinner table, we as lawyers can translate ideals to actions in big and small ways every day.

- **Combat bias and discrimination loudly and unequivocally.** To maintain the integrity of the legal system and fulfill its promise of working justice for all, a proactive stance against bias and discrimination is essential. Our ethical duty to serve as advocates demands that we stand up for others. Likewise, our ethical duty to serve as trusted advisors obligates us to advise against policies and practices that perpetuate exclusion.

To achieve this moral and ethical imperative, we must start by fostering an environment where open dialogue is encouraged, ensuring that all participants feel safe and supported in sharing their experiences. When we witness biased behavior or discriminatory practices, we must address it directly and promptly, using our voice to advocate for change. By standing firm against discrimination and consistently reinforcing a commitment to equality, we can challenge harmful norms and inspire others to join the fight.

- **Enhance cultural competence and self-awareness**. Cultural competence, or the ability to understand, communicate with, and effectively engage with people of different backgrounds, promotes equitable treatment of diverse clients and fosters a more thorough and empathetic approach to legal practice.

  To foster cultural competence, facilitate robust training that encourages group discussion and self-reflection, aimed at closing the understanding gap that can perpetuate existing inequalities and stifle the potential for allyship and collaboration across diverse groups.

  Cultural competence also can be achieved through the establishment of employee resource groups that empower individuals to connect, share experiences, and advocate for their communities. Encourage leadership to actively participate in these groups. Create a dedicated platform, such as a newsletter or internal blog, where employees can share articles, stories, and insights, fostering a culture of learning.
- **Recruit and retain talent from all backgrounds**. To effectively recruit all types of talent, begin by reviewing and revising job descriptions to ensure inclusive language that appeals to a broad audience. Expand recruiting by partnering with organizations and networks that

focus on underrepresented groups and utilizing diverse job boards. Implement a structured interview process that minimizes bias by using standardized questions and diverse interview panels.

To better retain talent from underrepresented backgrounds, create an onboarding experience that highlights the organization's commitment to inclusion and fosters a sense of belonging. Additionally, regularly solicit feedback from employees through surveys or focus groups to identify areas for improvement. Promote a culture of recognition that celebrates the contributions of all employees. Introduce flexible work arrangements that accommodate diverse needs, such as caregiving responsibilities, which can disproportionately affect certain demographics.

- **Support inclusive legal reforms.** Diverse legal professionals are more likely to champion and support reforms that address systemic issues and promote inclusivity. Their varied experiences and perspectives can drive important changes in laws and policies, aligning the legal system more closely with ethical principles of justice and equality. By publicly supporting diversity initiatives—such as sponsoring inclusive events or engaging in community outreach that emphasizes the importance of representation—lawyers can set a powerful example for their peers and clients.

  To support legal reform that will drive inclusion, start with education about existing laws and policies that impact marginalized communities, identifying gaps where reform is needed. Actively engage with advocacy organizations and coalitions that work on these issues, offering resources, volunteer support, or partnerships to amplify their efforts. Organize community forums or workshops that encourage public discussion and gather diverse perspectives on proposed reforms. Encourage colleagues to participate in civic engagement by providing paid time off for voting or attending public hearings related to legal changes. Lastly, consider communicating support for specific reforms through public statements or campaigns, demonstrating a clear commitment to social justice and inclusivity.

- **Demand continuous learning and improvement**. Law firms can leverage data to assess their inclusion efforts continually, setting measurable goals and holding leadership accountable. By prioritizing a data-driven approach to inclusivity, legal organizations can create a more equitable environment that not only attracts diverse talent but also maximizes the benefits that come from a genuinely inclusive workplace. A data-driven approach, however, requires monitoring progress and making necessary adjustments. It also depends on encouraging feedback and open dialogue. To that end, firms can conduct regular audits of firm policies, practices, and demographics to assess the effectiveness. These audits should result in actionable recommendations to improve inclusivity.
- **Cultivate curiosity and seek to understand**. True inclusivity begins with curiosity—the genuine desire to learn about experiences beyond our own. When we actively seek to understand others, we create space for empathy, connection, and growth. We can cultivate curiosity by asking thoughtful questions, listening to learn and not judge, and being open to perspectives that challenge our own. By approaching differences with curiosity rather than assumption, we break down barriers and build a culture where every voice is valued. When we deliberately cultivate curiosity within our homes, our workplaces, and our communities, we can move ourselves and others beyond passive acceptance and toward active inclusion.

## Call to Action

As the legal profession continues to evolve, so should our understanding of our ethical responsibilities. But through that evolution, we must remain tethered to the pursuit of inclusion as a moral and ethical imperative, as well as a practical necessity for achieving true justice and fairness. Inclusivity strengthens the legal system, enhances professional practice, and ensures that all individuals are effectively represented. It empowers us to address the needs of a diverse population, challenge systemic biases, and ultimately, it enriches our understanding of the law. In uniting our varied experiences and viewpoints, we are better equipped to serve justice and uphold the principles of equality and respect for all. It is time to meet the moment as leaders within our profession and our communities.

# Professionalism Begins in the Classroom: Building a Culture of Wellness

*Dominika Borek*

The ethical foundation of legal practice rests on two core duties: competence and diligence. As articulated in the American Bar Association's Model Rules of Professional Conduct, these are not aspirational ideals, but enforceable obligations.[1] Model Rule 1.1 mandates that "a lawyer shall provide competent representation," further defined as requiring "the legal knowledge, skill, thoroughness and preparation reasonably necessary for the representation."[2] Complementing this, Rule 1.3 stipulates that "a lawyer shall act with reasonable diligence and promptness in representing a client."[3] Together, these provisions establish the ethical expectation that attorneys will be intellectually prepared, responsive, and fully engaged in their legal work. However, the implicit assumption underlying both rules is that lawyers are psychologically capable of fulfilling these duties—of engaging with cases attentively, responding promptly to clients, and making reasoned judgments under pressure—a presumption that is increasingly untenable in light

---

1. *See* Model Rules of Pro. Conduct.

2. *See id.* r. 1.1 (adequate competence includes specific legal knowledge, skill, efficiency, thoroughness, and preparation employed in acceptable legal practice).

3. *See id.* r. 1.3.

of widespread burnout and mental health challenges across the profession.[4] The prevailing interpretation of Model Rules 1.1 and 1.3 fails to capture the reality that ethical competence is inseparable from psychological well-being. If mental fitness is a prerequisite for competent legal practice, then professional ethics must be revised to account for it.

The prevailing narrative in legal ethics places the burden of competence squarely on the shoulders of individual lawyers. The ABA Model Rules do not formally account for the fact that lawyers don't operate in isolation. Competence and diligence are not innate traits; they are cultivated and reinforced by the institutional structures in which lawyers are trained and employed. Responsibility for upholding these standards must be shared by lawyers and the institutions that shape legal identity. This includes not only law schools but also bar associations, licensing bodies, and the American Bar Association itself.

## The Shortcomings of Wellness Initiatives

Many law firms, law schools, and bar associations have adopted wellness initiatives aimed at mitigating psychological distress in the legal profession, such as mindfulness workshops, mental health webinars, CLE sessions on resilience, and employee

4. *See, e.g.*, Jessica R. Blaemire, *Analysis: Report Highlights Risks of Poor Attorney Well-Being*, Bloomberg Law (Sep. 20, 2024), https://news.bloomberglaw.com/bloomberg-law-analysis/analysis-report-highlights-risks-of-poor-attorney-well-being; Debra Cassens Weiss, *Surveyed Lawyers Report They Experience Burnout in Their Jobs More Than Half the Time*, A.B.A. J. (Mar. 9, 2022), https://www.americanbar.org/groups/journal/articles/2022/surveyed-lawyers-report-they-experience-burnout-in-their-jobs-mo; *see also* Edward J. Reich, *Interplay Between the Rules of Professional Conduct and the Reality of Attorney Mental Health Issues*, Dentons (Sep. 2019), https://www.dentons.com/en/pdf-pages/-/media/1c10e8fa1a5e4adb918a18db4e205a11.ashx.

assistance programs (EAPs).[5] While these efforts appear to reflect a growing commitment to mental health, they treat wellness as a matter of personal responsibility—something lawyers can manage through improved habits, stress reduction techniques, and greater emotional resilience. This individualist model misses the point; it ignores the structural realities that drive burnout in the first place: relentless billable hour requirements, unsustainable workloads, poor leadership, and a culture that discourages vulnerability and rewards emotional detachment.[6] These initiatives shift the focus away from the system and onto the individual, absolving institutions from making the structural changes that could reduce the prevalence of mental health issues in the legal profession.[7]

Psychologist and attorney Traci Cipriano calls this the "resilience myth"—the belief that psychological wellness can be achieved solely through personal effort, even within a toxic professional environment.[8] In *The Thriving Lawyer*, Cipriano critiques the culture of performative wellness in firms, where well-meaning initiatives like yoga classes and free meditation apps often serve as superficial fixes.[9] When wellness is treated as a personal responsibility, failure to maintain mental health

5. *See, e.g.*, *Wellness in the Legal Profession*, Penn Carey Law (June 12, 2023), https://www.law.upenn.edu/live/news/15899-wellness-in-the-legal-profession; *see also, e.g.*, The Well: Health and Wellness at HLS, Harvard Law School, https://hls.harvard.edu/student-life/the-well-health-and-wellness-at-hls.

6. Nicholas D. Lawson, *To Be a Good Lawyer, One Has to Be a Healthy Lawyer: Lawyer Well-Being, Discrimination, and Discretionary Systems of Discipline*, 34 Geo. J. Legal Ethics 1 (2021).

7. *Id.*

8. Traci Cipriano, The Thriving Lawyer (Informa Law, 1st ed., 2023).

9. *Id.*

becomes an ethical risk that falls entirely on the individual.[10] Cipriano argues that expecting lawyers to manage competing work and home life demands and to deal with their mental health issues on the side is unrealistic if the overall system and culture doesn't support them in doing so.[11]

This dynamic is particularly troubling in the context of ABA Model Rules 1.1 and 1.3, which require consistent competence and diligence.[12] Both rules presume a baseline of mental clarity, focus, and emotional stability—the traits most often compromised by common mental health conditions such as anxiety, depression, and burnout.[13] A lawyer experiencing burnout may struggle to meet deadlines, maintain attention to detail, or engage meaningfully with clients.[14] An attorney with depression may find it difficult to initiate tasks, process complex information efficiently, or advocate with sustained vigor.[15] A lawyer with anxiety can have trouble making decisions and resort to disregarding a problem as a way of avoiding it to avoid associated anxiety.[16] In other words, the symptoms of these

---

10. *See, e.g.*, Susan R. Martyn, *Lawyer Competence and Lawyer Discipline: Beyond the Bar*, 69 Geo. L.J. 705 (1981).

11. *See* Cipriano, *supra* note 9.

12. *See* Model Rules of Pro. Conduct r. 1.1, r. 1.3.

13. Marion Nickum et al., *Burnout Among Lawyers: Effects of Workload, Latitude, and Mediation via Engagement and Over-Engagement*, J. Psychiatry, Psych. & Law (Apr. 5, 2022).

14. *See* Karissa Wallace, *Recognizing and Combatting Lawyer Burnout: A Guide*, 100 Mich. Bar J. 48 (May 2021).

15. *See* Joann Mundin, *The Dark Side of Success*, Lawyers with Depression (Apr. 1, 2023), https://www.lawyerswithdepression.com/articles/the-dark-side-of-success-a-psychiatrists-exploration-of-depression-in-the-legal-profession.

16. *See, e.g.*, *Anxiety Disorders*, Mayo Clinic, https://www.mayoclinic.org/diseases-conditions/anxiety/symptoms-causes/syc-20350961 (last visited Apr. 20, 2025).

conditions are not merely incidental to legal practice as they directly undermine the very qualities that the rules demand.[17]

This system leaves lawyers caught in an impossible bind; it demands diligence and competence but remains silent on the institutional conditions necessary for its upkeep. Given the high stakes associated with violating the ABA Model Rules, lawyers facing mental health challenges are often incentivized to conceal their difficulties, fearing that disclosure may be interpreted as a professional weakness or an ethical failure.[18] This fear is not unfounded; disclosure may be perceived as a sign of diminished competence, professional instability, or even a potential ethical breach.[19] The system recognizes that mental illness can compromise performance yet provides no formal mechanism to separate and remedy mental-health-related shortcomings from willful wrongdoing.[20] In a number of cases, the court acknowledged mental illness as a mitigating factor, but not a justification; the underlying message was clear: Lawyers must manage their mental health privately, or risk being punished publicly.[21]

This culture of concealment has serious consequences. When lawyers suppress mental health issues out of fear, they are less likely to seek help, use available resources, or make necessary adjustments to their workload or case management.[22]

---

17. *See* Lyda Creus Molanphy, *Mindful Lawyering: Incorporating Mindfulness into the American Bar Association's Model Rules of Professional Conduct*, 15 St. Mary J. on Malpractice & Ethics 162 (2025).

18. *See* David Katner, *Normal: Revisiting Legal Ethics Rules with Mental Health in Mind*, 33 S. Cal. Rev. L. & Soc. Just. 427 (2024).

19. *See* Andrew F. Martin, *Mental Illness and Professional Regulation: The Duty to Report a Fellow Lawyer to Society*, Schulich Law, https://digitalcommons.schulichlaw.dal.ca/cgi/viewcontent.cgi?article=1580&context=scholarly_works.

20. *Id.*

21. *Id.*

22. *Id.*

Ironically, the very secrecy intended to preserve a lawyer's professional standing often puts both the lawyer and their clients at greater risk. The result not only perpetuates individual suffering but also undermines the goals of the rules themselves: to protect the integrity of the profession and ensure competent representation.[23]

Until the legal system acknowledges the link between mental health and ethical performance, it will continue to punish symptoms while ignoring causes.[24] Real change requires moving beyond symbolic gestures and confronting the roots of burnout embedded in legal culture.[25] And that work has to start early; law schools are where professional identities are first shaped, expectations are set, and norms are internalized.[26] To build a healthier profession, we need to begin with the institutions that train lawyers—not by offering more wellness workshops, but by rethinking the very structure of legal education itself.

## Law School: the Unacknowledged Breeding Ground

While mental health discourse in the legal profession often focuses on lawyers in practice, mental health issues resulting from the legal profession begin much earlier within the structure and culture of legal education.[27] Law schools play a formative role in shaping professional identity, yet they rarely equip students with the tools necessary for long-term ethical

---

23. *See* Model Rules of Pro. Conduct.

24. Cipriano, *supra* note 9.

25. *Id.*

26. *See* Barbara G. Fines, *Competition and the Curve*, 65 Univ. Miss. & Kan. City L. Rev. 879 (1997).

27. *Id.* at 880.

engagement.[28] Reforming the legal profession's approach to mental health cannot begin at the point of failure; it must begin at the point of formation in law school. If emotional detachment, overwork, and suppression are learned behaviors, then law schools must become intentional spaces for unlearning and reshaping professional identity. This shift requires cultural, curricular, and structural change, anchored in the belief that ethical competence is inseparable from mental wellness in the legal profession.

Law schools often foster environments that reinforce behaviors and mindsets that contribute to mental health issues.[29] Students are placed in a highly competitive atmosphere, where they are ranked relative to one another, and their success is largely defined by grades.[30] The initial four months of 1L are considered critically important, as students' first-semester grades are the main consideration for 2L job opportunities.[31] Furthermore, students often have little insight into their academic progress throughout the semester—a tool most have used to gauge their success in the past.[32] They receive no formal instruction on effective study methods or exam preparation strategies, leaving them uncertain about whether their approach to studying the law is effective or fundamentally misguided.[33] This all culmi-

---

28. *See, e.g.*, L. Silver, *Anxiety and the First Semester of Law School*, Univ. Wis. L. Rev., 1201–08 (1968).

29. *See* Matthew M. Dammeyer, *Anxiety and Depression Among Law Students: Current Knowledge and Future Directions*, Law & Human Behavior, 55–73 (1999).

30. *See* Kathryne M. Young, How to Be Sort of Happy in Law School (Stanford Univ. Press, 2018).

31. *See 2L Guide to Summer Jobs*, Harvard Law School, https://hls.harvard.edu/bernard-koteen-office-of-public-interest-advising/opia-job-search-toolkit/2l-guide-to-summer-jobs.

32. *See* Young, *supra* note 31; *see also* Silver, *supra* note 29.

33. *Id.*

nates in one end-of-semester exam worth 100 percent of the student's grade in each course—it's no surprise students in law school find themselves facing immense pressure from the start.[34] The result is that many first-year law students suffer from "failure anxiety"—a condition in which fear of performing poorly on final exams becomes so paralyzing that it interferes with their ability to concentrate, retain information, and engage in productive study habits.[35] Students begin to feel inadequate or out of place in the law school environment—an experience that often fuels imposter syndrome, undermines their sense of belonging, and exacerbates mental health issues.[36]

Soon enough, students who had been top performers are confronted with the realization that they may no longer be at the top of their class.[37] In an effort to outperform their peers, many sacrifice sleep, abandon self-care, and devote all of their time to studying.[38] This relentless work ethic, though often praised, creates a dangerous double bind. If students fail to achieve the desired outcome, the emotional toll of their efforts, amplified by exhaustion and isolation, can significantly worsen underlying mental health issues.[39] Conversely, if they succeed,

---

34. *Id.*; *see also* James M. Hedegard, *The Impact of Legal Education: An In-Depth Examination of Career Relevant Interests, Attitudes, and Personality Traits Among First-Year Law Students*, 4(4) AM. BAR FOUND. RSCH. J. (Autumn 1979).

35. *See* Silver, *supra* note 29; *see also* Benjamin et al., *infra* note 42.

36. *Id.*

37. *See* YOUNG, *supra* note 31.

38. *Id.*

39. *See, e.g.*, Ahana Gadiyaram, *How Academic Pressure and College Admissions Cause Student Stress*, N.Y. POST (Apr. 22, 2025), https://nypost.com/2025/04/22/lifestyle/how-academic-pressure-and-college-admissions-cause-student-stress; Thuy Dung Pham Thi et al., *Investigating Learning Burnout and Academic Performance Among Management Students: A Longitudinal Study in English Courses*, BMC PSYCH. 12, 219 (2024).

their success may inadvertently reinforce the belief that neglecting basic well-being is both necessary and rewarded.[40] In this cycle, overwork becomes the norm, rather than the exception.

Empirical data confirms the emotional toll of law school.[41] Law students exhibit significantly higher rates of anxiety, depression, and substance abuse than their peers in other graduate programs.[42] Over 40 percent of surveyed law students reported psychological distress, yet only a small portion sought treatment, with most citing fear of professional repercussions and stigma as reasons not to do so.[43] Although most law schools now offer counseling services, these are often underfunded, stigmatized, or siloed from academic support.[44] These findings point to a culture that normalizes psychological suffering as part of the training process, rather than recognizing it as a sign of systemic dysfunction.[45] This culture not only degrades mental health but also foster habits of detachment,

---

40. *See, e.g.*, Jenna Mittelmeier, *The Glorification of Overwork in Academia and Its Impacts on Our Collective Wellbeing*, Voices of Academia (Mar. 31, 2023), https://voicesofacademia.com/2023/03/31/the-glorification-of-overwork-in-academia-and-its-impacts-on-our-collective-wellbeing-by-jenna-mittelmeier.

41. *See* G.A.H. Benjamin et al., *The Role of Legal Education in Producing Psychological Distress Among Law Students and Lawyers*, Law & Soc. Inquiry 11, 225–52 (1986). *See also* Krill et al., *The Prevalence of Substance Use and Other Mental Health Concerns Among American Attorneys*, J. of Addiction Med. (2016).

42. *See id.*

43. *Id.*; *see also* Alan Reifman et al., *Depression and Affect Among Law Students During Law School: A Longitudinal Study*, J. Emotional Abuse, 93–106 (2000).

44. *See* Molanphy, *supra* note 18.

45. *See* Dammeyer, *supra* note 30.

perfectionism, and overwork that directly undermine the ethical standards attorneys are later expected to uphold.[46]

The pedagogical methods widely used in law schools further exacerbate this problem.[47] The Socratic method, curve-based grading, and lack of meaningful feedback create an atmosphere of chronic uncertainty and competitiveness.[48] Rather than fostering collaboration and intellectual curiosity, these methods promote self-isolation and internalized shame.[49] This educational style instills the belief that to succeed in law is to suppress personal emotions, disengage from affective experience, and master abstraction.[50] While these skills may serve analytical reasoning, they actively undermine relational competencies, such as empathy, attentiveness, and responsiveness, that are essential to ethical legal practice.[51]

It is perhaps no accident that this sorting process is prefatory to the professional sorting that follows.[52] Law schools gain institutional prestige by attracting students with high numerical

---

46. *See, e.g.*, Kennon M. Sheldon, *Does Legal Education Have Undermining Effects on Law Students? Evaluating Changes in Motivations, Values, and Well-Being*, Behav. Sciences & Law 22(2), 261–70 (2004).

47. *See* Martyn, *supra* note 11.

48. *See* Young, *supra* note 31.

49. *See id.*; *see also* Molanphy, *supra* note 18.

50. Toni Rempel, *The Mental Health Crisis in Law School: Improving Law Student Health Through Wellbeing-Focused and Trauma-Informed Legal Education*, Univ. of Saskatchewan (Mar. 28, 2024), https://harvest.usask.ca/items/4a80141c-123d-463d-b705-e30875d58a13; *see also* Jerome M. Organ et al., *Suffering in Silence: The Survey of Law Students Well-Being and the Reluctance of Law Students to Seek Help for Substance Use and Mental Health Concerns*, J. Legal Educ. 66, 116–40 (2016).

51. *See* Young, *supra* note 31.

52. *See* David N. Campbell, *On Being Number One: Competition in Education*, 56(2) Phi Delta Kappan 143 (Oct. 1974).

credentials and by placing those students in elite settings.[53] Given the increasing reliance of even public law schools on private funding by large firms, some professionals argue that, in a sense, the very survival of a law school hinges on its ability to sort students.[54] Relying on Big Law placement as a metric of success pressures schools to cater to the values of a narrow segment of the profession, often at the expense of student wellness and curricular innovation.[55] More importantly, while grading and ranking systems have traditionally played a role in law school prestige and employment outcomes, relying on them as essential to institutional survival is both short-sighted and increasingly incompatible with the evolving needs of the legal profession. As a result, law students are ill-prepared to manage the stressors of practice and carry unresolved psychological burdens into their professional lives.[56] Lawyers who begin their careers in a state of burnout are likely to commit ethical violations not out of malice, but out of depletion.[57]

## Legal Education as a Site of Ethical Formation

Curricular reform is a necessary starting point. Courses on professional responsibility must integrate concepts like trauma-informed practice, emotional intelligence, and mental fitness alongside traditional instruction.[58] Institutions must pioneer efforts to embed professional identity development into law school curricula to emphasize that legal ethics is not just about

53. *Id.*
54. *Id.*
55. *Id.*
56. *Id.*
57. *See* Young, *supra* note 31.
58. Rempel, *supra* note 51.

compliance but about cultivating the kind of person who can meet ethical demands over time.[59] Law schools should offer for-credit seminars on attorney wellness, communication under stress, and the psychology of decision-making—topics that directly impact one's ability to meet the standards of the Model Rules.[60] Treating these subjects as electives or optional support programs reinforces the false idea that mental well-being is *peripheral* to professional development.

Just as important as curriculum is a change in culture. Law schools must actively challenge the competitive, perfectionistic norms that valorize suffering and stigmatize vulnerability. One way to do this is by shifting from strict curve-based grading to collaborative, growth-oriented assessments that reward improvement and reflection.[61] Feedback-rich pedagogy, peer mentorship, and community building exercises should be embedded across the curriculum.[62] Faculty must be trained to model empathy and to recognize signs of burnout in students.[63] These shifts could send a clear message that being a good lawyer is not only about intellectual mastery.

Finally, structural supports must evolve to match these changes. Every law school should have dedicated mental health professionals who are integrated into academic advising—not siloed into inaccessible campus clinics; regular, anonymous mental health screenings could help destigmatize care-seeking behavior. Schools should track wellness indicators as seriously as they track bar passage or employment rates to recognize that

---

59. Neil W. Hamilton & Louis D. Bilionis, *Revised ABA Standards 303(b) and (c) and the Formation of a Lawyer's Professional Identity, Part 1: Understanding the New Requirements*, NALP Bulletin (May 2022).

60. *See* Martyn, *supra* note 11.

61. *Id.*

62. *Id.*

63. *Id.*

long-term professional viability is not captured by test scores alone. These changes are preconditions for building a profession in which ethical competence is sustainable. Law schools must take seriously their responsibility to shape not only skilled graduates but also ethical practitioners.

## Competence Requires Institutional Accountability

As discussed earlier, the fostering of burnout, depression, and chronic stress can compromise a lawyer's ability to think clearly, respond promptly, and engage meaningfully with legal matter.[64] When these impairments occur, the disciplinary system tends to treat them as private failures rather than foreseeable outcomes of a dysfunctional professional culture.[65] But institutional cultures that glamorize overwork while offering shallow solutions only deepen the ethical vulnerability of the profession.[66]

Although a number of states have added "mental wellness" to their professional responsibility frameworks, the Model Rules themselves have not evolved.[67] Current ethical standards

---

64. Jennifer Kirkpatrick Robbennolt & Jean R. Sternlight, *Behavioral Legal Ethics*, 5 Univ. Ill. L. Rev. 1181 (2013).

65. *Id.*

66. *See* Cipriano, *supra* note 9.

67. *See* Cal. Rules Pro. Conduct r. 1.1(b) ("'Competence' in any legal service shall mean to apply the (i) learning and skill, and (ii) mental, emotional, and physical ability reasonably necessary for the performance of such service"); Vt. Rules Pro. Conduct r. 1.1 cmt. [9] ("[a] lawyer's mental, emotional, and physical well-being may impact the lawyer's ability to represent clients and to make responsible choices in the practice of law"); Va. Model Rules Pro. Conduct r. 1.1 cmt. [7] ("[a] lawyer's mental, emotional, and physical well-being impacts the lawyer's ability to represent clients and to make responsible choices in the practice of law").

treat mental health issues as external to the concept of professional skill, failing to acknowledge that chronic stress or mental illness can erode performance just as surely as ignorance of the law.[68] The legal profession faces not just a mental health crisis, but a systemic ethical failure. Burnout and psychological distress aren't side effects—they're threats to a lawyer's ability to meet the ethical standards of competence and diligence. Yet the Model Rules ignore the reality that such standards are unsustainable in environments that erode well-being.

Accordingly, one of the most urgent reforms is the revision of the Model Rules themselves. The ABA should amend Rule 1.1 and its commentary to explicitly recognize psychological wellness and emotional resilience as components of ongoing competence. This would align with comment 8 to Rule 1.1, which already acknowledges that legal competence requires continued learning and adaptation.[69] Mental wellness and character development must be embedded directly into the definition of competence; This means amending Model Rule 1.1 to include ongoing psychological and emotional fitness as part of legal preparedness. It means viewing burnout not as a private weakness but as a public ethics issue—one that jeopardizes a lawyer's capacity to meet their professional obligations. And it means reforming law school curricula, cultures, and structures to align with these expanded ethical expectations.

Extending the definition of competence to include self-monitoring for mental well-being acknowledges a fundamental ethical truth: Lawyers cannot serve their clients effectively if they are unwell. As Molanphy notes, competence isn't a fixed body of knowledge, but a dynamic condition that necessarily

---

68. *See id*; *see also* Uchenna C. Ogbonnaya, Matthew S. Thiese & Joseph Allen, *Burnout and Engagement's Relationship to Drug Abuse in Lawyers and Law Professionals*, 64(7) J. Occup. Environ. Med. 621, 621–27 (2022).

69. *See* Model Rules of Pro. Conduct.

encompasses mental health. Institutional accountability must accompany this broader understanding.[70] Bar associations should issue clear ethical guidance on identifying impairment, offer tools such as burnout checklists, and implement safe, non-punitive systems for reporting concerns. Moreover, regulatory bodies should evaluate the ethical culture of law firms and law schools—not merely the conduct of individual practitioners.

Ultimately, the goal is not merely to reduce stress or prevent disciplinary action. It is to equip lawyers for a lifetime of ethical, sustainable practice. True competence extends beyond doctrinal knowledge and procedural skill; it also includes the ability to maintain presence, focus, and humanity in the face of pressure. Diligence is not just about endurance or efficiency but about showing up fully for clients with the clarity and care they deserve. The legal profession can no longer afford to treat mental health as a private weakness. It must be recognized as a foundational element of ethical lawyering.

---

70. *See* Molanphy, *supra* note 18.

# Professionalism in the Digital Age: The Ethical Use of Social Media and Artificial Intelligence

*Hon. John Browning (Ret.) and Jan L. Jacobowitz*

"Once you realize that you're in something that you've always wanted and you don't want to lose it, you behave differently. And that means the integrity, the professionalism, and knowing what's right from wrong and still making choices that you probably wouldn't have made."

— Paul Anka[1]

"Digital is really two things. It refers to a set of technologies, everything from artificial intelligence to the use of e-commerce. But digital is really about a different way of working, of making decisions, of partnering and reaching your clients, and so it's also about how you do things."

— Julie Sweet[2]

1. *Paul Anka Quotes*, Brainy Quote, https://www.brainyquote.com/authors/paul-anka-quotes.

2. *Julie Sweet Quotes*, Brainy Quote, https://www.brainyquote.com/quotes/julie_sweet_1104461.

## Defining Professionalism and Ethics

Paul Anka's quote refers to integrity, professionalism, *and* knowing right from wrong as three separate elements woven into conduct that supports and preserves a desired career. Professionalism in the legal profession is a much-referenced aspiration yet lacks a precise definition. Ethics, or the knowing of right from wrong, has a more accessible, widely accepted home in the American Bar Association (ABA) Model Rules of Professional Conduct (Model Rules) and the state bar legal ethics rules adopted from the Model Rules.

The literature often describes the legal ethics rules as the floor or minimum behavior required and professionalism as the ultimate behavior to which to aspire. Neil Hamilton and Verna Monson's definition of professionalism encompasses ethics as a significant element. They write:

> Professionalism is an internalized moral core characterized by a deep responsibility or devotion to others—particularly the client—and some restraint of self-interest in carrying out this responsibility. . . . Professionalism [may also include] these elements: ongoing solicitation of feedback and self-reflection, an internalized standard of excellence at lawyering skills, integrity, honesty, adherence to the ethical codes, public service (especially for the disadvantaged), and independent professional judgment and honest counsel.[3]

This description of professionalism and ethics provides a working focus for a discussion of lawyers' obligations in the digital world.

---

3. Neil Hamilton & Verna Monson, *Legal Education's Ethical Challenge: Empirical Research on How Most Effectively to Foster Each Student's Professional Formation (Professionalism)*, 9 U. St. Thomas L.J. 325 (2011).

## Ethics and Professionalism for the Digital World

Technology has impacted the legal profession since the 19th-century invention of the typewriter and the telephone. In fact, some lawyers were reluctant to use the telephone based both upon a perceived lack of professionalism and confidentiality concerns. Ultimately, the legal profession embraced the telephone; however, with each iteration—cordless, cellular, and smart phone—ethics issues emerged, often followed by ethics advisory opinions. The advent of the telefax and email generated similar as well as additional concerns about client communication and confidentiality.

In fact, a 1999 ABA Ethics Advisory Opinion provided email guidance to allay lawyers' concerns. The opinion advised that email was generally a reasonably safe method of communication without the use encryption. Fast forward to 2017, when the ABA released Opinion 477r, which explained that encryption had become much easier to employ and was now a worthy, reasonable consideration. ABA guidance had evolved in tandem with the advances in technology.

It is important to note that between the 1999 and 2017 opinions the ABA amended the notes to the Model Rule 1.1 "Competence" to include knowledge of the "benefits and disadvantages" of technology as a component of being a competent lawyer. Since 2012 at least 40 states have adopted this language or otherwise included technological competence in ethics advisory opinions or case law.

Thus, without dramatically amending the rules to discuss technological devices, social media, or artificial intelligence, the legal profession has acknowledged, if not always embraced, the fact that lawyers, as Julie Sweet notes, are engaged in "a different way of working, of making decisions, of partnering and reaching . . . clients . . . and doing things." Because technology evolves so rapidly, the ABA and state bars continue to release ethics advisory opinions and guidelines to provide advice on the ethical use of technological devices, social media, and, most recently, artificial intelligence.

The guidance aimed at technical devices and equipment includes cloud computing, encryption, virtual private networks, password choice and storage, device security, cybersecurity, and other aspects of technology. The focus is generally on the rules pertaining to competence, diligence, and confidentiality; in certain situations, communication with a client as to the use of technology is required. Many articles and books have been written to assist lawyers in understanding and employing technology. For the purpose of this essay, suffice it say that it has become both a professional and ethical duty to both understand and appropriately employ technology in the practice of law. A bit more nuanced are the obligations in some of the subsets of technology such as social media and artificial intelligence.

## The Professional, Ethical Use of Social Media

Social media networks were born in the mid-2000s and slowly but inevitably began to permeate the practice of law. The Philadelphia Bar Association released one of the first social media opinions in 2009 pertaining to the ethical guidance in researching a witness on social media. The Pennsylvania Bar Association followed with an advisory opinion in 2014 that defined knowledge of social media as a necessary component of competence.

There is no doubt, today, that the proliferation of social media platforms and their universal use has rendered social media an essential consideration in the effective, ethical practice of law. From jurisdiction and service of process to discovery to investigation of jurors and judges, social media acumen plays a role in litigation. In each of these areas, lawyers must follow the traditional legal ethics rules regarding contact with opposing parties, witnesses, jurors, and judges. The state bars and the literature in this area have done a good job of providing guidance such that violations have decreased over time.

Unfortunately, however, lawyers using social media continue to trip on both professional and ethical landmines. In fact, the social media landscape often gives rise to the online challenges of engaging with professionalism and legal ethics. The three main areas that illustrate the overlapping challenges of employing professionalism and ethics involve posts about cases, responses to client negative online reviews, and general commentary about current events or other personal matters.

As we often acknowledge, lawyers are human, too. Sometimes the emotion of the moment (or just a habit of sharing) results in a lawyer sharing an update on a case that may be of interest to others. Recently, a Massachusetts lawyer returned from a hearing at which he attempted to secure custody of a grandchild for the grandmother and posted "his day" on Facebook. Friends asked questions about why the government agency was opposing the placement and the lawyer explained that they did not trust that the grandmother could control her daughter, the mother. Seems that the lawyer did not focus on the fact that it was both unprofessional and a violation of the confidentiality rule to post in this manner.

The Massachusetts Bar notified the lawyer about the inappropriate nature of the post after the child's mother saw the posts and reported them to the grandmother who in turn informed the Massachusetts Bar. In other words, sharing is not caring, and the bar reprimanded the lawyer.

As opposed to lawyers generally posting about their cases, lawyers specifically responding to clients' negative online reviews comprises another challenging area for lawyers on social media. Defaulting to the premise that lawyers are human, too, it becomes easy to understand why a lawyer (or any human) has a natural inclination to defend themselves.

Unfortunately, the legal ethics rules do not provide an exception to client confidentiality to post an online defense. While the internet may serve as a court of public opinion, it does not constitute a tribunal under the rules. ABA Opinion 496 and several state bar ethics advisory opinions provide guidance that suggests that a lawyer may politely disagree with the client's opinion but may not share any confidential information in so doing.

It is important to note that a New Jersey lawyer's creative approach to avoiding a direct response by posting on his client's Yelp page did not avoid repercussions to his license. He posted, "Well, [client] is a convicted felon for fleeing the state with children. A wonderful parent. Additionally, she has been convicted of shoplifting from a supermarket. Hide your wallets well during a massage. Oops, almost forgot about the DWI conviction. Well, maybe a couple of beers during a massage would be nice."

The lawyer's defense to the posts before the New Jersey Bar included the argument that the convictions were public record and his belief that what was "good for the goose was good for the gander." He admitted that he had been quite upset.

The New Jersey Review Board distinguished public record from information that is generally known and did not appreciate the "goose/gander" defense. The attorney received a one-year suspension for this and various other violations.

Another prevalent area of concern involves lawyers posting "passionate" commentary on current events or other personal matters. (And in continuing with our "human" theme, psychological studies on online behavior have demonstrated that a primary motivation for posting may be anger that in turn often results in the use of highly emotional, biased, or profane language.) While these posts do not reveal the confidential information about a specific case, the unprofessional language or sentiment of a post may cause reputational damage, loss of employment, and violations of the legal ethics rules. When clients are publicly associated with the lawyer they may suffer because of that association.

Numerous examples exist of both prosecutors and public defenders losing both credibility and their employment after emotionally posting about events such as the George Floyd protests, the Orlando nightclub shooting, and other high profile current events. Prosecutors and public defenders admittedly practice under the additional challenge of public scrutiny of government offices and the requirement of the fair administration of justice in the legal ethics rules. However, lawyers in private practice have also been subject to reputational and job loss for commenting on current events. Law firms, government legal offices, and other legal organizations have developed social media policies to govern conduct and permit dismissal.

Of course, the unprofessionalism need not result from an emotional response to a current event. One lawyer posted negative comments about an ethnic community in the context of household employment. He found himself attacked online and deemed to be a terrible lawyer by those who were not clients, but sympathetic to the defamed ethnic community. He unsuccessfully sued for reputational damage perhaps further calling attention to his unprofessional posts ala the "Streisand effect."

Another lawyer felt compelled to post a video portraying himself screaming obscenities at a stowaway racoon on the lawyer's boat who appeared once the boat was underway. The video ends with the lawyer shoving the racoon into the water and leaving it to drown. The Florida Bar did not miss the viral nature of the video, launched a seven-month investigation, and then sent the lawyer to a diversion program that included a $750 professionalism workshop. One of the things we give up in exchange for the privilege of practicing law is the unfettered right to public self-expression.

## The Professional, Ethical Use of Artificial Intelligence

James McCarthy, a Dartmouth professor, coined the term artificial intelligence (AI) in 1956 as part of a proposal for a summer symposium to explore the proposition that machines *might* be able to perform human tasks. McCarthy's proposition has become a 21st-century reality and generative AI has taken the legal profession by storm. However, it is important to note that between 1956 and today, various forms of AI have become prevalent in society. Examples range from navigation systems, Siri, Alexa, and Netflix suggestions for movies to legal research, automatic word processing corrections to spelling and grammar, and various billing programs.

So, why has AI recently become the focus of so many CLE panels, news stories, state bar committees, and even disclosure orders by judges? Generative AI and open access provide the answer. Anyone can now download a generative AI application (think ChatGPT) and ask for information, drafting assistance, or legal research. While touted as efficient and inexpensive, for lawyers, ethics issues and parameters abound.

To date, Florida, California, Texas, North Carolina, Pennsylvania, Michigan, Missouri, Kentucky, New Jersey, Mississippi, and Washington, DC, have all issued ethics opinions regarding lawyers' use of generative AI. Like the early social media advice, the states are interpreting the traditional legal ethics rules to apply to the emerging generative AI technology. Competence and confidentiality, often the two predominant ethics concerns in the context of technology use may top the list. Competence (or the lack thereof) has made the headlines in several states. The need to understand the "benefits and disadvantages of technology" codified in the notes to the ABA Competence rule in 2012 has acquired new significance in the world of generative AI.

There are numerous examples of lawyers filing court documents with cites of nonexistent cases that ChatGPT provided as a result of "hallucinations." While not only unprofessional and violative of the legal ethics rules, some lawyers worsened their situations by engaging in a "cover up is worse the crime" scenario. In other words, by making various excuses and not immediately admitting their error to the court, they compounded the legal ethics issues by violating both the candor to the tribunal rule and the misconduct rule. The simple law school rule of reading every case before you cite it, would have saved these lawyers from both sanctions and reputational embarrassment.

Leaving these early incidents aside, some of the other ethics issues that emerge from the use of generative AI involve the duty to supervise, communication with clients, billing, and advertising. In other words, does a lawyer have to share with their client that they are employing generative AI? How does a lawyer bill for generative AI? When may it become incompetent not to employ generative AI? Does the use of an advertising bot risk the establishment of an attorney–client relationship? The list of questions continues to grow.

ABA Formal Opinion 512, issued in late July 2024, provides much-needed guidance regarding each of these questions and more. Like state ethics opinion counterparts, it addresses the issue of attorney competence and emphasizes that while lawyers are not required to become experts in this daunting new technology, they must have "a reasonable understanding of the capabilities and limitations of the specific [generative

AI] technology that the lawyer might use." The opinion also reminds lawyers that their duties in this regard are ongoing and not "a static undertaking." Even if lawyers do not necessarily expect to use generative AI in a given matter, they should still be aware of the tools relevant to their work so that "they can make an informed decision, as a matter of professional judgment, whether to avail themselves of these tools or to conduct their work by other means."

Formal Opinion 512 goes on to discuss the predictable ethical duties implicated by the use of generative AI, such as confidentiality, communication, candor to the tribunal, and the duty to supervise. But perhaps the most novel conundrum posed to lawyers involves billing. May an "AI surcharge" be added to a lawyer's invoice? Perhaps a more controversial question is whether the lawyer may be deemed to be charging an unreasonable fee if the lawyer legitimately bills 15 hours of her time when AI could have produced the same result in an hour. Here, too, Formal Opinion 512 offers guidance. It states that in determining the reasonableness of fees, lawyers should account for AI's potential to be "a faster and more efficient way to render legal services." The opinion also instructs lawyers to "analyze the characteristics of generative AI tools and how they will be used before deciding if each tool is part of the firm's overhead, or an out-of-pocket expense to be billed to clients."

Will lawyers' use of generative AI—full of fits and stumbles as it has started out—ever reach the point of becoming an expectation, part of the attorney's reasonable standard of care? While the profession is not there yet, we feel it will be—and that it will be at least in part client-driven. Formal Opinion 512 speculates that "robust client demand for [generative AI] tools as an efficiency or cost-cutting measure," along with increased acceptance, widespread availability of AI technologies, and "a track record of reliable results" will lead to the establishment of such an expectation.

## Conclusion

Whether it's the revolutionary advent of the typewriter, the telephone, the computer, or the smart phone, as technology evolves so too does the practice of law. Social media's arrival in the mid 2000s changed the practice of law—not only did smoking gun evidence find a new home, but also the requisite competence to discover it became a necessity. Moreover, unwary lawyers have found themselves stepping on ethical landmines as they publicly post thoughts that previously might have only been shared with a colleague over lunch.

Generative AI is the latest and perhaps most dramatic technological evolution. No doubt it is already both revolutionizing the practice of law and creating ethical challenges for lawyers. In fact, U.S. Supreme Court Chief Justice John G. Roberts, in his December 2023 Year End Report on the Federal Judiciary, sounded a warning about "the latest technological frontier: artificial intelligence (AI)." Even as this technology has "great potential to dramatically increase access to key information for lawyers and non-lawyers alike," he noted, it also "risks invading privacy interests and dehumanizing the law." The use of AI, Roberts observed, "requires caution and humility."

It is difficult to ignore the siren song that is generative AI. It is perhaps even more difficult to resist the lure of having a technological "sorcerer's apprentice" at a lawyer's beck and call, ready to generate a trial-ready motion or brief with just a few helpful prompts. Early experience with lawyers foiled by AI "hallucinations," however, reminds us that we must be more cautious. Such episodes are not mere tech problems, but ethical lapses.

The 21st-century trial lawyer must ensure not only that AI-generated content is accurate, but also that the lawyer's own use conforms to the ethical standards of our profession. Chief Justice Roberts was correct to be concerned about the risk of

AI "dehumanizing the law." With its immense potential to enhance efficiency and accuracy, generative AI is indeed transformative, but its output is no substitute for a lawyer's professional judgment and adherence to ethical duties.

Social media and generative AI are here to stay—the proverbial tech genie is out of the bottle. While the practice of law continues to adapt, the fundamental legal ethics requirements remain the same. Thus, lawyers must embrace technological evolution while remaining committed to ethically serving clients as the world continues to turn.

> "It is change, continuing change, inevitable change, that is the dominant factor in society today. No sensible decision can be made any longer without taking into account not only the world as it is, but the world as it will be."
>
> — Isaac Asimov[4]

4. *Isaac Asimov Quotes*, Brainy Quote, https://www.brainyquote.com/quotes/isaac_asimov_124394.

# Chapter 4

## Evolving Traditions, Enduring Principles

This chapter turns to the traditions that give our work its depth. It reflects on how lawyers learn from one another in ways no rulebook can fully capture, and how that guidance shapes the kind of practitioners we become. The essays in this chapter consider the quiet responsibilities that come with being part of a profession—to teach, to prepare others to step forward, and to keep growing ourselves. They also question whether the principles we point to as ideals should play a more deliberate role in how we practice each day. Together, these essays remind us that the strength of the profession is carried person to person, habit to habit, and that our shared commitment to those principles is what ultimately defines professionalism.

# Mentoring

*John M. Barkett, Bruce A. Green, and Paul Mark Sandler*

## Mentorship's Legacy

John W. Davis, one of America's most distinguished 20th-century lawyers, once remarked: "In the heart of every lawyer, worthy of the name, there burns a deep ambition so to bear themselves that the profession may be stronger by reason of their passage through its ranks, and they may leave the law itself a better instrument of human justice than they found it."[1] One way we have traditionally left the legal profession better than we found it has been by mentoring junior lawyers. The concept of a mentor is age-old. The term comes from the *Odyssey*: Mentor was one of the advisors to whom Odysseus entrusted his son when he went off to war. And, indeed, decades ago, the three of us were the beneficiaries of outstanding mentors in our early years as lawyers.

## Current Challenges

We take immense gratification in continuing this tradition by mentoring junior lawyers. But we are distressed by three phenomena. The first is the preoccupation of senior lawyers

1. https://www.nytimes.com/1926/08/05/archives/calls-jefferson-leader-of-thought-john-w-davis-says-he-had-greatest.html

with the business of law. The second is the COVID-induced trend to work from home and the accompanying loss of in-person "face time" that often results in spontaneous mentoring. The third is the attitude of some junior lawyers who question whether more senior lawyers—who may not be well-versed in technology or at the forefront of using artificial intelligence in legal practice—have much to offer as mentors.

The first two phenomena demonstrate shortsightedness by both senior and junior lawyers. The third demonstrates a naïve understanding of how to become a great lawyer.

It is true that pressures on senior associates and partners in firms, regardless of size, require them to bill gobs of hours and to be rainmakers, leaving no time for mentoring. This is nothing new. For more than a century, lawyers have been buffeted by economic pressures—pressures to focus exclusively on making money, not on practicing law as a profession. A 1916 volume by New York bar leader Julius Henry Cohen said it all: "The Law: Business or Profession?"

But investing in mentoring is just as important as billing more than 2,000 hours and seeking origination credit for new clients and matters. Mentors help young lawyers find gratification in professional service by connecting them to the profession's traditions and high ideals—what Maryland's code calls "the combination of the core values of personal integrity, competency, civility, independence, and public service that distinguish attorneys as the caretakers of the rule of law."[2]

Mentors can help inspire young lawyers to adhere to the highest level of excellence in serving the needs of clients, both paying and pro bono clients. They can impart knowledge. They can help junior lawyers avoid mistakes that stem from

---

2. https://govt.westlaw.com/mdc/Document/N52074AA4E29811EEA0E69D97D6A307F0?viewType=FullText&originationContext=documenttoc&transitionType=CategoryPageItem&contextData=(sc.Default)&bhcp=1.

inexperience while providing the wisdom that comes from experience. And they can assist junior lawyers in honing their judgment skills. Knowledge. Experience. Judgment. That's what makes a great lawyer. Mentoring creates great lawyers.

## Shared Rewards

The benefits go both ways. When a mentor helps mold a seasoned junior lawyer, a bond of trust is formed. The mentor knows that the junior lawyer can generate a work product that will require little to no editing, and, for example, have the confidence to take a good deposition alone; or produce an excellent contract draft; or communicate effectively with clients, co-counsel, or opposing counsel. Putting junior lawyers on the track to become mentors themselves one day must be the goal of every senior lawyer who wishes to perpetuate excellence in the service of clients.

And that's why the COVID-induced practice of working from home risks the proper development of junior lawyers. Sure, Zoom time is face time and it has its place in mentoring. But Zoom time is scheduled. There is no substitute for the in-person opportunities to mentor that arise spontaneously in a workday as junior lawyers are struggling with how best to solve a problem or address an issue.

We acknowledge the convenience of communicating by computer screen from one's home. We also acknowledge the productivity that is generated by avoiding a long commute to the office. Mentoring can tolerate these trade-offs—to an extent. But senior and junior lawyers who abdicate the mentoring process because of convenience do so at the risk of imperiling the bond of trust that mentoring creates and that is so important to the sustainability of excellence in a law firm.

Maybe it is true that old dogs cannot learn new tricks. Technology has made electronic discovery the province of the young lawyer, for sure. But trial strategy remains important in evaluating the evidentiary value of electronically stored information. And maybe generative artificial intelligence is or will be transformative. But generative AI is never going to replace the opening or closing statements in a jury trial, or the cross-examination of a party opponent or an expert witness. Lawyers will always have to stand up on their feet in a courtroom and speak to judges and jurors. What they say may be influenced by the output of technology, but how they say it and how they respond to questions from a judge or answers from a witness will always require quick, smart thinking that comes from—you guessed it—knowledge, experience, and judgment. That's what mentors teach mentees.

We speak from a combined nearly 150 years of experience. Yes, mentoring takes time for both the mentor and the mentee. But we promise you that if you make the time, the personal rewards will be lifelong and the professional benefits exponential.

# Succession Planning: Taking Care of Clients, Family, and Yourself

*David Seserman*

Succession planning embodies the best qualities of a true professional: foresight, accountability, and dedication to others. It ensures clients are protected, law firms remain stable, and families are spared unnecessary uncertainty if a lawyer unexpectedly cannot continue their practice. Although state bars have not yet mandated it, requiring every attorney to have a succession plan would provide critical safeguards for the public and reduce the burden on bar resources when a lawyer passes away or becomes incapacitated without a plan. Even without a formal requirement to do so, lawyers who put a succession plan in place demonstrate leadership, honor their ethical duties, and provide peace of mind to everyone who depends on them.

As lawyers, we are fully engaged in client matters, our active practices, and our communities. However, we often avoid thinking about what would happen if we were suddenly unable to practice law due to death or disability before our planned retirement. Succession planning addresses this critical "what if," yet it requires time and effort and is easily put off. Like disability and life insurance policies that we hope never to use, succession planning is a prudent and necessary safeguard for our practice, clients, and families.

Do all lawyers need a succession plan? The answer is unequivocally yes. For lawyers in medium and large firms, succession planning can be integrated into the firm's established operating procedures and policies. For example, firms that routinely implement fail-safe measures—such as assigning multiple attorneys and staff members to each client matter—also ensure continuity of representation. This built-in redundancy can act as an effective succession plan for attorneys in larger firms.

For sole practitioners and small firm lawyers, the need for a written succession plan is critical. Without the structural support of a larger organization, these lawyers rely entirely on their own planning to ensure client matters are appropriately handled in their absence.

## Protecting Clients, the Firm, and the Family

For lawyers in any size firm, a well-drafted succession plan can provide clarity, continuity, and peace of mind for the lawyer and their clients. For clients, the lack of a succession plan creates a risk of prejudice to their legal matters. Statutes of limitations may run hearings or hearings and trials could be missed. A carefully designed succession plan mitigates these risks, ensuring that clients are protected and their cases can move forward seamlessly in the lawyer's absence.

A succession plan is not just for clients; it also protects the firm by providing a framework for maintaining client relationships while minimizing financial harm. By ensuring operational continuity, a succession plan preserves the firm's reputation and economic stability, even during a difficult and unanticipated transition.

For their families, a lawyer's disability or death is a profound emotional and financial challenge. Without a succession plan in place, our loved ones—in a time when they are emotionally distraught—are left to navigate the complexities of dissolving a law practice along with everything else they have to deal with. They may not know where to begin or how to address urgent issues, adding unnecessary stress to an already difficult time.

## The Role of Succession Plans in Managing the Unexpected

The difference between having a succession plan and relying on appointed counsel because there is no plan is stark. A succession plan empowers a lawyer to dictate how their practice will be managed, providing stability for clients and protecting the lawyer's financial interests. Without such a plan, the practice is subject to dissolution by external authorities, leaving family members, colleagues, and clients to navigate a disorganized and often chaotic transition.

Without a succession plan, state bar programs step in to appoint counsel to oversee the dissolution of the lawyer's practice and the transfer of client matters. Appointed counsel's role, defined by state law or bar rules, is more limited than that of successor counsel, and focuses exclusively on dissolving a lawyer's practice and transitioning clients to new counsel. They do not take over ongoing cases or manage the financial aspects of the practice, which can leave gaps in closing the practice that must be filled by other colleagues or family members.

A succession plan, on the other hand, is a contract that names a successor and defines the scope of the successor's work. It can allow them to take over representation of certain client matters and collect outstanding invoices, ensuring continuity for both the practice and its clients.

## What to Include in a Succession Plan

There is no universal format or template for a succession plan, but most if not all state bars have plan resources and forms available online that can act as a starting point. Since the plan is a roadmap to managing and winding down the practice in the event of a lawyer's death or disability, a family member or trusted colleague should know how to access it and contact the designated successor counsel if it becomes necessary.

Once an initial succession plan is prepared, it should be reviewed annually (at a minimum) and updated to reflect changes in client information, matter status, and firm finances and operations. This should not be a burden since maintaining up-to-date client files, calendars, and records is already a core element of every lawyer's duty of competence and diligence. Staying on top of these law practice management issues is critical for a seamless transition of matters and winding down of the firm if the lawyer is suddenly unable to practice.

Depending on the needs of the practice and firm clients, succession plans can range from simple to highly detailed. A basic succession plan might consist of a list of active cases, file locations, deadlines, and essential financial details, such as information about operating and trust accounts. A more comprehensive succession plan goes further, addressing critical elements to ensure continuity and minimize disruption. A robust succession plan should include at a minimum:

- The location of all the electronic devices and cloud storage accounts that contain firm and client data.
- A current list of active matters and cases and access to the firm calendar with case deadlines.

- The location of all physical and electronic files.
- Up-to-date contact and contract information for clients, vendors, and service providers.
- Access to detailed financial records, including trust and operating accounts.
- Passwords and other access information for all of the firm's resources, such as email, software, websites, online storage, billing and accounting systems, to name a few.
- The designation of a successor lawyer who has agreed to wind up the practice and, where appropriate, take on client matters.
- Any documents necessary to give the successor lawyer access to all the assets and tools required to continue work for the clients or transfer their cases, files, and any trust funds to others without interruption.

When developing or updating a succession plan, it is a good opportunity to also audit electronic devices and storage files to confirm that client and personal files are not commingled. If personal and firm files are not kept separately, successor counsel will have to personally review and assess personal files that the lawyer may have intended or needed to keep confidential. Further, if regulation counsel or the courts oversee the dissolution of a law firm because there is no succession plan, while client files will be preserved, personal data on electronic devices will likely be forensically destroyed before devices are returned to family members. Rather than risk unwanted access to personal information or, worse, destruction and loss of that information, lawyers should take the time to separate all personal records and information from client and firm documents and assets and to keep them separate.

## Successor Counsel: Duties, Responsibilities, and Professional Considerations

An agreement with successor counsel can address undertaking representation of the deceased or disabled lawyer's clients (with the client's consent of course), concluding business aspects of the law firm including collecting outstanding receivables, disposing of or distributing tangible property associated with the law firm, ending vendor contracts, using firm assets to satisfy outstanding firm debt, and returning unearned client trust deposits. To ensure the successor counsel can perform their duties efficiently, it is advisable to grant them signature authority over financial accounts in advance. If granting full signature authority is not feasible, a limited power of attorney tied to specific contingencies can provide the necessary access to trust and operating accounts. Such provisions streamline the transition process and reduce delays in closing the firm's affairs.

When drafting a successor counsel plan, both parties to the plan must consider the ethical obligations associated with the role of successor counsel. Confidentiality and the avoidance of conflicts of interest are paramount. The lawyer establishing the succession plan and the successor counsel should both carefully evaluate any potential conflicts with current or former clients before entering into the agreement. An annual review of potential conflicts should be performed. Because serving as successor counsel can be time-consuming, the agreement should address compensation for the successor's time and expenses. Many sole practitioners address these concerns through reciprocal agreements, where they agree to act as successor counsel for each other, ensuring mutual protection for their practices.

## Considering a Request to Serve as Successor Counsel

If another lawyer asks you to act as their successor counsel, consider the request. Serving as successor counsel is a significant responsibility but also an opportunity to uphold the legal profession's integrity by ensuring that client interests are protected, even under challenging circumstances.

Before agreeing to be named successor counsel, you should evaluate the potential time commitment to determine if, given your own practice, you have the capacity to fulfill the role effectively. You should also assess any possible conflicts of interest and clarify the scope of your responsibilities in a formal agreement. By agreeing to serve, you not only help a colleague but also contribute to the broader mission of maintaining public trust in the legal profession. This act of service aligns with our ethical duties and strengthens the fabric of the legal community by fostering collaboration and mutual support among lawyers.

Lawyers are part of a noble profession built on trust and responsibility, and planning for the unexpected is essential to uphold these principles. Succession planning is an integral aspect of professionalism, and state bars should consider making it mandatory to protect all stakeholders in the justice system. Lawyers who take the time to plan for the future show not only competence but also an unwavering commitment to the values of the legal profession.

# Professionalism for the Next Generation: An Interactive Approach to CLE

*Gregory R. Hanthorn*[1]

"Don't tell me the moon is shining; show me the glint of light on broken glass."

— Anton Chekhov (generally attributed)

On February 6, 2017, the American Bar Association House of Delegates adopted a new "Model Rule for Minimum Continuing Legal Education and Comments," replacing the 1988 version of the Model Rule. The 2017 rule expressly called for mandatory "specialty" Continuing Legal Education, within the overall number of CLE hours, for professionalism, defined as "the tenets of the legal profession by which a lawyer demonstrates civility, honesty, integrity, character, fairness, competence, ethical conduct, public service, and respect for the rules of law, the courts, clients, other lawyers, witnesses, and unrepresented parties."[2]

---



2. Model Rule for Minimum Continuing Legal Education, Am. Bar Ass'n 1–2 (Feb. 6, 2017), https://www.americanbar.org/content/dam/aba/directories/policy/midyear-2017/2017_hod_midyear_106.pdf.

Many states soon fell in line with now having some form of separate CLE category exclusively for or including "professionalism." Of course, professionalism had been a concern and focus long before the revision of the Model Rule. For example, in Georgia, the Chief Justice's Commission on Professionalism had developed and promulgated *A Lawyer's Creed* and the accompanying *Aspirational Statement on Professionalism* as early as 1990, with the most recent amendments taking place in 2013.[3] The *Creed* and *Aspirational Statement* proved popular, and some form of professionalism standards, as distinct from the Model Rules of Professional Conduct,[4] have been adopted by one or more bar associations within at least 43 states (plus the District of Columbia, so effectively 44).[5]

3. *A Lawyer's Creed* and *Aspirational Statement on Professionalism*, CHIEF JUSTICE'S COMM'N ON PROFESSIONALISM, https://cjcpga.org/wp-content/uploads/2019/07/1-Lawyers-Creed-and-Aspirational-Statement-Clean-Copy-v-2013-new-logo-seal.pdf (last accessed Dec. 5, 2025).

4. Generally speaking, professionalism standards are "aspirational" in that breaching them will not result in discipline. In *Claypole v. County of Monterey*, Case No. 14-cv-02730 (N.D. Cal. Jan. 12, 2016), a magistrate judge imposed a separate "professionalism" sanction (in addition to discovery sanctions) for conduct occurring during discovery. Defense counsel's directive to plaintiff's counsel during a heated deposition—"[D]on't raise your voice at me. It's unbecoming of a woman. . . ."—was particularly singled out. *Claypole*, slip op. at 8. Florida also has noted that "professionalism" lapses can lead to discipline. Florida Bar v. Norkin, No. SC 11-1356 (Oct. 31, 2013) (ending, in footnote 5, "Members of the Florida Bar, law professors, and law students should study the instant case as a glaring example of unprofessional behavior.") (additional citation omitted).

5. A list of states with "Professionalism Codes" appears on the American Bar Association website, https://www.americanbar.org/groups/professional_responsibility/resources/professionalism/professionalism_codes (last accessed Dec. 5, 2025). This list was last updated March 2017, so please check your jurisdiction to see if it snuck in after that date.

Very well. CLE concerning professionalism should be mandatory. So what would that CLE look like?

While multiple jurisdictions have written standards for professionalism, CLE need not merely parrot those standards. For example, Georgia's Professionalism CLE rule notes, "[t]he text of *A Lawyer's Creed and the Aspirational Statement on Professionalism* need not be explicitly taught at every professionalism program. Promotion of the principles set forth in those documents includes coverage of the meaning of professionalism, recognition of obstacles to professionalism and techniques for overcoming them, and motivation to practicing with professionalism."[6] Early professionalism CLEs fell into two broad camps—(i) inspiring stories by attorneys who lived through era-defining and -changing events, and (ii) lectures, sometimes disguised by having the lecture split among "panelists." Inspiring accounts remain an important part of professionalism CLE, but are largely beyond the scope of this essay.[7] And, yes, there are times that it can be useful to have experienced practitioners explain "local" mores and hot takes on subjects such as: open-toed shoes, loud neckties, no neckties, bow ties, men's shoes that are (gasp) a color other than black or oxblood or brown, loud socks, and other items.[8]

---

6. Professionalism CLE Guidelines, Ga. Bar Ass'n (effective July 1, 2019), Rule 5 at 3, https://cjcpga.org/wp-content/uploads/2020/10/FINAL-COVER-ACKNOWLEDGMENTS-Revised-Professionalism-CLE-Guidelines-effective-07-01-19-link-corrected-10-12-20.pdf (last accessed Dec. 5, 2025).

7. The key word is "largely," because in fact inspiring accounts are a species of "showing, not only telling," as advocated more generally above.

8. Sadly, every example listed here comes from one or more CLEs that the author has attended. In the post-COVID era, one can add pretty much across all jurisdictions that swimwear or pajamas don't pass muster for virtual hearings in an any jurisdiction.

The classic lecture, however, is not how lawyers generally communicate when it matters. We "show" rather than "tell." The value of a lecture or series of lectures on "how to dress like a lawyer" or the clear need to "advocate for the rule of law among every lawyer's sphere of influence" is non-negligible, but we can aspire to more. This essay will present three approaches to engaging, interactive professionalism CLE that have all been battle-tested; and for the mnemonically minded, they'll follow the A, B, Cs as the use of Actors, Books, and Cinema are set forth and described.

But first, a diversion. Here's what all three approaches will have in common.

Each seeks to play with the CLE attendee's lenses. While the ultimate goal is for each CLE participant to examine that lawyer's own conduct and underlying attitudes, the examination will not start there. Instead, conduct will first be examined as portrayed by someone else, who happens to be fictional (either via watching scenes staged by Actors, interacting with familiar Books, or examining clips from Cinema). The play, book, or movie characters' approaches can then be discussed and examined, with the final move being to take what is learned from looking at the fiction and then applying that same lens to one's own conduct.[9] Simply put, we are more comfortable and better

---

9. The author was anticipated in this approach by several centuries by (okay, I stole this approach from) the prophet Nathan who confronted King David with charges regarding David adultery and murder by first having David critique a fictional "rich man" who had appropriated a "poor man's ewe lamb." Once David pronounced judgment on the "rich man," Nathan turned David's lens back to David's own conduct, declaring "You are the man!" 2 Samuel 12:1-9 (quoted material from NASB) (a similar account involving King David, but not Nathan, appears in the Quran at Surah S'ad 38:21-26, as David gleans lessons for his own conduct even as he judges between two litigants who had scaled the wall of the royal chamber to place their case before him).

at criticizing the conduct of fictional participants first and then moving on to apply the lessons.

Second, each of the suggested CLE examples seeks to make it easier for the attendees to participate by "showing" and then allowing all—the "panel" who knew what was coming and the people in attendance who did not—to comment. The moderator uses the "show" of the dramatic scene, or the account from a childhood book, or the account of a kind of familiar movie clip to "show" conduct than can then be dissected. And while, yes, of course, not everyone will have read the same childhood books, seen the same movies, or seen the plays containing the scenes, that's not the point. Enough material is presented up front by the Actors, a panelist summarizing an easy-reader Book, or a movie Clip[10] itself to "show" before the examination and "telling" begins.

Third, each interactive CLE can make it easier for the panelists and the attendees to track by specifying and citing (ah, yes, slides that can be sent to the appropriate local credentialling authority) the local professionalism standards. *A Lawyer's Creed* and *The Aspirational Statement on Professionalism* are sometimes used as examples, but the examples can readily be adapted to multiple codes in multiple jurisdictions.

Fourth, each interactive CLE is designed for an active moderator who will call on panelists and throw questions to the audience. This means that the moderator will have identified in advance with the panel who will be "first called upon" for each piece. A cheat sheet shared among moderator and panelists that shows the "first question" and to which panelist it will be addressed and also contains short notes for possible places to go in responding is an excellent way to get panelists thinking about the material in advance of the presentation. The

10. Yes, the author is overdoing the A, B, C emphasis, so please forgive the unusual capitalization.

moderator should also have the panel's permission, in advance, to jump in whenever a response moves too closely to becoming a "lecture," either by asking the panelist another, more focused question, or by throwing a question to a "back up panelist" also identified in the cheat sheet, or to the audience. Ideally, the presentation moves to a conversation among the panelists and away from a series of rotating lectures.

But enough generalities. How has each approach worked?

## Live Actors and the Plays of William Shakespeare

First, the author is a self-proclaimed Shakespeare nerd. But the choice of Shakespeare is justified in any event because Shakespeare's dramas provide an excellent lens through which to view human behavior on any topic; the works "hold, as 'twere, the mirror up to nature."[11] And Shakespeare was fascinated by law. "There was an unusual interest in things legal in later Tudor times, and Shakespeare fully shared in that interest. It will have been apparent, however, from his sketches of local justice and its officers that Shakespeare scrutinized our traditional benefactors—our amateur justices—with a shrewd eye, and that the defects of the system were fully apparent to him."[12] Because Shakespeare was Shakespeare, his outsider's view of

---

11. William Shakespeare, Hamlet, act 3, sc. 2. Throughout this essay references to Shakespeare are generally to the versions available online at www.shakespeare-online.com/plays, notwithstanding this author's idiosyncratic preference (for a variety of geeky reasons) for the texts published in the Applause First Folio of Shakespeare Comedies, Histories & Tragedies In Modern Type (Neil Freeman Ed.) (Applause 2001).

12. George W. Keeton, Shakespeare and His Legal Problems 55–56 (A&C Black Ltd. 1930, reprinted by The Lawbook Exchange Ltd. 2009).

our profession is more than skin deep. "[A] gesture in the plays that may at first look like a simple allusion to a legal concept or practice often points to a deeper engagement with how legal professionals organized the world, whether in relation to the law's technical workings or its underlying premises or its social effects. Even when Shakespeare seems merely to be decorating his dialogue with some legal word he has picked up (no specialist he!), Shakespeare is capable of great precision in his understanding of how law works and what it is for."[13]

So the material is clearly there. But how to present it?

Here, in addition to the moderator and panelists, the interactive CLE approach involves two actors who, scripts in hands, will present the cut-down scenes that set up each example. Professional actors work best,[14] especially if they are given the actors' note to "play up/exaggerate" the scenes and have some idea what talking points will follow. By happy accident, there are occasionally a few "extra" lines not attributable to the two main characters. Rather than cutting them, these provide great opportunities to have solicited volunteers before the program begins (seconds or minutes before, not days) and having the volunteers interact with the Actors.

So let's walk through the scene, the discussion, and the cheat sheet for one fairly detailed example, followed by a laundry list of other scenes from plays and points to be made.

---

13. Bradin Cormack, Martha Nussbaum & Richard Strier, *Introduction*, pp. 1–18, *in* Shakespeare and the Law: A Conversation Among Disciplines and Professions 2 (Bradin Cormack, Martha Nussbaum & Richard Strier eds., University of Chicago Press 2013).

14. The author has been spoiled enough to have had access to actors from the New American Shakespeare Company at the Atlanta Shakespeare Tavern. Shoutouts to the pairings of Jeff Watkins and Laura Cole (on multiple occasions); David Weber and Tiffany Porter; Andy Houchins and Laura Cole; and Jacob York and Tiffany Porter who have been the Actors at various CLE programs the author had the privilege to moderate.

The Shakespeare program begins best with Shakespeare's most famous line about lawyers: "The first thing we do, let's kill all the lawyers." This turns into a wonderful exposure (showing, then telling) of the importance of the rule of law and what will follow with the remainder of this particular CLE.

So here's the sample cut script,[15] with the two professional actors playing Jack Cade and Dick the Butcher, while the CLE audience is whipped up to cheer "God save your majesty" and audience members play Smith the Weaver and the Clerk of Chatham, the person on "trial" for the heinous crime of being able to read and write—

> CADE. Be brave, then; for your captain is brave, and vows reformation. There shall be in England seven halfpenny loaves sold for a penny: the three-hooped pot; shall have ten hoops and I will make it felony to drink small beer: all the realm shall be in common; and in Cheapside shall my palfrey go to grass: and when I am king, as king I will be,—
>
> ALL. God save your majesty!
>
> CADE. I thank you, good people: there shall be no money; all shall eat and drink on my score; and I will apparel them all in one livery, that they may agree like brothers and worship me their lord.
>
> DICK THE BUTCHER. The first thing we do, let's kill all the lawyers.
>
> CADE. Nay, that I mean to do. Is not this a lamentable thing, that of the skin of an innocent lamb should be made parchment? that parchment, being scribbled o'er, should undo a man? Some say the bee stings: but I say, 'tis the bee's wax; for I did but seal once to a thing,

---

15. I stress script because the Actors hold their lines in their hands. They can read and emote.

and I was never mine own man since. How now! who's there?

SMITH THE WEAVER. The clerk of Chatham: he can write and read and cast accompt.

CADE. O monstrous!

SMITH THE WEAVER. We took him setting of boys' copies.

CADE. Here's a villain!

SMITH THE WEAVER. Has a book in his pocket with red letters in't.

CADE. Nay, then, he is a conjurer.

DICK THE BUTCHER. Nay, he can make obligations, and write court-hand.

CADE. I am sorry for't: the man is a proper man, of mine honour; unless I find him guilty, he shall not die. Come hither, sirrah, I must examine thee: what is thy name?

CLERK OF CHATHAM. Emmanuel.

DICK THE BUTCHER. They use to write it on the top of letters: 'twill go hard with you.

CADE. Let me alone. Dost thou use to write thy name? or hast thou a mark to thyself, like an honest plain-dealing man?

CLERK OF CHATHAM. Sir, I thank God, I have been so well brought up that I can write my name.

ALL. He hath confessed: away with him! He's a villain and a traitor.

CADE. Away with him, I say! hang him with his pen and ink-horn about his neck.

Henry IV, part 2, Act IV, sc. 2.

After a quick round of applause, making sure to focus upon the two CLE attendees, the moderator then tees up the first question to a panelist, along the lines of—So what did we just see Shakespeare showing us?

The cheat sheet for this looks like—

Henry VI, part 2, Act IV, sc. 2 ("The first thing we do, let's kill all the lawyers")—(i) notice that in order for rebellion to succeed, with and without misinformation and lying, lawyers must be removed "first" as guardians of ordered liberty; (ii) notice that once lawyers are removed, crimes like "being able to read" or anything that appears to give any advantage suddenly come up; (iii) Cade's rebellion speech opens with a bunch of "campaign promises" depicting a virtual Eden but wholly left to his unfettered rule; and (iv) BONUS—if time, pull out the things lawyers did and do wrong, then and now, that make it easier for Cade to make this attack (i.e., lawyers should strive to avoid overly technical reliance upon "parchment, being scribbled o'er, [undoing] a man" and creating situation where "I did but seal once to a thing, and I was never my own man since."

Similar scenes and points follow by way of further examples:

The Tempest, Act II, sc. 1 ("no name of magistrate"). Gonzalo describes his imaginary kingdom while Antonio notes the contradictions, along with audience member cast as Sebastian. Discussion points—(i) Gonzalo realizes he can only be a dictator if there is "no name of magistrate"; (ii) without ordered liberty, "[t]he latter end of his commonwealth [inevitably] forgets the beginning"; (iii) tie back to Henry VI, part 2 discussion—even without a rebellion, building a new kingdom from the ground up as Gonzalo imagines he can be doing, requires laws and therefore lawyers; benign dictators (as Gonzalo imagines he would be) only benefit themselves.

Hamlet, Act V, sc. I (gravedigger speech)—(i) look at all of the exceedingly technical legal jargon Hamlet throws into his speech—quiddities, quillets, tenures, battery, recognizances, fines, double vouchers, recoveries, etc.; the lawyers have run roughshod over common folk with their multiple, hard to understand approaches; (ii) the hypothetical lawyer may well have been able to twist, mangle, convey, reconvey, and double-vouch his way through life; but none of "his quillets, his cases, his tenures, and his tricks" will serve to evade the leveling justice of death. However much land the lawyer conveyed (or perhaps even glommed from unsuspecting clients), "[t]he very conveyances of his lands will hardly lie in this box [i.e., a coffin]"; (iii) ordered liberty is well and good, but don't we see things going a bit far here; and (iv) in a BONUS moment of excessive geekiness, "double vouchers" appears to be a reference to a method of stripping title to a property by first filing a series of fictitious lawsuits.[16]

Measure for Measure, Act II, sc. 3 ("We have strict statutes and most biting laws"). While going into hiding, Duke Vincentio explains to Friar Thomas that the Duke has put Angelo in charge to enforce the law—let him take the fall and not the good Duke—and then step in later.—(i) laws that are not enforced are a bad idea, leading to a disrespect for the law; (ii) given how the play turns out, Duke Vincentio almost causes calamity and murder in his previously ordered kingdom; stepping away in order to let someone else clean up the mess before stepping back in is a dangerous approach; (iii) Friar Thomas's critique is justified—"It rested in your grace to unloose this tied-up justice when you pleased"; and a BONUS concurrence from the Supreme Court—Justice Stephen Breyer summarizes the situation neatly: "It's a mess. Nobody's doing the right thing. I mean the Duke is leaving, the whole city is poor, they're all running off to brothels, nobody gets married anymore, there are these little illegitimate children running all over. Instead of getting married, Isabella goes to a convent, and, my goodness, the Duke picks somebody who is really just terrible to run this

16. Cushman K. Davis, The Law in Shakespeare 269–70 (Washington Law Book Co. 1883).

city—Angelo, who can't control himself or anything else."[17] So the Duke decides to slip out of the dukedom and leave Angelo in charge in an executive capacity with Escalus to serve alongside as a magistrate. The Duke knows that Angelo will jump at the chance to enforce the least principle of the law to the utmost. Duke Vincentio of Vienna realizes that he has allowed the law itself to become a bit of a scarecrow. Because he was initially unwilling to enforce its harsher provisions, he is now unwilling to do so lest the people despair at receiving harsh treatment from him or, worse yet, turn upon him in rebellion.

Merchant of Venice, Act IV, sc. 1 (the "quality of mercy is not strained" speech). Portia and Bassanio are the Actors, with an audience member cast as the "on trial" Shylock. Throughout the scene the twists and traps in the supposed law of Venice that the supposed lawyer uses are exaggerated for comic effect.—(i) one lens, shows that Portia is actually manipulating the law to trap Shylock and set up a criminal charge; that is, the famous "quality of mercy" speech is ironic because Portia will show no mercy by the end of the scene, having forced Shylock to give up his possession and involuntarily convert religiously; (ii) taking the "quality of mercy" speech as written, it does provide a wonderful springboard for discussions of law and mercy.

Much Ado About Nothing, Act IV, sc. 2 ("O that I had been writ down an ass!")—Dogberry and Borachio are played by the Actors with the Watchmen (First and Second combined), Sexton, Conrade, and Verges played by audience members.—(i) Dogberry's hash of legal proceedings and misuse of legal language, and language in general, highlights the need for professional advocates and counselors; (ii) Dogberry simply

---

17. Stephen Breyer, *Roundtable, Shakespeare's Laws: A Justice, a Judge, a Philosopher, and an English Professor*, pp. 301–22, *in* Shakespeare and the Law: A Conversation Among Disciplines and Professions 302 (B. Cormack, M. Nussbaum & R. Strier, eds., University of Chicago Press 2013).

will not take hints on how to proceed, ignoring the Sexton and even the members of the watch.

Henry IV, Part 2, Act V, sc. 2 ("use the same with like bold, just and impartial spirit"). Henry V and the Lord Chief Justice.—(i) the Chief Justice was terrified that former Prince Hal, whom the Lord Chief Justice had upbraided frequently, is now king; Henry thanks the Lord Chief Justice for his prior work for Henry's father and. Hopes that when Henry has children the Lord Chief Justice will be equally impartial and just in his dealings with them; (ii) applying the law equally and justly served the Lord Chief Justice well, however uncomfortable it was at the time and certainly as he contemplated his first meeting with the new King, former ruffian prince; (iii) BONUS point—the Lord Chief Justice in Henry V's time was William Gascoigne, whose "tenure of office was also notable for the introduction of examinations as a preliminary to admission to practise as an attorney; and the same statute also provided that an attorney should cease to practise on conviction for fraud."[18] So Lord Chief Justice Gascoigne was a forefather of both the bar exam and disbarment proceedings.

Henry V, Act I, sc. 2 ("in right and conscience" can Henry "make this claim"). Henry V asks the Archbishop of Canterbury a straightforward question—"in right and conscience" can Henry claim to be the hereditary ruler of certain lands in France. If the answer is yes, then war with France is likely to follow. Canterbury's long, tedious, meandering response drives the scene, as Henry becomes more and more frustrated with Canterbury's failure to get to the point and address the question. Summing up the "advice," Henry has a legal claim to the lands in France so long as the lands in France are actually considered to be lands of Germany (where females may

---

18. George W. Keeton, *Shakespeare and His Legal Problems* 159–60 (A & C Black, Ltd. 1930).

inherit the throne) and, anyway, the land has been illegally seized by rulers before.—(i) the failure to address the client's request for legal analysis in a straightforward, simple manner is pretty stark; (ii) Canterbury puts a finger on the scale to both tell Henry what he wants to hear (go ahead and seize the land) and, quietly, to benefit Canterbury and other church leaders by distracting Henry with a war so that Henry will stop seizing monasteries (as seen Act I, scene 1 of the play); (iii) the advice itself can be used of an example that not every argument that can be made "should" be made.

## Books, Books, Books

This CLE approach owes much to Robert Fulghum's *All I Really Need to Know I Learned in Kindergarten* (1988). The point is simple, some of the earliest lessons are the simplest and most profound.

So for this CLE, three to five panelists will alternate presenting a description of a title, giving a brief plot summary, and then taking a first question from the moderator. If you have purchased copies of the books in advance there can be further "interactivity" by giving one copy of each title to a member of the audience either by way of drawing (yawn) or with a quick trivia question thrown out by the moderator to the crowd.

Titles that can work well (and authors) follow, along with a brief portion of cheat sheet notes.

Dr. Seuss, *The 500 Hats of Bartholomew Cubbins* (Vanguard Press 1938; renewed 1965). This provides an excellent jumping off point for the varied roles lawyers play. *A Lawyer's Creed* and the accompanying *Aspirational Statement*, for example, note duties owed/hats worn with respect to the lawyer's own clients, opposing parties and their counsel, the courts, the lawyer's colleagues in the practice of law generally, to the profession itself, and to the public and our system of justice. Just as Bartholomew struggles with balancing multiple hats, lawyers have entered a profession uniquely calling for that ability.

Robert McCloskey, *Make Way for Ducklings* (Viking Press 1941). After a perilous and risky journey, Mrs. Mallard and eight ducklings are reunited with Mr. Mallard in the Public Garden. Along the way, Mrs. Mallard teaches the ducklings what it means to be a duck, and also along the way, many kindnesses are provided by others (including policemen closing a road so the ducklings can cross). Here the need for mentorship of each succeeding generation of lawyers is pictured writ large.

P.D. Eastman, *Are You My Mother?* (Random House 1960; renewed 1988). More fowl! This time a hatchling bird is in search of its real, avian mother. The hatchling quizzes a kitten, hen, dog, and cow, while not bothering to ask several machines, before mistaking a steam shovel for the hatchling's mother. All ends well, as the steam shovel returns the hatchling to the nest. Again, the professionalism points include knowing what role is being played when (i.e., which hat the lawyer is wearing) and also recognizing to whom various duties (especially client duties) are owed.

Maurice Sendak, *Where the Wild Things Are* (Harper & Row 1963). Max dresses in a wolf suit and misbehaves, as one does. He is sent to bed without supper. His room is transformed into an island with beasts that try to scare him. They don't, so they make him their king. Once Max gets lonely, he returns home and, surprise, discovers a hot supper waiting in his bedroom. From a professionalism standpoint, we have a story of redemption, including a "hot supper" waiting for Max's return to non-wild behavior. And being fed a hot supper, the book suggests, even trumps being the king of all the wild things. These lessons can be applied to persons reentering society at large after time in prison, victims of trafficking reentering society after abuse, and even lawyers benefiting from the wake-up call of a disciplinary action.

Margaret Wise Brown, *Goodnight Moon* (Harper & Brothers 1947). In a series of rhyming couplets, a young bunny says "goodnight" over the course of a single hour and ten minutes to the multiple objects, inanimate and living, in the bunny's room. First, each object is identified. Then, each object is separately told "goodnight," setting up repetition. Finally, the "goodnights" are taken beyond the room to the stars, air, and noises everywhere. In sum, *Goodnight Moon* somewhat pictures "mindfulness" and relaxation techniques decades before they became hot topics among stressed professionals. The book also evidences a quiet thankfulness and gratitude. While the limited vocabulary certainly does not expand to include, "[i]n our practices we should remember that the primary justification for who we are and what we do is the common good we can achieve through the faithful representation of people who deasire to resolve disputes in a peaceful manner and to prevent future disputes" (prologue to *Aspirational Statement on Professionalism*), the sense is certainly pictured in the book's portrayal, particularly the final move to stars, air, and noises everywhere.

## Cinema: Sherlock Holmes on the Silver Screen

One common professionalism topic is unconscious bias. In that regard, the Sherlock Holmes movies over the years provide wonderful opportunities to compare/contrast legitimate inductive and deductive reasoning over against leaning upon bias, excessive generalization/stereotyping, confirmation bias, and the like. For this type of CLE program, the stories themselves could be used but short clips from movies across decades work better.

Arthur Conan Doyle describing Holmes—you can pull down from YouTube and edit Arthur Conan Doyle's 1929 interview. In the clip, Doyle describes how his Sherlock Holmes works. In doing so (from about the two-minute mark forward of the interview), he notes the gathering and observation of specific facts and drawing conclusions from those facts, as opposed to jumping to conclusions.

With respect to a variety of actors portraying Sherlock Holmes with widely differing approaches, a good representation that also allows for drawing out professionalism points follows (with the professionalism cheat sheet points following each particular film/television episode):

"The Adventure of the Red-Headed League" from "The Adventures of Sherlock Holmes" (Granada TV 1985) (Jeremy Brett as Sherlock Holmes and David Burke as Dr. John Watson) (DVD MPI Home Video 2000)—"You have been to Afghanistan, I perceive"—(i) contrast the conclusions Homes does draw with those he does not; without a preconception, he notices Watson's soldiery bearing, tan, and limp; thus, service in Afghanistan. Holmes's conclusions are narrow and observation based. He does not, for example, note that Watson was at the Criterion Bar and conclude that because Watson is looking for a roommate to share expenses Watson is an alcoholic and unreliable.

"The Case of the Cunningham Heritage" (Guild Films 1954) (Ronald Howard as Sherlock Holmes and Howard Merion Crawford as Dr. John Watson) (Episode 1 of 39-Episode Television Series) on "Sherlock Holmes: The 1954–55 Television Series") (DVD Mill Creek Entertainment 2005). This otherwise non-canonical account "lifts" the "You have been to Afghanistan, I perceive" scene as it was the opening episode in a 39-episode television series.

"The Hound of the Baskervilles" (20th Century Fox Film Corporation 1939) (Basil Rathbone as Sherlock Holmes and Nigel Bruce as Dr. John Watson) (DVD MPI Home Video 2004). This one is kind of meta. The scene to pull is the one where Holmes draws conclusions from the walking stick left behind at 221B Baker Street by Dr. Henry Mortimer. In addition to the run of observation-to-conclusion material, in the 1939 movie Dr. Mortimer is played by Lionel Atwill, a frequent "bad guy" in numerous films leading up to and including 1939. Why? The screen version of "Hound of the Baskervilles" ran into the problem that there were so few characters to suspect. So they case Atwill, whom the audience had repeatedly seen as a villain, as a bit of a red herring. Thus, the professionalism point of not relying overly much on past observations or "facts," especially when it comes to people. Incidentally, Atwill went on to play the ultimate Holmes universe bad guy—James Moriarty—in "Sherlock Holmes and the Secret Weapon" (Universal Pictures 1943), also opposite Rathbone and Bruce.

"The Problem of Thor Bridge" from "The Casebook of Sherlock Holmes" (Granada TV 1991) (Jeremy Brett as Sherlock Holmes and Edward Hardwicke as Dr. John Watson) (DVD Granada Media 2004). The Sergeant Coventry examination with Holmes and Watson at the outset and then later as Holmes explains that this was not murder by Mr. Gibson but suicide point out the Sergeant's willingness to employ stereotyping (all Americans have lots of guns and use them) and giving past observations undue weight (after all, many husbands have been guilty of violence against wives) instead of noticing the actual facts presented. A great quote comes in from Holmes to Watson—"you have seen me miss my mark before, Watson. I have an instinct for such things, and yet sometimes it has played me false." In short, Holmes is always letting new facts/observations advance his conclusions.

"Sherlock Holmes and the Case of the Silk Stocking" (BBC One 2004) (Rupert Everett as Sherlock Holmes, and Ian Hart as Dr. John Watson) (DVD BBC Video 2204). This non-canonical outing shows Holmes determining that the corpse presumed to be of a streetwalker is instead that of a kidnapped and murdered heiress.

"The Sign of Four" (RKO Pictures 1932) (Arthur Wontner as Sherlock Holmes and Ian Hunter as Dr. John Watson) (DVD Alpha Video 2003).

"A Study in Pink" from "Sherlock" (BBC One 2010) (Benedict Cumberbatch as Sherlock Holmes and Martin Freeman as Dr. John Watson) on "Sherlock: Season One") (DVD BBC Worldwide Americas 2010). "RACHE". This one's kind of fun. Compare the conclusion that Cumberbatch's Holmes draws regarding "RACHE" with that in Doyle's original and in any of the other "A Study in Scarlet" clips you may wish to pull (I prefer Peter Cushing's for the contrast). The professionalism point involves, at a minimum, humility. Within each version of the story's universe Holmes is correct, yet the conclusions contradict one another.

"A Study in Scarlet" from "Sherlock Holmes" (BBC 1968) (Peter Cushing as Sherlock Holmes and Nigel Stock as Dr. John Watson) on "The Sherlock Holmes Collection" (DVD A&E Television Networks 2009). In addition to contrasting with the Cumberbatch "A Study in Pink," Cushing's discussion with Lestrade and Gregson sets up the difference between clear bias—Lestrade and Gregson—and Holmes's observation-based approach.

And some closing points for any of the Holmes clips.

Notice Holmes's intense, manic concentration. Is he, perhaps, on the autism spectrum? And even if he is not, the Holmes clips can lead to a rewarding discussion of how different people perceive differently.

Notice that while Holmes can be "dismissive" of policemen, he is rarely dismissive of the usually-dismissed-or-ignored-in-Victorian England economically disadvantaged.

And as an elephant in the room, Holmes's dismissive attitudes and remarks regarding women, including recognizing and being astonished that he was outsmarted and outmaneuvered by "the Woman" Irene Adler in "A Scandal in Bohemia," show that Holmes was unaware of his own blind spots. Other examples of blind spots abound, but let's leave them for your future panels to find, discuss, and apply.

## Conclusion

Hopefully the main takeaways for thinking about and putting together this type of Professionalism CLE are obvious, but just in case:

- The moderator bears the burden of preparation with the panelists being able to focus and dig in deeper on each of their respective primary and secondary pieces upon which they will be called.
- Conversations trump lectures. And modeling solid, respectful disagreement is terrific.
- Each type of CLE uses a lens—a way into a conversation by looking at a piece of fiction—that will then be turned on the lawyer's own conduct. So multiple other varieties not discussed here are possible, including music clips (which can begin with a name that tune contest among the attendees), arias from famous operas, famous art that is in the public domain or readily licensable for educational purposes, and the like.
- A variety of perspectives on the panel is critical, including diversity of current role (prosecutor, criminal defense attorney, civil litigator, family law practitioner, trial court judge, appellate judge), lived life experiences, stages of practice (relatively senior/relatively new), and the like. If all of the panelists "look like" the moderator (and therefore all look like each other), find other qualified

panelists. Frankly, the easier "lift" on panelists can make it more attractive for panelists otherwise reticent about jumping into presenting (as opposed to only attending) CLE.

- Have fun. Seriously, have fun. That's also part of "professionalism"; the more you enjoy being a lawyer the more the desire to give back will simply well up.

# Professionalism Guidelines: More Than Aspirational

*D. Alicia Hickok*

Reading the essays that precede this one is inspiring, moving, encouraging. If the reader was discouraged, this book is a godsend. If the reader was uncertain, this book strengthens resolve and hope. But what about the person who does not pick up the book because of skepticism or cynicism or apathy? Professionalism cannot be important only to those who are committed to being professional and to practicing in an honorable profession. It must be a shared commitment that characterizes the profession and shapes how those outside see the profession. That it currently is not raises the question: How do the skeptics and cynics and those who do not care become convinced to become professionals in an honorable profession in service of justice and equity?

The perhaps instinctive response—legislate or regulate—is itself greeted with skepticism and cynicism. Who legislates? Congress? What about the three branches? Who regulates? Courts? Does that provoke an evaluation of the advocate rather than the advocacy, contrary to the duty of a lawyer to represent a client and advance a client's cause rather than to be a focal point individually? But having ideals out there for those who choose them is equally flawed. Fundamentally, professionalism asks for a commitment by a lawyer to have conduct emanate from and reflect character, and that sits uneasily both with traditional rules and precatory standards. The problem is exacerbated by the need to have standards for the profession as a whole, instead of individual, or even local, laments about this or that shortfall. When the public thinks of "judges" or "lawyers" it may have a more vivid picture of the judges and lawyers in local news, but that picture feeds a broader image that extends from the local to the national. This essay proposes that the antidote to the current perception of a broken system needs to be systemic, and that the system needs to say with one voice that it seeks justice and equity and upholds certain basic values and principles, and that it relies on having professionals before it to do the same. In turn, that commitment needs to be accepted and reflected back by the professionals themselves.

The one vehicle that currently expresses commitment is the oath each lawyer takes as an officer of the court in order to receive a license to practice. Without much fanfare, jurisdictions have begun to integrate key principles of professionalism into the oath each lawyer swears. Some, like California or Massachusetts, do so with brevity.

> I, (licensee name) solemnly swear (or affirm) that I will support the Constitution of the United States and the Constitution of the State of California, and that I will faithfully discharge the duties of an attorney and counselor at law to the best of my knowledge and ability. As an officer of the court, I will strive to conduct myself at all times with dignity, courtesy and integrity.

Or, for Massachusetts,

> I (repeat the name) solemnly swear that I will do no falsehood, nor consent to the doing of any in court; I will not wittingly or willingly promote or sue any false, groundless or unlawful suit, nor give aid or consent to the same; I will delay no man for lucre or malice; but I will conduct myself in the office of an attorney within the courts according to the best of my knowledge and

> discretion, and with all good fidelity as well to the courts as my clients. So help me God.

A significant minority of states enumerate core principles of professionalism in their oath. South Carolina's oath is an example.

> I do solemnly swear (or affirm) that:
>
> I am duly qualified, according to the Constitution of this State, to exercise the duties of the office to which I have been appointed, and that I will, to the best of my ability, discharge those duties and will preserve, protect and defend the Constitution of this State and of the United States;
>
> I will maintain the respect and courtesy due to courts of justice, judicial officers, and those who assist them;
>
> To my clients, I pledge faithfulness, competence, diligence, good judgment and prompt communication;
>
> To opposing parties and their counsel, I pledge fairness, integrity, and civility, not only in court, but also in all written and oral communications;
>
> I will not pursue or maintain any suit or proceeding which appears to me to be unjust nor maintain any defenses except those I believe to be honestly debatable under the law of the land, but this obligation shall not prevent me from defending a person charged with a crime;
>
> I will employ for the purpose of maintaining the causes confided to me only such means as are consistent with trust and honor and the principles of professionalism, and will never seek to mislead an opposing party, the judge or jury by a false statement of fact or law;

> I will respect and preserve inviolate the confidences of my clients, and will accept no compensation in connection with a client's business except from the client or with the client's knowledge and approval;
>
> I will maintain the dignity of the legal system and advance no fact prejudicial to the honor or reputation of a party or witness, unless required by the justice of the cause with which I am charged;
>
> I will assist the defenseless or oppressed by ensuring that justice is available to all citizens and will not delay any person's cause for profit or malice;
>
> [So help me God.]

Indeed, some law schools ask for oaths as a student undertakes to study law. Atlanta's John Marshall Law School, for example, has the following oath:

> As I begin the study of law at Atlanta's John Marshall Law School, I acknowledge and accept the privileges and responsibilities inherent in my becoming a lawyer, and the high standards and ideals that accompany such an undertaking.
>
> Accordingly, I pledge that I will at all times conduct myself with the dignity befitting an advocate and counselor in a learned profession.
>
> I commit myself to service without prejudice, integrity without compromise, and the diligent performance of my duties with the utmost good faith.
>
> I acknowledge that I will be a zealous advocate, but will act with courtesy and cooperation toward others, and I will at all times, personally and professionally, conduct myself in a professional manner.
>
> I will remember that my responsibilities to the legal profession should control my conduct both as a

> student of the law and, therefore, as a member of the bar.
>
> I hereby accept my new status as a professional, and I will approach my colleagues and adversaries alike with the same integrity, professionalism, and civility that the practice of law demands.
>
> I pledge to conduct myself in accordance with and abide by Atlanta's John Marshall Law School's Code of Student Responsibility.
>
> This pledge I take freely and upon my honor.

Oaths are also required of the judges and justices who are the ones before whom the lawyers practice. Indeed, the justices of the United States Supreme Court take two oaths, a constitutional oath and a judicial oath.

> I, ________, do solemnly swear (or affirm) that I will support and defend the Constitution of the United States against all enemies, foreign and domestic; that I will bear true faith and allegiance to the same; that I take this obligation freely, without any mental reservation or purpose of evasion; and that I will well and faithfully discharge the duties of the office on which I am about to enter. So help me God.[1]

> I, ________, do solemnly swear (or affirm) that I will administer justice without respect to persons, and do equal right to the poor and to the rich, and that I will faithfully and impartially discharge and perform all the duties incumbent upon me as ________ under the Constitution and laws of the United States. So help me God.[2]

---

1. 5 U.S.C. § 3331.
2. 28 U.S.C. § 453.

At the moment, however, nothing links the two, let alone aligns the two. There is no vocalized mutuality of commitment.

An oath is preferable to a standalone set of professionalism ideals for three reasons. First, ideals are frequently expressly aspirational. For example, according to a compilation posted by the American Bar Association (with the caveat that the website notes it was last updated in 2017), there is a document that encourages (or admonishes to) "professionalism" or "civility" in 44 of the 50 states, as well as in the District of Columbia but, while some refer to a "creed" (which only Texas couples with "mandate") or "code," "pillars," "tenets," or "standards," others have "guidelines" or "principles"—or even more explicitly, "voluntary standards," or "aspirational statement" or "statement of professional aspirations," or just "statement" or "aspirations." The precatory nature is even more emphasized when the call to professionalism is an expression of a state or local bar association—in which membership itself is voluntary.

Even for Texas, the one state to use the word "mandate," the message is mixed. In 1989, when the Texas Supreme Court adopted by order its Creed and Mandate for Professionalism, it explained first that lawyers owe duties to clients within the context of the profession's broader duty to the legal system. It then said that tactics by a minority of lawyers, ranging from "lack of civility to outright hostility and obstructionism" do not serve justice but rather delay or deny it. With all of that said, and despite the use of "mandate," the Texas Supreme Court explained:

> These rules are primarily aspirational. Compliance with the rules depends primarily upon understanding and voluntary compliance, secondarily upon reinforcement by peer pressure and public opinion, and finally when necessary by enforcement by the courts through their inherent powers and rules already in existence.

> These standards are not a set of rules that lawyers can use and abuse to incite ancillary litigation or arguments over whether or not they have been observed.[3]

Texas's observation points to the second weakness of standalone professionalism standards. In an adversarial system, tools become weapons when "adversarial" replaces the "truth-seeking" it was meant to facilitate, and particularly when adversarial is viewed not just as lawyer opposed to lawyer but lawyers opposed to courts or to an abstract system. Indeed, it may be the rise of "adversarial" (replacing "truth-seeking") as the keyword to describe the entire judicial process that has highlighted the need and outcry by so many for professionalism and civility. Without a common mission to find, promote, and protect truth and justice, there is no core to bolster public confidence, and the malfeasance is readily generalized as a feature and product of the justice system.

As a result of the perception (or, perhaps, self-fulfilling prophecy) that the profession is dishonorable and not only tolerates but promotes injustice and inequity, "professionals"—those who embody professionalism—are seen as exceptional, which feeds the clamor crying that everything to do with courts requires control from outside the court system. That perception is unwarranted and dangerous, but the reaction to it points out the weakness of standalone ideals, which may be peculiar to the American ethos.

This country mythologizes independent thought through tales of underdogs and mavericks who singlehandedly shape history—or change law. Elsewhere, independence is not independent thought so much as independent judgment, a strength of character in service of a system, not in opposition to it. In Germany, for example, the *Bundesrechtsanwaltsordnung*

3. https://www.txcourts.gov/media/276685/texaslawyerscreed.pdf.

(BRAO) starts with the understanding that a lawyer is an independent agent of the administration of justice.[4] Similarly, the International Bar Association's International Principles on Conduct for the Legal Profession begin with independence and explain:

> A lawyer shall maintain independence and be afforded the protection such independence offers in giving clients unbiased advice and representation. A lawyer shall exercise independent, unbiased professional judgment in advising a client, including as to the likelihood of success of the client's case.

As alluded to earlier, the oaths of the judiciary and the oaths of lawyers exist in tandem, to a certain extent parallel, but they are not reciprocal, or even cross-referenced. And yet there would be great value in incorporating the sense of this and other precepts, that there is an obligation for a justice system to protect those who protect what the system protects. That sense of protectiveness may in itself explain the reluctance of Texas and others to weaponize professionalism. Linking and aligning the two may be as simple as transforming a lawyer's entry into the bar from a one-sided oath to a two-sided covenant or compact, much like a call and response. A hypothetical example might be:

> COURT: We have sworn to administer justice and equity, with fidelity to truth and without undue delay, and we recognize your role to advocate with an honest purpose, sharing with us your knowledge and discretion, for us to consider and weigh. In return, we ask only that you serve your clients, our courts, and the

4. BRAO, pt. 1, § 1.

law, with integrity and fidelity and treat all within and without the system with respect and courtesy.

RESPONSE: I, (licensee name) solemnly swear (or affirm) that I will support the Constitution of the United States and the courts and the law, that I will come before the court with studied knowledge and independent judgment and will serve with fidelity and integrity and without prejudice, zealous for my client and committed to assisting the defenseless or oppressed by ensuring that justice is available to all citizens. I will not delay any person's cause for profit or malice but will at all times conduct myself with the dignity, courtesy, and integrity befitting an advocate and counselor in a learned profession to maintain the respect and courtesy due to courts of justice, judicial officers, and those who assist them.

This distills and combines many of the principles in the preceding oaths into a concise oath. Think of the powerful message a vocalized and unified shared commitment to the mutual quest for justice and equity, through candor and mutual respect, fidelity and independent judgment, would communicate throughout the profession and to the public.

To be sure, individual states will need to consider both the concept and language of any such compact, and the result will likely look different than the preceding example, but there is already a burgeoning consensus both that there is a need for professionalism and on what a lawyer's oath should contain, and there are already a significant number of uniform laws and model acts that demonstrate a shared understanding of various facets of the law across multiple jurisdictions.

The observation that there are already model acts and uniform laws raises the obvious question that many principles of professionalism (most notably, candor) are already in the Model

Rules of Professional Conduct, variations of which have been adopted throughout the country, and it might be simpler to expand the Model Rules. If professionalism could be reduced to conduct, expanding the Rules of Professional Conduct could lead to largely consensus rules, or at the least, to conscious decisions by each jurisdiction to adopt, modify, or decline to adopt the new rules. Certainly, the Model Rules and many professionalism standards overlap. As an example, Oregon's Statement of Professionalism speaks in terms of a "professional standard of conduct that goes beyond merely complying with ethical rules" but some of the enumerated commitments are to communicating with clients, written fee agreements, preparation, and the pursuit of nonfrivolous claims, each of which is already found in the Rules of Professional Conduct.

As noted, however, key aspects of professionalism are more about character than conduct, and those are not amenable to inclusion in rules of conduct. The hypothetical oath set forth earlier is not redundant of the Rules of Professional Conduct. Its principles are, however, foundational to the rules. Said differently, while it is possible to reward candor and punish a lack of candor, it is difficult to measure integrity. The merit of claims can be assessed more readily than the judgment exercised to articulate them. Whether one has refrained from ad hominem attacks is objective; whether one treats others with respect requires more than observation or analysis of a certain interaction. Certainly, if lawyers serve with integrity, exercise judgment, and view and treat others with respect, the demands of the Rules of Professional Conduct will be satisfied as well.

Likewise, there are Rules of Judicial Conduct, again existing parallel to instead of linked with the Rules of Professional Conduct. It would be even more incongruous to impose upon a judge a rule that he or she must welcome lawyers to practice before them, so long as they practice professionally.

Rules, whether of professional or judicial conduct, are externally imposed and externally enforced, and external sight lines require conformity of conduct rather than serving as a call to commitment, let alone a joint commitment by the agents of the administration of justice to the profession of law. The profession, the justice system, and the public and justice that both serve would be better for the speaking of shared commitment.

# Professionalism and the Business of Law

*Hon. Christopher C. Conner (Ret.)*

"Civility costs nothing and buys everything."

— Mary Wortley Montagu

Shortly after I passed the bar exam in the fall of 1982, I met with two senior partners of my new employer—a medium-sized private law practice—to discuss the firm's rules on professionalism. Looking back, I view this meeting as a very timely, basic introduction to rules of civility in my nascent litigation practice. At the time, however, it was an eye-opening lesson to the complexities of personal interaction in an ever-changing profession.

## Seniority, Communications, and Billing

The partners emphasized civility and deference to seniority. They explained that an attorney's reputation is paramount—and that I should carefully protect my reputation and, concomitantly, that of the firm by being honest, courteous, and professionally competent in all interactions with opposing counsel and court personnel. If I crossed the line of civility with opposing counsel, word of my misdeed would spread like a brush fire in the wind. Similarly (and presciently, I might add), I was admonished that at some point in my future litigation practice, clerks in the prothonotary's office may be critical to a filing deadline, so treat them with the same respect given to counsel. If circumstances require an in-person meeting with opposing counsel, the less-experienced lawyer (referencing me, of course) should always offer to meet at the office of the more senior lawyer or otherwise defer to the senior lawyer's location preference.

Our discussion also included guidance on communications with the court. For example, they advised me to reference an order as "the court's order" or "your Honor's order" and conclude correspondence with "Respectfully submitted." In court, always shake hands with opposing counsel at the beginning and the end of every hearing, stand as soon as the judge enters the courtroom, attempt agreement on matters of procedure and scheduling, and avoid seeking court intervention for mundane requests that should be resolved by counsel. I took copious notes during this meeting and took their advice quite seriously.

I would be remiss if I did not mention that my meeting also included a description of ethical billing practices and the client appreciation curve. Revenue generation has always been a part of the practice of law. Lawyers in the private sector generate income by virtue of expertise in various practice areas, and timely payment of fees is the *sine qua non* of a successful law firm. Productivity, client generation, and billable hours are appropriate measuring sticks for compensation. Accounts receivable must be regularly analyzed and addressed. Managing partners have long pursued a law firm structure that maintains low overhead with streamlined billing practices and profit incentives. In other words, to survive, private law firms must operate as business entities.

My law firm was typical. I had an annual billable hour goal of 1,800 hours and pro bono expectations of another 150 hours. Associates were expected to network and appropriately establish themselves in their respective communities. The firm encouraged both volunteer work and bar association activities.

In sum, the firm had a holistic view of associate development, guiding us to immerse ourselves professionally both in our work and in our communities. I became a partner in 1989 and endeavored to grow my commercial litigation practice with the help of partners in transactional areas of the firm whose clients frequently needed litigation assistance. As my litigation practice grew, I received greater responsibility for the management of associates, which provided me with opportunities to pass along those early lessons on professionalism in the business of law.

## Changes in the Legal Profession

In the 1990s, our profession suffered a crisis of incivility, capturing the attention of bench and bar. Judges observed a decline in professionalism and expressed concern about its ethical implications.[1] Law review articles considered the merits of emerging "Rambo tactics," which treated civil litigation as war and opposing counsel as enemy combatants.[2] Bar associations and individual courts, including my own district court, hurried to promulgate new standards and guidance.[3]

Law firms, meanwhile, began to computerize files, maintain websites, and forgo the formality of letterhead for the

---

1. *See, e.g.*, Hon. Sandra Day O'Connor, *Professionalism*, 76 WASH. UNIV. L.Q. 5 (1998); Hon. Warren E. Burger, *The Decline of Professionalism*, 63 FORDHAM L. REV. 949, 953 (1995).

2. *See, e.g.*, Jean M. Cary, *Rambo Depositions: Controlling an Ethical Cancer in Civil Litigation*, 25 HOFSTRA L. REV. 561, 563 (1996); Judith S. Kaye, *Lawyering for a New Age*, 67 FORDHAM L. REV. 1, 8 (1998).

3. *See* Christopher J. Piazzola, Comment, *Ethical Versus Procedural Approaches to Civility*, 74 UNIV. COLO. L. REV. 1197, 1199–200 (2003); *see also* U.S. Dist. Court for the Middle Dist. of Pa., Local Rules of Court, at app. C (2014).

convenience of email.[4] Lunch meetings became conference calls. Long-standing rules that I had learned as a young attorney about seniority, handshakes, and whose office would be the forum for a meeting all faded in importance. The practice of law looked a lot different the day I became a judge from what it had been the day I became an attorney. More importantly, the practice of law today looks very different from only a few years ago.

The *business* of lawyering continues to evolve with advances in technology, promoting efficiency in serving clients, processing information, and resolving disputes. But with new paradigms come new challenges; and a rapid shift away from in-person legal work has revived concern for standards of professionalism, courtesy, and how we interact with one another.[5] While I am not compelled to frame this discussion in the language of a renewed crisis, a sense of thoughtful alarm would not be—if you'll pardon the phrase—out of order.

The scale of the new normal is undeniable. A recent ABA survey found that a vast majority (about 87 percent) of workplaces allow lawyers to work remotely to some extent. Meanwhile, 30 percent of lawyers reported working from home almost all the time, and 44 percent of young lawyers indicated that they would consider leaving their current jobs for a greater ability to work remotely.[6] In response to the COVID-19 pandemic, American courts at every level conducted

---

4. *See* Tracey Baetzel & Carl W. Herstein, *Virtual Memory: Looking Back at the Changing Relationship Among Lawyers, Law Firms, and Technology*, 77 Mich. Bar J. 422, 425 (1998).

5. *See, e.g.*, Gary L. Gassman et al., *Defining Civility as an Attorney*, 55 Tort Trial & Ins. Prac. L.J. 557, 570–72 (2020).

6. *See* Stephanie A. Scharf et al., *Practicing Law in the Pandemic and Moving Forward: Results and Best Practices from a Nationwide Survey of the Legal Profession* (Am. Bar Ass'n 2021).

proceedings using videoconferencing applications like Zoom and Webex. Many jurisdictions have altered their rules to allow for remote proceedings on a more permanent basis. Face-to-face interaction, it seems, is no longer an essential component of practicing law.

What do we risk in this brave new world? For one thing, the absence of personal interaction and connection opens the door to informality and ultimately unhelpful (if occasionally entertaining) expressions of frustration. In the old days, discussions about settlement prospects or a discovery dispute ordinarily would have been handled face-to-face over a cup of clam chowder or in a law firm's conference room. Today, it is commonplace for such exchanges to take place online, often with extempore, informal, and ambiguous language.

As a trial judge, I have been exposed to increasing informality in all manner of communications between counsel. Oftentimes, discovery disputes frame the issues with an exhibit of email threads that reflect mutual frustration more than problem-solving dialogue. Many emails lack basic courtesies or proper grammar, let alone insight. My view is that the pressure of law practice, together with the ease of instantaneous communication, cultivates informality and discourtesy. I do not mean to suggest that in-person interaction alone guards against all manner of unprofessional behavior. All the same, we are bolder behind keyboards than we are in courtrooms, and more vocal with the imagined security of a mute button than we would be otherwise. Our brains literally function differently during online exchanges than they do during face-to-face conversations.[7] New research casts what some might dismiss as a minor pleasantry—the handshake—as something "deeply biological in origin," a shared practice with our closest evolutionary relative, the chimp,

---

7. *See* Bill Hathaway, *Zooming in on Our Brains on Zoom*, YaleNews (Oct. 25, 2023).

and an inimitable way to build connection.[8] One might wonder how the legal profession will fare in adapting to this increasingly remote paradigm.

## Enduring Professionalism

Will the business of law supplant all remnants of professionalism? I take great comfort in the fact that ours is an adversarial system of justice. Good-faith negotiation, respectful argument, and civil discourse are more than passing strategies or tools to be wielded in one instance and then discarded in the next. They are the fundamental building blocks of a successful law practice in a system that aspires to resolve matters under the rule of law. These fundamentals are the key to effective lawyering, and they will outlive both current and future evolutions of law firm business practices driven by technological intervention and economic pressures. In a nutshell, adherence to basic tenets of professionalism and civility makes you a better lawyer.

To the members of bench and bar who remember what it was like to practice before the world of virtual hearings and rapid-fire emails, I encourage you to reflect upon what we have lost and what we have maintained. True, changing that meeting with opposing counsel next week from a Zoom call to a lunch might seem frivolous. It might even take more time out of your day. But think about what you might gain with an in-person exchange of perspective. A more personable interaction could mean a new or improved professional connection or simply a more enjoyable working relationship; it could mean some insight into the case that would not otherwise be communicated by ones and zeros; or, admittedly, it could just mean a cup of clam chowder. Until we remember what it was like to sit as

8. *See* Jake Kerridge, *The Handshake Is Deeply Biological—We Can't Let Covid Kill It Off*, TELEGRAPH (Mar. 28, 2021).

lawyers across the table from one another, and to see our colleagues as more than a talking head on a computer screen or a disembodied voice on speakerphone, it is difficult to say just how impactful this small gesture could be.

To the young lawyers, for whom the remote-work environment is all you know, a word of caution. Law is not a profession about convenience and reflexive decision-making. It is deliberative, yeoman-like work inescapably bound up in the complexity of human relationships. Embrace that. Master that. Think twice and three times before you press "Send." Beware the all-too-common temptation to shed your sense of civility and professionalism in the digital world because it will follow you back into the real world. I promise that you will be a better advocate for it.